The Novels of Kurt Vonnegut

ABSOLUT VONNEGUT.

Absolut Vonnegut, silkscreen by Kurt Vonnegut, © 1995, 22 × 30 inches. Used by the kind permission of Kurt Vonnegut.

The Novels of Kurt Vonnegut

Imagining Being an American

_____ DONALD E. MORSE

Contributions to the Study of Science Fiction and Fantasy, Number 103
Donald Palumbo, Series Adviser

Westport, Connecticut
London

Library of Congress Cataloging-in-Publication Data

Morse, Donald E., 1936–
    The novels of Kurt Vonnegut : imagining being an American /   Donald E. Morse.
      p. cm.—(Contributions to the study of science fiction and fantasy, ISSN 0193–6875 ;
    no. 103)
    Includes bibliographical references and index.
    ISBN 0–313–31914–6 (alk. paper)
      1. Vonnegut, Kurt—Criticism and interpretation.   2. Science fiction, American—History
and criticism.   3. National characteristics, American, in literature.   I. Title.   II.   Series.
PS3572.O5Z786   2003
813′.54—dc21   2002192775

British Library Cataloguing in Publication Data is available.

Library of Congress Catalog Card Number: 2002192775
ISBN: 0–313–31914–6
ISSN: 0193–6875

First published in 2003

Praeger Publishers, 88 Post Road West, Westport, CT 06881
An imprint of Greenwood Publishing Group, Inc.
www.praeger.com

Printed in the United States of America

The paper used in this book complies with the
Permanent Paper Standard issued by the National
Information Standards Organization (Z39.48–1984).

10 9 8 7 6 5 4 3 2 1

For Csilla Bertha

We should impart our courage, and not our despair, our health and ease, and

not our disease, and take care that this does not spread by contagion.

Henry David Thoreau

Imagine being an American.

Kurt Vonnegut

Contents

Preface

Life "must be lived forward but can only be understood backward," as Søren Kierkegaard famously remarked. The same backward understanding holds true for Kurt Vonnegut's novels from *Timequake*, published in 1997 back to *Player Piano*, published some forty-five years earlier in 1952: each novel can only be fully understood in light of all the others preceding it. Like Kathryn Hume in her *American Dream, American Nightmare*, I place my focus "on the possible responses of nonprofessional readers who read primarily for pleasure and information, for escape and consolation, for answers to problems in their own lives, for a sense of learning about themselves or about those different from them" (8).[1] The emphasis of this study falls, therefore, on the value of reading Vonnegut's novels, their relation to American experience, and their distinguishing features as fiction. Such interests are widely shared among Vonnegut's readers. I have attempted to draw parallels between and distinctive affinities with Vonnegut's work and that of other American authors, especially Ralph Waldo Emerson, Henry David Thoreau, and Mark Twain. Emerson, Thoreau, and Walt Whitman in the nineteenth century attempted to imagine a new American literature and culture free from the influence and constraints of Europe—one that would sound its "barbaric yawp over the rooftops of the world." Vonnegut imagining being an American in the second half of the twentieth century does so against the backdrop of their partial, if considerable, achievement.

The literature and culture created in the nineteenth-century American Renaissance continued to flourish in the twentieth century, "America's Century" until by century's end the entire world eagerly read an American book.[2] Still, the United States, as all nations and cultures, remains unfinished with many of its most sacred promises still unfulfilled, such as equality of status and opportunity for all and the creation of an aristocracy of virtue and merit This unfinished quality so palpably reflected in Vonnegut's novels helps differentiate his work from that of his nineteenth-century counterparts. Those nineteenth-century writers focus on beginnings—the promise of America inherent in creating a new nation and on the concomitant failure to set significant goals. Vonnegut from his vantage point of the second half of the twentieth century focuses on the failure of America to keep its promises, especially those relating to social justice, while achieving far too many trivial objectives. Vonnegut's work, therefore, reads more like Whitman's newspaper articles and stories of political failure and corruption than it does like Whitman's "Preface to the Leaves of Grass" or "Leaves of Grass" itself with its idealization of democracy and the promise of America. "Stories about what a nation has been and should try to be are not attempts at accurate representation, but rather attempts to forge a moral identity," as Richard Rorty so astutely observes (13). His remark is as true for Vonnegut's fiction as for Whitman's poetry or Abraham Lincoln's addresses.

My discussion of Vonnegut's imagining being an American owes much to dozens of scholars upon whose work I have relied. I have attempted to take into account most of the previous scholarship on Vonnegut, while contributing to the ongoing discussion of his fiction. To better elucidate the complex world of Vonnegut's novels, I deliberately employ a variety of approaches, including literary criticism, biography, and other disciplines where I thought they would clarify his work. As a matter of deliberate choice, however, this study is a *reading of* Vonnegut's novels rather than a *theorizing about* them. While I have not hesitated to use critical theory where applicable, especially in discussing *Breakfast of Champions*, like most critics writing on Vonnegut, I have found biography, history, psychology, art criticism, and so forth more immediately useful. I strongly prefer conclusions inductively arrived at in reading both literature and criticism rather than deductively dictated. I agree with J. Hillis Miller that "A theory is all too easy to refute or deny, but a reading can be controverted only by going through the difficult task of rereading the work in question and proposing an alternative reading" (21). And that is the goal of *Imagining Being an American*: to send us all back to read and reread Vonnegut's novels. His novels are, therefore, both the occasions for this study and its end. I hope this book will appeal both to long-time and to first time readers of Vonnegut as well as to my fellow Vonnegut scholars.

Kurt Vonnegut began his writing career at the top of his trade with impressive early sales of short stories to the high-paying popular slick magazines.[3] From 1950 to 1963, or for about one-quarter of his long, prolific fiction-writing career, he published over forty stories in a variety of magazines, including *Collier's*, *Saturday Evening Post*, *Cosmopolitan*, *Redbook*, *Galaxy Science Fiction*, and the *Magazine of Fantasy and Science Fiction*. He first collected a dozen stories in *Canary in a Cat House* (1961). Later, well after he stopped writing short stories, he reprinted eleven of the original twelve and added another dozen for a total of twenty-three and published the collection as *Welcome to the Monkey House* (1968).[4] After 1963, Vonnegut concentrated his energies on writing novels, occasional pieces, and reviews.[5] Peter J. Reed in *The Short Fiction of Kurt Vonnegut* (1997) focuses on the short stories, public speeches, reviews, and essays. In his authoritative final chapter, "The Short Fiction and the Canon," he deploys his considerable knowledge of the Vonnegut *oeuvre* concluding that "[t]he short fiction remains complementary to the earlier novels much as the short *non*fiction, in essays, speeches and collections, complements the later novels. They are an essential part of Vonnegut's extraordinarily versatile literary creativity, and arguably more central to it than his ventures into drama, poetry, libretto and requiem" (154). Vonnegut himself is not so charitable. He says that "My own stories may be interesting . . . as relics from a time, before there was television, when an author might support a family by writing stories that satisfied uncritical readers of magazines, and earning thereby enough free time in which to write serious novels" (*Bagombo Snuff Box* 3). The stories remain Vonnegut's apprentice work and, therefore, will not be discussed here.[6]

As a professional writer, Vonnegut has experienced both extremes of the reception spectrum. For the first twenty years of his career he suffered obscurity and neglect then almost overnight enjoyed celebrity and wealth. Either obscurity or fame is familiar to many American writers, but rarely, if ever, do they occur to the same writer as dramatically as they have to Vonnegut. Vonnegut used his fame to further the public good in becoming a spokesperson of conscience speaking out against "show biz wars," racism, amoral profiteering, drug abuse, meaningless work, and public, corporate, and private abuses of power. (He also on occasion used his fame for private profit in doing advertisements.) At the same time, he has consistently advocated investing in the future of the planet, practicing individual decency, and recognizing the necessity of establishing a viable human community. He has done so with almost unfailing good humor and a surprising amount of grace. His career now spans fifty years and clearly warrants the kind of serious extended criticism he now enjoys.

Although Vonnegut's fiction before *Slaughterhouse-Five* was ignored, denigrated, and chastised by reviewers and a few essayists, he was fortunate in having some critics who early on appraised his work in book-length studies. These were almost uniformly favorable, such as the mostly introductory books by Richard Giannone, Jerome Klinkowitz, James Lundquist, Clark Mayo, Donald E. Morse, Peter J. Reed, Stanley Schatt, and John Somer. At the same time superb individual essays or chapters in books were published by Kathryn Hume, Robert Merrill, John Irving, Leslie A. Fiedler, and Robert Scholes. Many of these have been collected and published together with reviews and sometimes interviews. Leonard Mustazza's *The Critical Response to Kurt Vonnegut* (1994) has proven the most useful and certainly the most complete of these compendiums. Mustazza brings together forty years of scattered reviews and articles grouping them by novel. His work supercedes Robert Merrill's *Critical Essays on Kurt Vonnegut* (1990). In that earlier compilation, a majority of the essays and all of the reviews were reprinted from mostly still accessible newspapers, magazines, and scholarly journals. Merrill's introduction did, however, provide a thorough and much-needed chronological review of Vonnegut scholarship from its beginnings through 1988.

Besides collections of reviews and essays, readers of Vonnegut's novels now have the distinct advantage of Marc Leeds's comprehensive *The Vonnegut Encyclopedia: An Authorized Compendium* (1995) and William Rodney Allen, *Conversations with Kurt Vonnegut* (1988). Leeds's impressive volume—an obvious labor of love and homage to Vonnegut and his works—combines an encyclopedia of every named character, institution, place, and most frequently appearing images with a concordance. The references include all the fiction and nonfiction through *Hocus Pocus* (1990) and *Fates Worse Than Death* (1991). A prolific interviewee, Vonnegut's interviews have appeared on film, radio, and television, in newspapers, magazines, and scholarly journals, and Allen conveniently collects many, including substantial ones by David Standish, Robert Scholes, Charlie Rielly, and Robert Musil.[7]

In contrast to the earlier criticism of Vonnegut's work, more recent full-length studies by Kevin Alexander Boon, Mustazza, and Lawrence R. Broer have begun the process of insightfully reading Vonnegut's work in light of a compelling thesis. Boon's *Chaos Theory and the Interpretation of Literary Texts: The Case of Kurt Vonnegut* (1997) explores the body of Vonnegut's fiction in light of chaos theory. According to chaos theory, we cannot predict *when* any event may occur but we can predict *that* it will occur. Billy Pilgrim, for instance, cannot predict when he will come unstuck in time, "he only knows that at some point he will inevitably be uprooted from a particular moment in time and thrust into another without warning" (Boon 96). Boon concludes that human beings in Vonnegut's novels are necessarily "boundary creatures, [and therefore] both order and chaos are necessary in order for life to continue" (169). Life becomes "both determinate and indeterminate" (96)—as exemplified perhaps most clearly by Billy Pilgrim's coming unstuck in time and by Kilgore Trout becoming a timequake victim. Boon contends that "Vonnegut is a story teller in the scientific age—a post-Nietschean, post-Einsteinian sage writing in a time of long-dead Gods and inhumane science" (168). As Vonnegut himself describes in some detail in "How I Lost My Innocence" (*Palm Sunday* 69–70), science became tainted, lost its innocence, and became part of the problem once the atomic bomb was used against civilian populations. No longer could science be seen as the solution to all problems, as has so often been maintained in science fiction and in much of twentieth-century science. "For Vonnegut, things cannot be nailed down no matter what kind of hammer you use" (Boon 24). Vonnegut's work, therefore, "is complex because it describes a world that is complex, a world where systems stabilize and destabilize unpredictably, yet with certainty" (24). Characters must fail when believing that they have discovered a real purpose (for instance, Constant in *The Sirens of Titan*, 1959), or found the key to understanding the universe (Bokonon, for example, in *Cat's Cradle*, 1963), or invented a system for predicting events (as O'Looney does in *Jailbird*, 1979).

One of Boon's important contributions to the discussion of Vonnegut's works lies in his going beyond the usual debate over the roles of free will and determinism in the novels as, perhaps, most clearly exemplified in the work of the late Tony Tanner. Chaos theory offers "a fresh theoretical frame which explains how both [free will and determinism] can exist without the apparent contradiction," Boon claims (28). "Chaos is not the obliteration of natural order" but rather artificial systems of order become "the obliteration of natural chaos" (47). " 'Man created the checkerboard; God created the *karass*,' " boasted *The*

Books of Bokonon (*Cat's Cradle* 12). The *karass*, a group of people of no clearly defined form, is a fractal reflecting natural chaos such as that found in tornadoes, earthquakes, or volcanic eruptions. Vonnegut has always been suspicious of all systems of whatever kind, preferring natural chaos to human creations of order. "Let others bring order to chaos. I would bring chaos to order," boasts the narrator of *Breakfast of Champions* (1973, 210). But the world prefers order. Therefore, as Boon points out, "[m]arginal characters are the focus of Vonnegut's fiction" (97).

Typically, the "Vonnegut protagonist has had a troubled childhood [and] . . . irresponsible parents," rightly contends Mustazza (157) in his chronological study of Vonnegut's novels, *Forever Pursuing Genesis: The Myth of Eden in the Novels of Kurt Vonnegut* (1990). He develops the viable thesis that the novels through *Bluebeard* (1987) portray a loss of innocence while pointing to the paradox of "the cause of human suffering . . . [as] . . . [what] most . . . [people] consider the cause of human greatness . . . our own inventiveness" (169). But as most of us discover about ourselves and about others—as well as about societies and cultures—our strengths are our weaknesses. Vonnegut understands this truth as may be seen in several novels, such as *Galápagos* (1985), *Hocus Pocus* (1990), and *Timequake* (1997)—the last two appeared after Mustazza's book. Mustazza places Vonnegut within a tradition of the novel or literary work of ideas where familiar propositions are challenged. "What good is free will, Vonnegut suggests, if it makes only for death?" (122).[8] His central thesis—one that Boon refined further—is that Vonnegut's fictional world is a fallen world "in which human beings are essentially slaves to forces they cannot . . . control" (23).

In *Sanity Plea: Schizophrenia in the Novels of Kurt Vonnegut* (1989, revised edition 1994) Broer maintains that each Vonnegut novel deals with schizophrenia in characters, plot, and/or theme. Although he has read widely in contemporary social and literary criticism, he often cuts Vonnegut's novels to fit his thesis.[9]

The state of Vonnegut criticism at the turn of the century could be gauged by three books: *The Vonnegut Chronicles* (1996) edited by Reed and Leeds, *Kurt Vonnegut: Images and Representations* edited by Leeds and Reed (2000), and Klinkowitz, *Vonnegut in Fact: The Public Spokesmanship of Personal Fiction* (1998).[10] All three reflect Vonnegut's growing international reputation as novelist and commentator as they do his increasing importance as a public spokesperson, his continued dedication to painting, and various film directors' growing interest in adapting his novels. Vonnegut once remarked "that public speaking is almost the only way a poet or a novelist or a playwright can have any political effectiveness in his creative prime" (*Wampeters, Foma & Granfalloons* xvi). One of America's best public spokespersons for humane values, his clear-headed discussion of complex issues reminds his audiences again and again of the fragility and the sacredness of human beings and of their considerable foolishness. Much of the power of what Vonnegut says derives from his naïf pose as a speaker who sees familiar things directly and freshly—a technique borrowed from his fiction. For instance, Vonnegut in his "Palm

Sunday Sermon" examines Jesus's often quoted—and misquoted—statement about the poor that "you always have with you." Jesus is making a joke, claims Vonnegut. He is saying "about what Mark Twain or Abraham Lincoln would have said under similar circumstances"—when tired, foreseeing great pain, and exasperated by the phoniness of someone like Judas. So Jesus turns to Judas and says, in Vonnegut's refreshing translation of the Aramaic seen through the New Testament Greek: " 'Judas, don't worry about it. There will still be plenty of poor people left long after I'm gone' " (*Palm Sunday* 1981, 328–29). This, Vonnegut hastens to explain, becomes the equivalent of "a divine black joke," describing the circumstances exactly saying much about the pretenses of piety and nothing at all about the poor (329). Simple, brilliant, to the point, and—I suspect for those in Vonnegut's immediate audience—an unforgettably etched phrase. Such nuggets are buried in all the best of Vonnegut's public addresses.

Vonnegut's claim on critical and scholarly attention remains significant. All of his books continue in print—a most remarkable phenomenon at a time when publishers look for the instant best-seller and reluctantly maintain skimpy backlists or none. The steady sales of his novels and collections of stories and essays attest again and again to his continued popularity as writer and as public figure. In addition, he has received significant honors including numerous honorary doctorates, election to the American Academy of Arts and Letters, and been chosen as New York State Author for 2001–2003. Now, fifty years after his first publication as a fiction writer, he appears, in part, to have found and, in large measure, to have created the audience he deserves. "Why is Vonnegut an excellent writer?" asks John Mills. His answer points to that special attribute readers identify in Vonnegut's best work: "Because he displays that quality Sir Philip Sydney called *energia*—a total involvement of the imagination with the material whose by-product is a series of delightful inventions expressed with a kind of nonchalant grace" (149–50). Each of his inventions focuses on imagining being an American.

ACKNOWLEDGMENTS

This book has been a long time in the making and I owe several friends a considerable debt for their generosity over the years. I wish to thank Ed Marman, Robert Adolph, and Csilla Bertha who generously read and commented on earlier drafts. Each made invaluable suggestions for improvement. I have benefited greatly from numerous conversations about Vonnegut's fiction with the Hungarian scholar, Zoltán Abádi-Nagy who, in his capacity as editor of the *Hungarian Journal of English and American Studies*, has been both generous and rigorous. His interview with Vonnegut remains essential reading for anyone engaged with Vonnegut's work. I am also grateful for Len Mustazza's early encouragement and for Matthew Wolf-Myer's generous assistance.

My work was greatly facilitated by several librarians, those necessary angels of all scholarship. I wish to thank, especially, Barbara Somerville, Oakland University in Michigan, and her Inter-Library Department for providing extraordinary service over many months and thousands of miles. Grateful thanks also to Ilona Péter Kovácsné, English Department Librarian, University of Debrecen in Hungary, for innumerable helpful suggestions of books and journals; to Robert Gaylor, Reference Librarian, Oakland University, for confirming arcane facts, book titles, and review sources; and to Teréz Szabó, Associate Department Librarian, for generous assistance. Part of this study was generously funded by an Oakland University Faculty Research Fellowship that gave me several glorious months for research and writing.

Special thanks go once again to Kurt Vonnegut for giving generous permission for me to quote from all his published works and his unpublished letter to me and for supplying the painting, *Absolute Vonnegut*, while graciously granting me permission to reproduce it.

Finally, I wish to thank the several editors who read, criticized, and published earlier versions of various chapters in this book: Zoltán Abádi-Nagy, Martha Bartter, Jenö Bártos, Tamás Bényei, Kevin Alexander Boon, Berg Bowers, David Hartwell, Donald M. Hassler, Mária Kurdi, Rob Latham, Marc Leeds, R. Meiner, Agnés Péter, Peter Reed, Walter Rix, Péter Szaffkó, Roger Schlobin, W. A. Senior, C. W. Sullivan III, and Lehel Vadon as well as my permissions editor, Audrey Klein and copy editor Terri Jennings. Any errors remaining are my own.

I dedicate this book to my wife Csilla Bertha who wonderfully energizes my life and work.

NOTES

1. Like Hume, I am not writing for "the theorist who reads by means of Lacanian psychology or postcolonial formation in multiple subjectivities." I agree with her that such a person "is not a typical reader, and I am not trying to reproduce all those reading responses" (8). Also, I disagree with Carl Freedman, *Critical Theory and Science Fiction* (2000) that "the conjunction of critical theory and science fiction is not fortuitous but fundamental" (23). Freedman's assumption rests on an assertion that Marxism is "privileged" (8). Clearly he practices what Rorty calls the "nostalgic piety" of those who "still speak of themselves, for what seem to me purely sentimental reasons, as 'Marxists'" in so claiming such a "privileged" position for Marxism (Rorty 46). While most people would agree with Freedman that there is a significant problem in seeing "[e]xactly how the proletariat can seize control of the means of production when the latter are, to an ever-growing extent, organized on a transcontinental basis" (9), most would not view such seizure as either desirable or remotely possible. The democratic labor union movement, for example, would appear a far more viable way of conferring dignity on labor, while significantly advancing labor's economic interests. While I certainly do agree with Freedman that "Marxism is undergoing a certain crisis today" (8), I remain unconvinced by his argument that the various critical theories derived from Marxism remain immune from or untainted by that crisis. By specifically linking his discussion of science fiction literature to an anticipated revolution premised by Marxist utopian thinking—more nostalgic piety—Freedman completes his circular reasoning arriving back where he began with the claim that "Marx must inescapably be counted (if implicitly and even unconsciously) one of the major theorists of science fiction" (86). There is also the attendant difficulty of Freedman's employing the work of György

Lukács who had the highest praise for realistic novels while loathing nonrealistic fiction. One must sympathize with Freedman's problem when he allows as how "any use of Lukács's theory of realism in science-fiction criticism must proceed . . . indirectly" (46). Very indirectly, if at all, I would have thought. For a detailed examination of the weaknesses and strengths of Freedman's argument, see John Fekete's extensive review essay (especially 79, 85–86, 89–90, and 92). Of the many specific objections Fekete makes to Freedman's sweeping assumptions, none may prove more devastating than his observation that "at the level of literary criticism, Freedman has given himself unrestricted power to construct any text any way he likes" (89). For a review of Vonnegut criticism at the end of the twentieth century, see my "Bringing Chaos to Order." For full bibliographic information on citations, see the "Works Cited and Consulted" chapter in this book.

2. "In the four quarters of the globe, who reads an American book?" famously wrote Sydney Smith in the *Edinburgh Review* in 1820.

3. "By 1949 he [Vonnegut] had published more words than Norman Mailer, Saul Bellow, Grace Paley, or any other fiction writer his age" (Klinkowitz, "Essayist" 2).

4. In 1968 Vonnegut dropped "Hal Irwin's Magic Lamp" in favor of "EPICAC." For a discussion of Vonnegut's stories collected in *Welcome to the Monkey House*, see Morse, "Upbeat and Slick" in *Reader's Guide* (101–09).

5. Vonnegut did, however, write two additional stories on request. The first, "Welcome to the Monkey House" written on assignment from *Playboy* that also suggested borrowing the plot outline from the previously published novel, *The Sirens of Titan*, is reprinted as the title story in *Welcome to the Monkey House*. The second, which he noted would probably be his last short story, he wrote on assignment from Harlan Ellison for inclusion in his "Dangerous Visions" series (1971). Ten years later, it was reprinted in *Palm Sunday* (226–33). Vonnegut published no stories in 1959, 1965–1971, or from 1972 to the present.

6. "Looking back at them in the magazines in which they were originally published," Reed argues, "they often appear strikingly less dated than the advertisements and illustrations that decorate their pages" (*Short Fiction* 153). He bolstered his argument by gathering together the uncollected short fiction for Vonnegut to publish in *Bagombo Snuff Box* (1999). For a detailed review of Reed's book on Vonnegut's short fiction, see my "Repetition and Generalities." For a defense of the intrinsic worth of the short fiction, see Jeff Karon (105–17). I have also not discussed any of the film or television versions of Vonnegut's works for the simple reason that they are not works by Kurt Vonnegut. With the exception of George Roy Hill's direction of Stephen Geller's script for *Slaughterhouse-Five*, virtually all of the film and television productions fail even to approximate the unique qualities of Vonnegut's fictional worlds. For the best discussion thus far of the various film and television versions of Vonnegut's fictional works, see Boon and Pringle (167–96).

7. I have checked the text of all criticism and interviews as originally published, but have cited these and other collections of essays and interviews as more readily available to readers and scholars, except where the reprinted version contains serious errors or omissions.

8. He traces Vonnegut's elaboration of this dilemma through several novels but develops it at length in his discussion of *Breakfast of Champions* and *Slaughterhouse-Five*.

9. For example, in his chapter on *Cat's Cradle* Broer conspicuously ignores the end of the world—an event that dominates Vonnegut's novel and, if considered, might have led him to modify his argument. For a fuller examination of the limitations of the first and revised editions of Broer's book, see my review essay "Bringing Chaos to Order."

10. Since *At Millennium's End: New Essays on the Work of Kurt Vonnegut* edited by Kevin Alexander Boon appeared in 2001, while this book was in press, I regretfully could not make use of its several excellent essays except in a few content notes.

Introduction

We are healthy only to the extent that our ideas are humane.

—Kurt Vonnegut, *Breakfast of Champions* (16)

"Who . . . can be said to represent an age? Not the grandfathers or the children, but the middle generation" answered the literary historian Van Wyck Brooks at the beginning of the last half-century (115). It is precisely that generation that came of age in World War II that Kurt Vonnegut's novels speak to and about. Those who survived returned home, carried with them the memory of World War II and the Bomb, married high school sweethearts, started a career, and raised a family. That is *the* representative generation of twentieth-century Americans. As their writer, Vonnegut may well be *the* representative American writer of the latter half of the twentieth century. His novels reflect that generation's experience of the major traumatic private and public events that have gone into imagining the unending saga of being an American during the twentieth century. Those public events preeminently include the Great Depression, World War II, the invention and use of the atom bomb, the Vietnam War, and the weakening of social bonds and institutions after the 1960s. Equally representative private events include marrying, having a family, establishing a career, divorcing, remarrying, growing old, and experiencing loss. In between these two poles of the public and private, Vonnegut's novels also treat the particularly American brand of isolation and loneliness, the confrontation with internal rather than external evil in the prevalent question of means and ends, and the omnipresent suffering life inevitably brings. Like Ralph Waldo Emerson's writing, Vonnegut's assures us we are not alone. Like Henry David Thoreau at Walden Pond, he also reminds us that "the same questions that disturb and puzzle us have in their turn occurred to all the wise men; not one has been omitted" (75). Yet each question must be asked again by each new generation. Like Mark Twain, he casts a jaundiced eye on what his neighbors call "progress"—even when that progress is spectacular as in the achievements of the space program. The *Chicago Tribune* book critic Joseph Coates summarized many of Vonnegut's best qualities when comparing him to Twain:

Only a man so ready both to mock and enjoy the antics of his own and others' minds, and whatever they are capable of, could be less mad; and I am convinced once again that America has had no writer so cheerfully, entertainingly and less hectoringly sane—hence truly subversive—since Mark Twain. (4)

Like all significant American writers, Vonnegut, too, has imagined what it means to be an American—recalling the country's great promises and its equally great failures.

Among Vonnegut's major preoccupations perhaps the single, most obvious one is his undeviating ethical stance from *Player Piano* (1952) through *Timequake* (1997). "If there is a literary moralist writing today, it's Vonnegut," emphatically declares Loree Rackstraw ("Diviner" 53). And Kevin Alexander Boon predicts that "fifty years into the twenty-first century, when future scholars look back at Vonnegut's work, . . . they will certainly recognize him as [the] . . . conscience [of the post-nuclear twentieth century]" ("What to Do" ix). Vonnegut's ethically oriented fiction deals with important contemporary problems in American life thoughtfully and at length. If his attitude toward their solution remains skeptical, that does not negate the seriousness with which he addresses them. Arthur M. Saltzman once defended Vonnegut against the charge of taking important problems lightly. He concluded:

Whoever accuses Vonnegut of taking important problems lightly should be reminded of the platitudes his characters are forced to resort to—for example, "God damn it, you've got to be kind," in *God Bless You, Mr. Rosewater*, and the emphasis on the Sermon on the Mount in *Jailbird*—which are delivered in desperation by people who have nothing more substantial than outworn sentiments and clichés to cling to. One tends to envy that presumably less jaded audience of the past who may have been able to believe in such sentiments as viable alternatives. (101)[1]

The Irish philosopher, Richard Kearney, in the *Poetics of Imagining: Modern to Post-Modern*, identifies three main headings under which he believes "the ethical potential of narrative imagination may be summarized" (255). Vonnegut's novels fit well under each of Kearney's headings. "(1) The *testimonial* capacity to bear witness to a forgotten past; (2) the *empathic* capacity to identify with those different from us (victims and exemplars alike); and (3) the *critical-utopian* capacity to challenge official stories with unofficial or dissenting ones which open up alternative ways of being" (255). Each of Vonnegut's early novels through *Slaughterhouse-Five* (1969)—with the exception of *Player Piano*—does "bear witness to a forgotten past"—a past that official versions of the history of World War II wished to repress. *Slaughterhouse-Five*, in addition to reanimating a forgotten, buried past, also "open[s] up alternative ways of being" as illustrated in its introduction and Tralfamadorian sections. The intermediate or transitional novels from *Breakfast of Champions* (1973) through *Deadeye Dick* (1982) emphatically "identify with those different from us" (Kearney 252) whether they are in jail or out, active street people or passive pharmacists, exceptionally gifted intellectually or impoverished socially. *Player Piano* challenged the received wisdom that "the business of America is business" and, therefore, if businesses or international corporations do well enriching the top layer of society everyone below will benefit from the wealth as it trickles down. *Player Piano, God Bless You, Mr. Rosewater* (1965), *Jailbird* (1979), and *Hocus Pocus* (1990) all suggest how false this notion is. *Timequake*, on the other hand, explicitly tackles the problem of meaningless work in Vonnegut's proposed constitutional amendment "*Article XXIX:* Every adult who needs it shall be given meaningful work to do, at a living wage" (152). The late novels from *Galápagos* (1985) through *Timequake* then go on to "challenge official stories with unofficial or dissenting ones which open up alternative ways of being" (Kearney 255), whether those "official stories" boast of the progress of human evolution, the value of twentieth-century art, the United States' successful extrication from Vietnam, the value and use of the Information Highway, or the illusion of immortality.

Vonnegut's fiction, overtly ethical in its treatment of the great moral, social, and political issues of his time, attacks genocide, racism, and the destruction of nature; defends first amendment rights and the sacredness of all life; advocates viable forms of human community; and accepts inevitable loss. His heroes and role models are Abraham Lincoln, Eugene Debs, and Jesus of Nazareth. His novels, because of their consistent ethical stance, may be usefully viewed as the kind of stories that Richard Rorty describes as "[s]tories about what a nation has been and should try to be." Such stories "are not attempts at accurate representation, but rather attempts to forge a moral identity" (13). In imagining being an American, Vonnegut has forged a moral identity composed of a mosaic of bits and pieces of experience and history, such as witnessing the Dresden massacre and taking seriously Eugene Debs's clarion call to arms to end poverty. Like Rorty, Vonnegut, too, believes that democratic institutions can serve social justice (Rorty 36). In recalling the greatness of President Lincoln and social activist Debs as moral touchstones for political and social action, Vonnegut performs a useful public service. Rorty contends that "it would be a big help to American efforts for social justice if each new generation were able to think of itself as participating in a movement which has lasted for more than a century, and has served human liberty well. . . . Each new generation . . . should be able to see, as Whitman and Dewey did, the struggle for social justice as central to their country's moral identity" (51). Vonnegut is intricately bound up in that struggle.

If Kathryn Hume is right and "[t]he current generation of American writers—from 1960 into the 1990s—can usefully be characterized as the Generation of the Lost Dream" (*Dream* 292) in part because they "intuit no grand answer" and "most of the writers of this generation no longer feel that they can dream for the whole nation," then Vonnegut stands somewhat apart. Although disillusioned, he tenaciously clings to his dream of a better society, with a genuine culture and a real community. In doing so, he offers alternatives for American society in the twenty-first century. Unlike many of his contemporary fellow novelists, Vonnegut is—to borrow Rorty's terms—no *spectator* but an *agent* for change. As such, he has greater affinity with not only nineteenth-century but also early twentieth-century American novelists and intellectuals than he does with most of his nihilistic contemporaries. Rorty maintains, I believe correctly:

The difference between early twentieth-century intellectuals and the majority of their contemporary counterparts is the difference between agents and spectators. In the early decades of this century, when an intellectual stepped back from his or her country's history and looked at it through skeptical eyes, the chances were that he or she was about to propose a new political initiative. (9)

Vonnegut does propose new political and social initiatives in his novels and that certainly sets him apart from the vast majority of late twentieth-century science fiction writers. "The only social change presented by most SF has been toward authoritarianism," argues Ursula K. Le Guin. She continues her indictment by pointing to a prominent science fiction motif of "the domination of ignorant masses by a powerful elite—sometimes presented as a warning, but often quite complacently. Socialism is never considered as an alternative, and democracy is forgotten. Military values are taken for ethical ones. Wealth is assumed to be a righteous goal and a personal virtue" ("American SF" 95). Vonnegut's science fiction—like all his novels—is a clear exception to her description. From *Player Piano* to *Timequake*—as well as in all his public speeches, most of his reviews, and in his autobiographical writing—Vonnegut consistently and continually argues against authoritarianism and in favor of democracy, against military values and in favor of individual freedom, against imparting virtue to the accident of wealth and in favor of radically altering the conditions of the poor. As an active agent for change, he proposes new political initiatives that culminate in *Timequake*'s proposed two constitutional amendments and in the utopian possibility of community and genuine work, celebration and love represented by Xanadu, the ideal writers' retreat.[2]

A second related, but still-distinct, characteristic of Vonnegut's novels lies in their preoccupation with relations between people and machines.[3] Like Lewis Mumford before him, Vonnegut "has never had any use for this nineteenth-century dream of a liberation of mankind by mechanical invention, for the values that count for him are inner values; and he well knew that the planet on which we live may become an extermination-camp at any moment" (quoted in Brooks 146). Technology remains important for Vonnegut especially in its potential for abuse, but far more important for him is the seminal question "What are human beings for?" A partial, if negative, answer given in novel after novel is that human beings should not serve, emulate, or worship machines but instead strive to create a viable human community. Behind Dwayne Hoover's maniacal murderous spree in *Breakfast of Champions*, for instance, lay his faulty assumption that everyone in the world was a machine except for himself. A truly mad presupposition, yet one closely allied to any of the myriad of racist beliefs that led to many of the terrible twentieth-century massacres. In a less extreme form, however, Hoover's view corresponds to what Vonnegut in *Slapstick* calls "the American machine" with its human "interchangeable parts" (7). And this leads to a third characteristic of much of Vonnegut's fiction: that it is rooted in anthropological methods.[4]

"[A]ll of Vonnegut's works are anthropology theses—or more precisely, drafts of a single one, which has not yet reached a hopeful conclusion," judged James Whitlark a few years before the publication of *Timequake* (85). Anthropology and especially anthropology as taught at the University of Chicago when Vonnegut attended, figures distinctly and directly in several novels. "Anthropology taught him about kinship groups and about how people without writing depended on memory for their information. In *Breakfast of Champions*, he links memory and kinship," Hume maintains (*Dream* 260).[5] Three years later, with the publication of *Slapstick* (1976), "Vonnegut was still chewing on this notion that extended family could be a solution to our rootless and emotionally numb existence" (Hume, *Dream* 261). Vonnegut remains one of the very few American writers who have addressed directly both in his fiction as well as in several of his public addresses this issue of radical mobility resulting in loneliness. "Vonnegut's solution has the advantage that it could be made available to everyone and is not invalidated by telephones, television, or drastic economic collapse. A simulacrum of an extended family may, for many, be better than no family at all. As a thought experiment, at least, it is interesting, if only semiserious" (Hume, *Dream* 262). While *Slapstick* proposes a national solution to the problem, *Timequake* offers a more local one and, perhaps, ultimately a more viable one in Xanadu, the utopian writing colony in Rhode Island.

"One feels a powerful impact of vision and soul. . . . We feel his presence as an author," wrote James Wood, reviewing *Fates Worse Than Death* (9). Peter J. Reed, among others, testifies that "[e]ven where the authorial voice is not heard, the author's presence is felt and his attitudes are frequently conspicuous" ("Lonesome" 120). Intimacy noticeably characterizes Vonnegut's fiction. Readers know and identify with Kurt Vonnegut the author of these novels and in this, as in so much else, he is truly the Emersonian writer. Wood perceptively compares the two: "The more Vonnegut writes, the more American he seems—a kind of de-solemnized Emerson, at once arguer, doubter, sermonizer and gossip. . . . Like that other great essayist, Vonnegut's prose seems radically accountable: a man lives behind it" (9). That de-solemnized feeling derives in large measure from his sense of humor. A sense of humor that is at once self-deprecating and borders often on sentimentality, but that continually enables a listener to come up smiling after a pratfall. "Jokes . . . are a minor art form," rightly claims Vonnegut (*Playboy* 91). Tears, like laughter proves a legitimate answer to being frustrated or exhausted, to being in a state where both thinking and striving appear futile. Laughter also has an added advantage over crying in that it takes far less time to recover from laughter so a person is able to begin reasoning and getting on with life.

Like many other American novelists of the latter half of the twentieth century, there is a noticeable absence of children as characters in Vonnegut's fiction unlike in his autobiographical works and public addresses, which are brimful of references to his family and, especially, to his children. With the exception of *Timequake*, his novels for the most part are marked by silence about his children and the only references to children as characters are to disastrous parent-child relations and calamitous child-rearing practices. This lack reflects—at least in some part—not just Vonnegut's choices in writing but also the over-arching central trauma of the twentieth century. Van Wyck Brooks, writing in 1953, described what became Vonnegut's experience of the world as reflected in all his fiction:

There has never been an age that moved so swiftly from summer into winter,—or from what appeared to be summer,—as the age we have lived through the "century of the child," as Ellen Key called it in its hopeful opening years that turned into the century of Moloch, the eater of children. (159)[6]

Finally, within Vonnegut's fiction there is a noticeable shift from the early novels' terrible pessimism to the relative optimism of *Galápagos* and *Bluebeard* (1987) through to the acceptance of a life lived with loss in *Timequake*. John Irving is surely right that Vonnegut's clarity is indeed "brave work" in a domain where muddy thinking often passes for profundity (214), and David Andrews warns that his "verbal clarity entails neither compositional nor intellectual simplicity" (42). This becomes especially pertinent as Vonnegut moves to that most necessary, if terribly difficult, position of accepting late in life what has been and what must be.

If adolescents must establish their personalities and begin a life's work, while those in mid-life evaluate what they have accomplished or failed to accomplish, then those at the end of life face the urgent tasks first of accepting life as already lived and second of facing the inevitable, approaching end. Those elderly unable to accept the life they have lived may become withdrawn, bitter, despairing. Those able to accept their life, on the other hand, often become serene. For many, such acceptance can be extremely difficult and—for someone with Vonnegut's biography—could easily have been impossible. Frank McConnell places Vonnegut's style within that acceptance of what is:

Wounded and saddened by the chaos of his age, Vonnegut retreats to *fiction*. . . . His simplicities are disingenuous simplicities, and all the more affecting for that, since they are chosen and ferociously held *precisely* to make a separate peace with a disgusting century. . . . [F]rivolity in his tales . . . is precisely the strong moral point of the work. It is a frivolity *chosen* . . . because any attempt to confront the unspeakable in terms of conventional "moral seriousness" is foredoomed to trivialize the enormity of horror by its very pretence to "explaining." (208–09)

Although McConnell was speaking mostly of *Slaughterhouse-Five* and the early novels, his discussion of frivolity as a response to horror applies equally well, if not more so, to *Timequake* and the last novels. One of the most attractive features of *Timequake*—besides the omnipresent Vonnegut humor—is Vonnegut's acceptance of the life he has lived with all its pain, dread, vagaries, and losses. In this acceptance may be found most of the enumerated characteristics of Vonnegut's fiction: its intimacy, emphasis on what it means to be human, the importance of community and family, the necessity for courtesy, and the importance of ethical behavior. Kilgore Trout's healing mantra serves as the watchword not only for this last novel but also for all of Vonnegut's novels, "You were sick, but now you're well again, and there's work to do" (*Timequake* 169). Moreover, for only the second time in a Vonnegut novel a daughter of his appears as Lily participates in her class's production of Thornton Wilder's *Our Town*.[7]

Emerson suggested that Americans belong either to the party of hope or the party of memory. Clearly Vonnegut belongs to the party of hope, but hope restricted to this world. Like Lewis Mumford, he believes "It is better to face chaos courageously than to cherish the dream of returning to an outworn synthesis" (quoted in Brooks 134). Vonnegut's writing loudly proclaims that we humans are alone on Earth, that no transcendent or extra-galactic force will intervene to save us from our own folly—not even from our own cheapness when faced with self-induced ecological catastrophe. Yet, his novels also reflect the party of hope's belief that individuals do make a difference, that society, while never advancing, can nevertheless be changed for the better, that the job of imagining, then creating America must of necessity remain forever unfinished yet at the same time must be reimagined, recreated by each individual in each generation. Ideals such as a viable human community, courtesy, creativity, caring, are goals not to be achieved but to be aimed at. For Vonnegut, there is little to be gained in denial, in proclaiming the futility of reform, or abandoning ideals. He stands with Eugene V. Debs of Terre Haute, Indiana and with Abraham Lincoln of Illinios—both from the Midwest and both of the party of hope (*Bagombo* 292). Having been the canary in the coal mine warning of poisons in the national atmosphere, then becoming the gadfly on the body politic, Vonnegut ends his career as a novelist where Walt Whitman ended his as a poet, John Dewey his as a philosopher, Emerson his as a prophet, and Thoreau his as a meditator-mediator: Like each of his American writer-predecessors, Vonnegut, too, affirms his role as the sojourner who observes, participates, reports.

"In going down into the secrets of his own mind, he has descended into the secrets of all minds," said Emerson speaking of the poet in his address, "The American Scholar" (64). Vonnegut shares Emerson's belief in the universality of our questions and feelings, while at the same time he does not insist on a universality of history or value. An American pragmatist, he again and again reminds us of the unfinished nature of America—"You were sick, but now you're well again, and there's work to do." Assuring us that we are not alone in our questioning, puzzlement, and pain, Vonnegut offers an alternative vision to John Winthrop's apotheosis of America as a City set on a Hill—isolated, alone—and to the United States as the post-Cold War enthusiasts' global hegemonic power. His more modest vision centers on a country populated by extended families whose citizens are committed to fulfilling the promise of meaningful work for all. Profit-driven, free-booting corporations, such as RAMJAC in *Jailbird*, would no longer control the country nor would it be patronizingly guided by wealthy, well-meaning philanthropists, such as Senator

Rosewater. Such a nation would not be characterized by self-aggrandizement—whether in war or in love affairs—but would be pervaded by courtesy. A world not erased by television, but one animated by playful art where children put on plays to amuse their parents and friends rather than going on crusades to save the world. Although this would be a world where people must work to prevent massacres from occurring, life itself would still come to a natural end in "plain old death" (*Slaughterhouse-Five* 4). In Vonnegut's novels, the ripe fruit does fall,[8] loss becomes terribly real and omnipresent, but equally real is that most wonderful of all human qualities: human awareness that comes into existence "only because there are human beings" (*Timequake* 213).[9] Finally, as Vonnegut imagines being an American, the alternative world he envisions in his novels is one where the best and the brightest are remembered and revered as are Lincoln and Debs in his novels. A democratic world of radical equality and no special pleading—where Lincoln and Debs are at one with Laurel and Hardy and where, if there must be original sin, then it is balanced out by "original virtue" (*Timequake* 211)—a transient world at once both forever mysterious and forever new. "Imagine being an American."

NOTES

1. Saltzman's perceptive essay contrasts *Slaughterhouse-Five* with *War and Peace*. He concludes that each novel exhibits strengths possible only in their respective times and places. "I do not doubt . . . that Vonnegut envies Tolstoy his confidence in his convictions; the point is, modern technological warfare is even more devastating and dehumanizing than its nineteenth-century equivalent, and its fictional products, Billy Pilgrim and Heller's Yossarian, approximate the consequences of modern warfare better than Tolstoy's Pierre and Prince Andrew could" (97).

2. Vonnegut borrowed the name of the ideal writers' retreat from the opening lines of Coleridge's poem "Kubla Kahn." Those two lines Vonnegut says are the two best lines in poetry in English. "In Xanadu did Kubla Kahn / A stately pleasure-dome decree" (Coleridge 255).

3. As John J. Pierce points out "Dehumanization through the overdependence [sic] on technology had been a theme in anti-utopian science fiction since Forster's 'The Machine Stops' " (177).

4. The University of Chicago rejected an early version of *Cat's Cradle* as his thesis in anthropology but then much later that same university awarded him a master's degree for the published novel.

5. Hume then gives an elaborate analysis of Cyprian Ukwende and Eddie Key (two characters in *Breakfast of Champions*) who know both by name and at least by some anecdote or a scrap of history some 600 living relatives (Ukwende) or ancestors (Key). The result is that they are "able to have deep, nourishing feelings about [strangers and those outside their family]" (*Breakfast of Champions* 271).

6. As part of her examination of traditional values and themes missing from late twentieth-century American novels, Hume discusses various novelists' treatment of children under the provocative sub-heading "Where Are the Children?" (268–71).

7. See *Slaughterhouse-Five* (11–12, 18). Vonnegut's children are mentioned in *Timequake*'s opening paragraph that echoes the beginning of *Cat's Cradle* (and that, in turn, echoes the opening line of *Moby-Dick*). His children also are mentioned in the penultimate chapter as absent because they "had other fish to fry" (207). The point of the

clambake is not to honor Vonnegut, but his fiction and, therefore, since his and all children are absent from his fiction there would be no point in having them there. *Slapstick* describes briefly, but in detail, the idyllic childhood of Wilbur and Eliza whereas in *Timequake* Lily and her class figure as actual children studying and putting on their school play for their parents.

8. "Is there no change in paradise?" asked Wallace Stevens in "Sunday Morning." His answer was to question rhetorically whether ripe fruit ever falls from the trees in paradise.

9. Apparently, this represents Vonnegut's version of the Weak Enthropic Principle

2

Uttering Our Painful Secret

> Novel writing doesn't breed serenity.
> —Kurt Vonnegut

"Imagine being an American," Kurt Vonnegut exclaims not altogether ironically in *Fates Worse Than Death* (131) and as if in wonder at all that the United States could be, as well as in mock horror at all it has become. I have taken liberties with this exclamation shifting the focus from *imagine* being an American—that is, being a privileged citizen of the richest, most powerful nation on Earth where the accident of birth confers seemingly unlimited possibilities for life—to *imagining* being an American—that is, actively participating in the unfinished tasks of building a culture, creating a literature, fashioning a country. Vonnegut's novels focus on such ongoing tasks so familiar to readers of American literature. Almost alone among contemporary American writers, Vonnegut, like Mark Twain before him, attracts a remarkably wide range of readers from old to young, academic to popular, technologically sophisticated to naïve. His novels serve an impressive range of purposes—social commentary, philosophical and theological discourse, ethical argument, parody, satire, prophecy—all focusing on what it means to be an American living in the United States in the second half of the twentieth century.

A preeminent American storyteller with a sharply critical, satiric vision, Vonnegut may be seen—as I have argued—as *the* representative American writer of the latter half of the twentieth century in that the concerns articulated in his writing are the great moral, social, and political issues of his time, such as genocide, racism, the destruction of nature, endangered first amendment rights, the need for human community, and the sacredness of all life. When asked what in the world was really sacred, Bokonon, Vonnegut's ingenious religious teacher in *Cat's Cradle* (1963), replies: "Man . . . That's all" (143). Did any other public figure, for instance, in 1986 speak up for the child killed during the American air raid on Libya? Typically, it was Vonnegut who challenged the Pharisaical

Christians, such as Jerry Falwell who proudly quote biblical verses that "make murder acceptable" to justify the slaying of Qaddaifi's baby daughter. Vonnegut himself offers as his explanation that "the little girl, by allowing herself to be adopted by a dark-skinned Muslim absolutely nobody watching American television could love, in effect committed suicide" (*Fates Worse Than Death* 161–62). But Falwell and his followers remained silent, as did the vast majority of Americans most of whom were probably ignorant that any moral issue might be involved beyond the United States superior firepower. Again and again in his writing, public speeches, and novels Vonnegut, however, insists on raising such embarrassing issues about questionable means used to effect unclear ends as in this example where both means and ends prove upon reflection morally and ethically doubtful.[1] Vonnegut "rejects cant, imposed solutions, and utopias without rejecting a hope for justice," as R. B. Gill observes (86).

In October 1987, when Vonnegut published *Bluebeard*, his twelfth novel in thirty-five years, he listed fifteen of his other seventeen published books opposite the title page, after which he exclaimed: "Enough! Enough!" Ten years later he labels *Timequake* his final novel (xiv) and goes on to record his leave-taking of writing. So *Timequake*, that bittersweet melange of reminiscence, fiction, and opinion may be read as Vonnegut's valedictory, as more than one reviewer and interviewer astutely observed. In a less prolific, less tireless writer such statements might clearly imply he was ready to call it quits back in 1987 having reached the traditional retirement age of sixty-five and having survived as a professional writer longer than most of his generation. But with Vonnegut one should never bet on him following such traditional actions. In the decade after *Bluebeard*, he produced two more novels, *Hocus Pocus* and *Timequake*, along with another autobiographical collage, *Fates Worse Than Death*. During this same fertile period, in addition to the books, he wrote numerous uncollected reviews, essays, speeches, commencement addresses, a liturgical mass, and gave and rewrote several interviews. His wife, Jill Krementz, remained skeptical about the various announcements that accompanied *Timequake's* publication—such as "Let someone else write the books" (Stone 78) or "I've been able to say everything I possibly could say" (Siegel, "Interview"). "I don't believe for a moment that he's giving up writing," she asserted (quoted in Stone 80). Time will tell. Other novelists have published well into their eighties and some into their nineties. So Vonnegut may yet surprise himself and discover that he has not only more to say, but that in *Timequake* he found a new form, a kind of hybrid mixture of biography, opinion, and fiction, which would allow him to continue entertaining and teaching through writing.

Vonnegut's serious writing begins in 1952 with *Player Piano*, a satiric look at a future where automation takes over the world, leaving no room for human creativity or responsibility. From that beginning, he moves through a series of highly original creations in *The Sirens of Titan* (1959), *Mother Night* (1961), *Cat's Cradle* (1963), and *God Bless You, Mr. Rosewater* to *Slaughterhouse-Five*—his best-known novel. His next two novels proved crucial as transitional works: the comic masterpiece, *Breakfast of Champions* and the fantastic autobiography, *Slapstick*. The six novels that follow these two, while definitely recognizable as Vonnegut's, move into new imaginative territory. The Watergate novel, *Jailbird*, views that nadir in American political life not as an isolated phenomenon but as a kind of culmination of other gross violations of constitutional rights in, for example, turn-of-the-century labor warfare that included the Sacco and Vanzetti trial. *Deadeye Dick*'s 1982 tale of an American isolato continues in that tradition so well begun by Herman Melville in "Bartleby, the Scrivener." The joyful, imaginative *Galápagos* that he claims as his best novel (*Fates Worse Than Death* 131) presents a wry view of human beings a million years in the future against a backdrop of the best that has been thought and said by them. The hoax-autobiography, *Bluebeard*, on the other hand, completes the process of accepting the inexplicable begun in *Slaughterhouse-Five* by affirming both the value of unique individual experience and the value of all truly creative art. The narrator of *Hocus Pocus*, a Vietnam veteran now in jail, played the ignominious role of the last U.S. soldier to leave the American Embassy on the last helicopter out of Saigon. That novel confronts various American failures in education, foreign policy, and celebrity. *Timequake*, on the other hand, utilizes fluctuations in time—much as *Slapstick* earlier utilized fluctuations in gravity—to raise issues familiar from all the earlier novels, such as determination and free will, the nature of and basis for human community, the place and importance of imagination in culture. What is substantially different from previous novels, however, is *Timequake*'s recurring accent on accepting continuous, inevitable loss.

Besides his fiction, Vonnegut began publishing collections of his speeches, reviews, sermons, essays, interviews, and even advertising copy beginning in 1974 with *Wampeters, Foma & Granfalloons*. His second collection, *Palm Sunday: An Autobiographical Collage* (1981) stands out as an exceptionally entertaining and revealing contemporary autobiography by an American writer, using—in addition to published speeches, reviews, interviews—letters and other family writings. *Fates Worse Than Death*, a notably illuminating collection of musings, speeches, and insightful recollections of the 1980s, appeared ten years later. Vonnegut's play, *Happy Birthday, Wanda June* (produced 1970–1971), despite its problematic ending, received remarkably good reviews, ran for a respectable five months in New York, and has since enjoyed many university and college productions.

Like W. H. Auden who late in life returned to writing serious, light verse (which, paradoxically, perhaps only a mature poet can do well), Vonnegut late in his career turned to writing serious, varied, often innovative fiction—yet all with a surface lightness. He appears somewhat dazed by the volume of his later work: "I always thought, if I could ever get something down about Dresden, that would be *it*. After *Slaughterhouse-Five* I'd already done much more than I ever expected to with my life. Now, since I don't have to do anything any more, I've gotten more personal, freer to be idiosyncratic" (quoted in Amis 137). All true, but not at the price of sacrificing his trademark indignation at human stupidity, short-sightedness, and parsimony, especially as reflected in America's lost opportunities. Also continually present in his late novels is his alarm over the neglect of responsibilities, the denigration of imagination, and the disregard for community.

Vonnegut's dominant themes derive from his having experienced the major private and public traumatic events characteristic of twentieth-century Americans. Born in 1922 in Indianapolis, Indiana of German immigrant parents, he arrived just in time to feel the crushing effects of the Great American Depression. For many children born during, immediately before, or right after the Great Depression, their own experience, as well as the scars the Depression left on their parents, often marked them for life. The era caused a shift in the Vonnegut fortunes from quite well-to-do—where the children, for example, went to private schools and colleges, the family lived in a large residence with plenty of servants, and enjoyed the freedom to travel at will—to penury. "By 1930," Vonnegut mused, "it was obvious everything was gone and wasn't going to come back. I got pulled out of an elitist private school—that would be, third grade, I guess" ("Interview," Allen and Smith 270). So he attended first Public School No. 43 and then Shortridge High School in Indianapolis. A family historian testifies that the family finances became really difficult at about the same time as young Kurt entered adolescence. When he enrolled in Cornell University his father told him in no uncertain terms "to be a scientist or nothing" ("Serenity" 35, reprint 30).[2]

The Great American Depression and its aftermath left its imprint on Vonnegut's sensibility, prose style, sense of humor, and values. He several times has characterized himself as a child of the Great Depression. His early experience also appears to have led him to appreciate the value of comedy as a palliative in life: Jerome Klinkowitz believes that "the great popular comedians of the American 1930s gave Vonnegut the basis for his artistic style" ("Vonnegut in America" 11). In interviews and essays, Vonnegut extensively praised both comedians and jazz musicians who have provided him with far more consolation and food for thought than any number of contemporary novelists, poets, painters, philosophers, politicians, or preachers. Vonnegut believes that future historians "will congratulate us on very little other than our clowning and our jazz" (*Palm Sunday* 140). The long-term effect of the Great Depression on those he describes as the "last recognizable generation of full-time, life-time American novelists" was to make them "edgy and watchful" (*Palm Sunday* 1).

Of the second major national and international event in Vonnegut's life, World War II, he somewhat disingenuously claims it left him unchanged. What did change, however, was that he "became entitled to converse as a peer with other combat veterans of any army, of any war" (*Fates Worse Than Death* 156). Taken prisoner by the Germans during the Battle of the Bulge, Vonnegut had the extraordinary good fortune to survive the fire-bombing of Dresden as a prisoner of war. From *The Sirens of Titan* to *Bluebeard*, World War II and the role of the United States in it is never far from the surface of his fiction, while in *Mother Night* and especially in *Slaughterhouse-Five* that war lies at their very center. Paul Fussell, an historian of the two twentieth-century world wars, documents the uniqueness of *Slaughterhouse-Five* when read against silence—the almost universal response of Allied soldiers to the brutality, inhumanity, and repetitiveness of World War II. "So demoralizing was this repetition of the Great War within a generation that no one felt it appropriate to say much, either to understand the war or to explain it," he concludes (*Wartime* 132–33). American poet and critic, Karl Shapiro, speaking specifically of those writers such as Vonnegut and himself who had actually been in the World War II fighting, adds "We all came out of the same army and joined the same generation of silence" (quoted in Fussell, *Wartime* 134). "Kurt Vonnegut was of this group," continues Fussell. "When he returned from the war, he says, he wanted to tell everyone about the destruction of Dresden, which he had witnessed. . . . But found that it took him twenty-three years to overcome his urge to say nothing and to tell finally . . . what had happened in Dresden in 1945 and the way it had affected his own life" (134). When Vonnegut did finally break that silence with *Slaughterhouse-Five*, he brought the disquieting message that the United States was complicit in the destruction of an unarmed city and the massacre of thousands of civilians.

Other equally, if not more influential events for Vonnegut's fiction occurred in his family and domestic life. These include the deaths of his parents and sister, his marriage, fathering three of his own and three adopted children, eventual separation, divorce, ensuing remarriage, and beginning another family late in life. When he has assessed the relative importance of all these events on forming his character, he ranks the trauma of witnessing the devastation of Dresden below that of his mother's suicide, the adoption of his dead sister's children, the flight of his children away from home, and his divorce (*Palm Sunday* 301). While it is often difficult, if not impossible, to gauge the shock of such events in another person's life, because Vonnegut writes out of the events of his life, many of their consequences are observable in his works. He has also discussed many of them in interviews, essays, and the prefaces to his novels. Such consequences include his inability to write for a year after his father died and the difficulties and joys he experienced as a parent. Vonnegut adopted three of his sister Alice's four children after an unforgettable day of horrendous, tragic events where the train carrying his brother-in-law to work plunged into a river and his sister shortly after died of cancer (*Palm Sunday* 244).[3] Of these events perhaps the one with the greatest long-term consequences was the doubling in size of his family and the great increased responsibilities that brought with it. Clearly, Vonnegut is proud of all his children and delights in their various choices in life, and, in retrospect at least, looks with a certain pride at the notoriety they enjoyed growing up in West Barnstable, Massachusetts where it appears they had their own special policeman assigned to monitor their activities. Yet, no one went to jail and no one was busted for dope.

Of his separation and subsequent divorce Vonnegut is understandably discreet, yet surprisingly open. In interviews and essays he attempts to account for what happened, sometimes focusing on the shift in belief his first wife underwent that led her to practice a form of religion that he found intolerable (*Palm Sunday* 192–218). Other times he becomes painfully aware of the phenomenon of two people once close growing further and further apart as the years pass until, at last, there is little or no communication between them: Eventually, he chose to separate from Jane, his wife of twenty-five years. (They had known one another longer than that, having grown up together and been high school sweethearts.) "It does not hurt to be wounded . . . it hurts afterward," Vonnegut declared in an interview ("The Novelist"). If his separation and divorce was the wound, then clearly he hurt terribly afterwards, and what was even worse found he would receive neither support nor sympathy from his family. As only the second Vonnegut to get a divorce, he discovered that he had not only offended his relatives by the kind of books he chose to write, but also had compounded his offense by getting a divorce. These strong feelings, which he sums up in the confession "I am embarrassed" (*Palm Sunday* 71), or in the guilt-loaded phrase, "I await the police" (191), underlie, particularly, the narrative and characters in *Breakfast of Champions*, *Slapstick*, *Deadeye Dick*, and indirectly *Hocus Pocus*.[4] His work in the theater on *Happy Birthday, Wanda June* became part of his "running away from home" and his search for a viable community or family ("About This Play" vii–xvi).

His second marriage to the professional photographer, Jill Krementz, in 1979 and their adoption of their daughter Lily in 1982, may, on the other hand, underlie the joy of *Galápagos* and *Bluebeard* as well as the urgency with which he confronts public issues.[5] Clearly, Vonnegut has taken his own good advice to student writers: "Find a subject you care about and which you . . . feel others should care about. . . . [T]his genuine caring, . . . not your games with language, . . . will be the most compelling and seductive element in your style" (*Palm Sunday* 77). Not only did he take his own advice but he also followed it scrupulously.

One of the attractions Vonnegut's novels hold for most readers lies in their sensing the depth of feeling underlying all the good fun and jokes. Readers become convinced that behind the books there exists a real Kurt Vonnegut—a private human being with well-considered concerns, thoughts, and feelings about himself, his work, world, and friends. "In Vonnegut's fiction the distinctive manner includes the closeness of the author to his material and the intimacy he achieves with his reader through his personalized style. Even where the authorial voice is not heard, the author's presence is felt and his attitudes are frequently conspicuous" (Reed, "Lonesome" 120). This intimacy helps account both for Vonnegut's distinctive voice and the devotion of his readers. "He [Vonnegut] will go on being important to those for whom enthusiastic intimacy remains a plausible response to literature; he will continue to be denigrated by those for whom such a response is irrelevant" (Rampton 25). Drawing upon his experience and feelings, he writes novels about subjects he cares about with predominately two major themes: the difficulty or, perhaps, impossibility of coming to grips with the magnitude of evil and short-sightedness experienced in the modern world, and the necessity for establishing a viable human community in that fragmented world. The context Vonnegut provides for exploring both themes is drawn directly from his experience of growing up in Indianapolis, leaving it for college and the armed forces, and then finding himself somehow unable to return. Vonnegut and his sister Alice left Indianapolis after World War II.

And, of all the relatives we left behind, not one could think of a reason why we should come home again.

We didn't belong anywhere in particular any more. We were interchangeable parts in the American machine. (*Slapstick* 7)

Vonnegut believes loneliness in the United States occurs primarily because Americans lack relatives and friends. His family history is a case in point: both his father and grandfather "grew up in a huge extended family which is no more" ("Art of Fiction" 193). For Vonnegut, this loss remains crucial to late twentieth-century American experience and leads to a sense of instability and rootlessness. He returns to this subject in interview after interview. In a typical instance he laments that "people don't live in communities permanently anymore. But they should: Communities are very comforting to human beings" (*Playboy* 79).

Vonnegut's work thus reflects the isolation Americans experience living in their highly mobile, atomistic society. Alexis de Tocqueville remarked on this phenomenon over 150 years ago, when he wrote: "Democracy does not create strong attachments between man and man, but it does put their ordinary relations on an easier footing" (*Democracy in America*, quoted in Bellah 117). Vonnegut focuses on, however, not simply the ordinary relations of everyday social or political life in America. He also dwells on "the unbelievability of life as it really is" (*Palm Sunday* 297), especially in those difficult times when a person needs the kind of strong attachment which offers understanding, warmth, and comfort in order to be "lonesome no more."

Because he cares about his subjects, Vonnegut's books have an immediacy that often compels, yet he never preaches—not even in his most bitterly satiric novel, *Cat's Cradle*. That satire examines the human capacity for greed and duplicity, which leads inevitably to the destruction of the world. It takes as pessimistic a view of humankind as the Latin satirist Juvenal did in his Tenth Satire, "On Prayer."[6] Vonnegut, too, like Juvenal, satirizes the vanity of human wishes, but instead of Juvenal's laceration of human thick-wittedness, he quietly mourns its ubiquitous presence. Nor does he rely on Juvenal's invective and threat to carry his satire in *Cat's Cradle*. Instead, he employs jokes, parody, playful invention, and the fiction of an objective, if slightly puzzled narrator.

Given his reliance on humor and jokes—he several times described his novels as "mosaics of jokes"—Vonnegut more closely resembles that other great Latin satirist, Horace, who attempted "to tell the truth laughing," and for whom there were "no real knave[s] in his world," but only fools (Paulson 21). Although Vonnegut does tell the truth through laughter, and does see most villains as simply fools, unlike much of Horace he does not rely on *savoir faire*, urbanity, and understatement or make extensive use of false praise and irony. Nor are his moral and artistic values those of an urbane intellectual—such as Horace— whether of ancient Rome or contemporary New York, but instead are those of an unsophisticated American pragmatist. His voice is that of the Middle West with its essentially conservative outlook and beliefs. "I trust my own writing," he concedes, "when I sound most like a person from Indianapolis" (*Palm Sunday* 79). "The key to Kurt Vonnegut's genius, what indeed may have made him the foremost serious writer in America today, is his unique ability to fashion a work of art out of an ordinary middle-class life . . . when all he had to work with were the common experiences of his generation," concluded Klinkowitz ("Vonnegut in America" 33)[7] Despite his focus on "the noblest study of mankind," Vonnegut is no American Alexander Pope believing in reason as the keystone of human nature. From *Player Piano* to *Hocus Pocus*, human beings in his novels and stories appear motivated by everything *but* reason, and for ten years in *Timequake* they are completely bereft of reason, being totally determined without any shred of free will. In *Galápagos*, the narrator, from his perspective of a million years in the future, asserts that most of the problems on planet Earth have been caused by human beings having brains too big for their and everyone else's good. Evolution, therefore, steps in and over the next million years, helps the fittest, that is, the small-brained to survive. Whatever else they may be, human beings in Vonnegut's novels are neither portrayed as reasonable nor are they adept at reasoning.

Rather than emphasizing a clearly defined view of the world based upon reason, such as that shared by most people since the Enlightenment, Vonnegut emphasizes the uncertainty human beings experience. "No respecter of evidence has ever found the least clue as to what life is all about, and what people should do with it," he maintains (*Palm Sunday* 196). Nevertheless, he remains a moralist committed to humane values and perspectives who gives us a brilliant satiric portrait of his society with its failures and its negative values in the second half of the twentieth century. He does it not with Juvenalian invective and threat nor with Horacean laughter or Popean mock heroic deflation, but through carefully formed, often fantastic comic stories—a choice that places him in the company of such fantastic classic satirists as Lucian and Apuleius.

Lucian of Samosata, often credited with writing some of the first science-fiction stories, is generally acknowledged as one of the earliest fantasy writers who combined a marvelous literary invention with a fine comic sense and a keen satiric vision in order to criticize his society. In his most famous story, *Lucius, or The Ass*, he created an ideal narrator for his satire by adapting the folk tale of the man-in-an-ass's skin who becomes like the famous fly-on-the-wall: an invisible person before whom people will reveal their true values and beliefs, hiding nothing. Vonnegut in *Breakfast of Champions* invents a similar narrator who behind his mirror-sunglasses not only observes, but also claims to control events and characters. As creator of his fictional universe, he can foretell the future and tell fortunes, including the most amazing, if the most trivial events, such as who will succeed in obtaining radial tires for her car!—much as Swift earlier had his narrator in the "Bickerstaff Papers" issue similarly exact predictions about equally inconsequential events.

Apuleius, another of Vonnegut's literary ancestors, adapted, in his turn, Lucian's story for his delightful early novel, *The Golden Ass*. Apuleius gave the basic story of the man-transformed-into-an-ass an elaborate astrological and religious framework, and used it to criticize his society from top to bottom. From the professions to the slaves, from the courts to the bandits, from the educated to the ignorant, some form of greed motivates everyone in the fantastic world of Apuleius—whether for money, sex, or power. And, no one escapes his satiric criticism. Similarly, Vonnegut satirizes people's greed for money, sex, and power in *Cat's Cradle, Player Piano, The Sirens of Titan, God Bless You, Mr. Rosewater, Jailbird, Galápagos*, and *Hocus Pocus*. Vonnegut also employs a narrator in *Cat's Cradle* similar to Apuleius's: An uninvolved reporter writing a book on the day the world ended observes firsthand the selfish, self-centered values that then lead to the destruction of the world.

In American literature, the satirical Mark Twain comes closest to being Vonnegut's literary foster father. Vonnegut named his first-born son after him (*Palm Sunday* 172) and paid him a writer's true compliment by using the conclusion of *A Connecticut Yankee in King Arthur's Court* (1889) as part of a contemporary war story inserted into his first novel, *Player Piano* (219-20). The basic premise of *A Connecticut Yankee in King Arthur's Court* also underlies Kilgore Trout's first short story where Merlin as Arthur's Court Magician magically "equip[s] the Knights of the Round Table with Thompson submachine guns and . . . 45-caliber dumdums" (*Timequake* xiii).[8] Vonnegut also built at least one of his novels, *Mother Night*, on Twain's exploration in *Huckleberry Finn* (1884) of the "tendency for . . . impersonators to get carried away by their impersonations, to become what they impersonate, and therefore to live in a world of illusion" (Berkove 295)[9]—a sentence that exactly describes Howard Campbell as well as Tom Sawyer and Huck Finn. Extensive echoes and references to Twain and especially to *Huckleberry Finn* with its child narrator occur within many of Vonnegut's novels.

[T]he haunted and wonderful imagination of Huckleberry Finn . . . is the prototype for many of Vonnegut's narrators: a child marked by the loss of parents, not ready yet for marriage, love, or responsibility, but lighting out for the territory with a mind haunted by images of death and destruction. The territory ahead . . . is . . . the great river of life with fugitives and charlatans. (Berryman, "After the Fall" 102)

Vonnegut, a moralist like Twain, remains profoundly disturbed by the values of the society in which he finds himself. He, too, wrestles with the major moral and religious issues of his time, while employing humor to deflate pomposity and mock pretension. Also like Twain and Apuleius, Vonnegut uses the fantastic in the service of his satire. Finally, like late Twain in *Connecticut Yankee*, he often despairs over humanity's inability to realize what our planet could be or should be, and its apparent willingness instead to settle for despoiling the Earth through war and the misuse of technology. Vonnegut also criticizes the negative values he finds around him, values that Twain had earlier satirized including greed, the lust for power, and the willingness—sometimes—even eagerness to destroy people and nature. At the end of *Cat's Cradle*, Bokonon gives his response to the end of the world when he writes the last sentence in *The Books of Bokonon*. Given the almost total destruction of the planet and the poisoning of the earth, the only appropriate response is to die "thumbing my nose at You

Know Who" (191). "Vonnegut's literary idol Mark Twain, he of the sayings of Pudd'nhead Wilson and the historical satire of *The Mysterious Stranger*, would have loved that irreverent finale," rightly claims Kermit Vanderbilt (150).

To be convincing, however, Vonnegut, as a normative satirist, must include in his work a set of positive values or a clearly articulated standard against which the reader can measure the evil or the human shortcomings under satiric attack. In the first six novels, for instance, Vonnegut maintains that human beings miss their potential to be happy and to love—his positive values—for several different though related reasons that become the objects of his satire. In *Player Piano*, human beings, having nothing useful to do, settle for inhuman work. In *The Sirens of Titan* they engage in meaningless relationships and activities. In *Mother Night* they give up their lives to an evil cause, while in *Cat's Cradle* and *Slaughterhouse-Five* they irresponsibly play with the toys of death. The positive standard against which he asks readers to assess such evil and waste becomes clearly articulated in most of these novels. At the end of *The Sirens of Titan*, Malachi Constant having spent most of his life roaming the solar system concludes that "a purpose of human life, no matter who is controlling it, is to love whoever is around to be loved" (313). Similarly, in the preface to *Mother Night* Vonnegut reflects on one of the morals for his novel: "Make love when you can" (vii). Eliot Rosewater, the improbable hero of *God Bless You, Mr. Rosewater, or Pearls Before Swine*, operates not according to the world's values but according to the imperative to love "all creatures great and small" that he discovered in a William Blake poem. He, however, carefully divides up the lines so he can paint them on his stair risers for all those who visit him to see:

> The Angel that presided o're my birth
> Said Little creature form'd of Joy & Mirth,
> Go love without the help of any Thing on Earth. (Blake 614)

Within Vonnegut's first six novels, *Player Piano, The Sirens of Titan, Mother Night, Cat's Cradle,* and *God Bless You, Mr. Rosewater*, this positive standard of holding, giving, sharing, and experiencing human love during good times and bad, during peace and war, remains constant, and against this standard all actions are measured. When the action becomes evil beyond comprehension, as in the Dresden massacre, where 135,000 unarmed civilians were incinerated almost overnight or in the Holocaust, where the Nazis attempted to annihilate the Jews, then the novels understandably turn dark. Lurking in the background and all around the edges of the pre-*Slaughterhouse-Five* novels are all the unanswerable questions left over from World War II—the equivalent of a worldwide moral hangover. Questions such as: How could people hate so unreservedly that they would attempt to annihilate another race or another group of people simply because they found them different from themselves? Why this terrible inhuman hatred that leads to massacres, firestorms, death camps, and/or atomic incineration? Why? As the main character in *Mother Night* says,

There are plenty of good reasons for fighting . . . but no good reason ever to hate without reservation, to imagine that God Almighty Himself hates with you. . . . Where's evil? It's that large part of every man that wants to hate without limit, that wants to hate with God on its side. . . . [T]hat finds . . . ugliness so attractive. . . . [T]hat punishes[,] . . . vilifies and makes war gladly. (190)

These words acquired even more profound depth on 11 September 2001.

"Given such evil what is the purpose of history?" Vonnegut, in effect, asks in *The Sirens of Titan* and *Cat's Cradle*. Both novels suggest, through their satiric view of the world, that what history records remains void of meaning unless it is "the complicated futility of ignorance"—to borrow a sentence from *Hocus Pocus* (14). What then is the purpose of life? Vonnegut has God himself answer this question through the Bokononist creation myth in *Cat's Cradle*:

> "Everything must have a purpose?" asked God.
> "Certainly," said man.
> "Then I leave it to you to think of one for all this," said God.
> And He went away. (177)

In the pre-*Slaughterhouse-Five* novels, the bitterest satire occurs unsurprisingly in *Cat's Cradle*, where the purpose of human beings to love is completely thwarted. On the day the world ended, the question—"Who is left for me to love?"—becomes as meaningless as a bird's call at the end of a massacre, "Poo-tee-weet." In its place is another terrible question: "How can I, in this . . . empty world, find some neat way to die?" (*Cat's Cradle* 190). Vonnegut, so clearly passionate about the sacredness of human life, thus comments trenchantly on human shortsightedness and folly. His view of humanity culminates—at least in his fiction—neither in continued bitter reproaches nor in invective and threat, but in the acceptance of human limits. It does not partake, however, of the quietism embodied in the Tralfamadorian total view of all time that eventually Billy Pilgrim, the hero of *Slaughterhouse-Five*, appropriates as his own.

Vonnegut, unlike Billy, accepts both the universal reality and pivotal place of suffering in human experience—suffering that may be as total as the fire-bombing of Dresden or the atomic bombing of Hiroshima and Nagasaki. He does not, as some critics argue, reduce all suffering and all forms of inhuman brutality including massacres to the lowest common denominator of ubiquitous death (see, for example, Chabot 46–47). Human beings love "what vanishes," wrote W. B. Yeats. To which he added: Is there anything "more . . . to say?" indicating that he, like Vonnegut, had been forced to accept human limitations and mortality ("Nineteen Hundred and Nineteen"). Yet, both Yeats and Vonnegut contend that there is much, much "more . . . to say" and both attempt to say it. Central to that saying is their wrestling with the unanswerable question, Why do the innocent suffer? "Suffering is the chief equalizer of human experience, and the authority of suffering . . . goes far on the way toward convincing us that there is such a thing as a 'human community.' Whatever the anthropologists tell us about human differences, a touch of suffering makes the whole world kin" wrote Donald Shriver (2).[10] This "authority of suffering" underlies all of *Slaughterhouse-Five*.

Having accepted suffering as a necessary part of life Vonnegut became free in the novels after *Slaughterhouse-Five* to satirize particular evils in the modern world rather than, as earlier, wrestle with the question of evil itself. *Galápagos*, his eleventh novel, for example, makes brilliantly, satirically clear what many of his other novels—along with a Kilgore Trout short story, "The Planet Gobblers" (*Palm Sunday* 209)—had implied. Human beings are a danger to the planet, and if they are not controlled in some way, they will destroy all forms of life. Alvin B. Kernan might well have been describing the satire of *Galápagos*, when, several decades before, he identified the object most frequently attacked by modern satirists as "an uncritical and simple belief in infinite progress, based on the improvement of material conditions, on the development of science and on an ultraoptimistic assumption about human nature and its potentials" (iv). Once, responding to a question about whether he felt there was progress or if things were getting better, Vonnegut asserted: "I don't have the feeling [that we are going somewhere]" ("The Novelist Talks").

The acceptance of suffering, as central to humanity as well as the experience that assists in defining the human community, also helps account for the shift in those positive values against which Vonnegut implies we should measure his satiric attacks. The emphasis in *Slapstick, Deadeye Dick, Jailbird, Galápagos, Bluebeard, Hocus Pocus,* and *Timequake*, therefore, falls on the necessity for establishing human community, for seeing "the whole world kin" (Shiver 2). In *Bluebeard*, for instance, Vonnegut satirizes the disastrous disassociation of head and heart, and the distortion of values that occurs with the puffing up of a particular style of painting through excess wealth, which, in turn, leads to all the problems associated with sudden fame and riches for obscure artists. (If Jay Gatsby had lived into the 1950s and collected art, instead of period rooms, then he, too, might have had a Karabekian on his wall in West Egg.) Some critics go so far as to maintain that "The notion of building a new religion organized around the depiction of human suffering in art, however naïvely conceived, duly becomes a central idea in *Bluebeard*" (Rampton 17). After wandering in the world of art as far as Malachi Constant had roamed in *The Sirens of Titan*'s solar system, Rabo Karabekian returns home to the human community to celebrate life, and—most miraculous of all—to "love whoever is around to love," which, in his case, as in that of so many, turns out to be himself (*Bluebeard* 300).

The difference, therefore, between Vonnegut's early and late novels derives not so much from a major change in values or theme, as it does from a shift in attitude and tone. Vonnegut himself acknowledged this shift in his commencement address to the graduating class at Hobart and William Smith Colleges in 1974, where, somewhat bemused, he admitted that he had abandoned the pessimism that had governed his life up to then in favor of optimism (*Palm Sunday* 209). The compelling idea underlying the novels up to and including *Slaughterhouse-Five*, might be described as the necessity of accepting evil as part of human experience along with the concomitant realization that a touch of suffering makes the whole world kin and the moral imperative to love. Underlying the last eight novels—*Breakfast of Champions* through *Timequake*—is a similar idea, although one distinct enough to be distinguished from the first. Human kinship and love could lead to a vision of the wholeness of life and human beings—a true answer to the deepest human needs. This resolved vision of human life, underlies the shift in Vonnegut's satire from the bittersweet wisdom of Bokonon in *Cat's Cradle*, the desperate wanderings of Malachi Constant in *The Sirens of Titan*, and the dissection of American values in *Breakfast of Champions*, *Jailbird*, *Deadeye Dick*, and *Hocus Pocus* to the gentle chiding of humanity by Leon Trout in *Galápagos*, the happy resolution of Rabo Karabekian's life in *Bluebeard*, and the tender treatment of the conclusion of Kilgore Trout's and "Kurt Vonnegut's" careers as writers in *Timequake*. This resolved vision may also underlie as well Vonnegut's description of his own shift from pessimism to optimism.[11]

This shift in attitude and tone is accompanied by a shift in plot and character that Vonnegut himself predicted as early as 1973. When he was asked what he thought would happen in his work in the future, he replied with characteristic understatement that he guessed his "intuition will pooh out—my creative craziness; . . . I'll become more of an explainer[;] . . . I may finally have to become more of an educated man. . . . How could anybody have come this far with so little information?" (*Wampeters, Foma & Granfalloons* 284). Typical self-deprecating Vonnegut. Yet, in one sense, he did become "more of an educated man." Besides his earlier research in World War II for *Mother Night* and *Slaughterhouse-Five*, he later did research in labor history and the Sacco and Vanzetti trial for *Jailbird*,[12] Darwinian evolution for *Galápagos*, art theory and history for *Bluebeard*, and the history of the Vietnam War for *Hocus Pocus*. Vonnegut's one-of-a-kind novels may have some similarities one with another but they do not duplicate one another. He attributes much of that originality to being the son of an architect, for it is the dream of every architect to construct a truly original building in which people will feel perfectly comfortable (*Fates Worse Than Death* 55). Clearly, that has been Vonnegut's goal in his fiction.

In both early and late novels Vonnegut often employs a fictional future to help clarify negative as well as positive values. Whether in *The Sirens of Titan* or *Galápagos*, *Player Piano* or *Slaughterhouse-Five*, *Hocus Pocus* or *Timequake* the fictional future reflects back upon the present. Vonnegut's anti-utopian future runs counter to many of the themes and values found in some of the more traditionally optimistic science-fiction writing. According to literary historian James Gunn, science fiction is rooted in the belief that through thinking humans can save the planet and themselves. Through technology, humans will indeed find a way out of the current ecological dilemma. Progress for Gunn becomes not only possible but also highly probable, thanks to science. He believes that "the farther into space one travels the less significant become the passions and agonies of man, and the only matter of importance in the long morning of man's struggle to survive is his survival so that his sons could be seeded among the stars" ("Science Fiction" 199). Sounding somewhat like those science-fiction writers that Gunn described, several contemporary scientists enthusiastically postulate that technology will continue to rise exponentially over billions of years, constantly accelerating in proportion to existing technology. The more star systems that intelligent beings have colonized, the more star systems they can colonize. . . . [O]ver several billion years, intelligent beings will have completely colonized vast portions of the visible universe. (Kaku 308 summarizing Barrow and Tipler, *The Anthropic Cosmological Principle*)

To all such speculation Vonnegut responds with a resounding "No!" "That Humanity is going somewhere really nice was a myth for children under 6 years old, like the Tooth Fairy[,] . . . the Easter Bunny and Santa Claus" writes Eugene Debs Hartke in *Hocus Pocus* (206)—and, clearly, Vonnegut agrees. From *Player Piano* and *The Sirens of Titan* to *Galápagos* and *Timequake* he satirizes such absence of value, neglect of the heart, and mistaken shift in focus away from the human individual to the indifferent cosmos. Nor is Vonnegut impressed by those "human children who take the heavens for their playground . . . [as] substitutes for the traditional gods" (Parrinder 73) featured in so much contemporary science fiction. Besides clearly rejecting any notion of progress that underlies both the scientists' and science-fiction writers' assumptions about humans conquering the universe, Vonnegut also avoids the cliché-ridden staples of American science fiction embodied in imperial adventures. Ursula K. Le Guin, among others, rightly labeled "incredibly regressive and unimaginative"

[a]ll those Galactic Empires, taken straight from the British Empire of 1880. All those planets—with 80 trillion miles between them!—conceived of as warring nation-states, or as colonies to be exploited, or to be nudged by the benevolent Imperium of Earth toward self-development—the White Man's Burden all over again. The Rotary Club on Alpha Centauri—that's the size of it. ("American SF" 94)

All of Vonnegut's work, like all of Le Guin's, goes against this grain.[13] In contrast, within his novels science fiction becomes an effective method for asking the truly important questions about the nature of humans and their universe (see, for example, *Slaughterhouse-Five* 101). "Science fiction has flowered and prospered in our troubled and fast-evolving century in part because it alone among contemporary literatures consistently deals with the big questions: What are we here for? Where are we going? How much worse can things get?" contends David Hartwell (25). Hartwell also claims that exactly such questions help account for the recent substantial and growing popularity of science fiction (25). Vonnegut's work constantly asks these and related questions whether he is writing science fiction or writing within other genres or modes.

Vonnegut's six early novels from *Player Piano* to *Slaughterhouse-Five* have been labeled alternately science fiction, black humor, satire, schizophrenic fiction, fabulation, fantasy, and so forth. While there is some truth behind each of these labels, depending upon which novel or group of novels one reads and from what perspective one reads it, a conclusion more relevant to these novels might be that Vonnegut's work escapes easy classification. He has written successful science fiction, as he has some black humor; he definitely is a satirist and he surely is a fantasist, but each novel remains unique. *God Bless You, Mr. Rosewater*, for instance, differs from the other four early novels in its highly traditional form with those truly fantastic parts incorporated as Kilgore Trout science-fiction novels and stories—a device which will become a staple of Vonnegut's later fiction. Also, unlike the other early Vonnegut novels, its hero, Eliot Rosewater, although in an insane asylum, neither dies nor faces death and has some modicum of hope at the end that he has at least frustrated, if not overcome, the evil forces arrayed against him.

Vonnegut's willingness to tackle major moral, social, and political issues central to American life and thinking from genocide to automation, from the significance or lack of it in history to the possible end of the world, also becomes clearly visible in the five novels preceding *Slaughterhouse-Five*. He examines evil in our time in the schizophrenic mentality of the double agent, of those who invented and staffed the death camps, and of those that developed and deployed the atomic bomb. He warns against valuing automation and efficiency over human variety and inefficiency, and against evaluating people by their uniforms of race, color, creed, or nationality rather than by their flesh-and-blood human desires and needs. Finally, he rejects the discarding of some of humanity as useless and unworthy of love. Vonnegut's positive vision of the fragility and worth of each human being is then juxtaposed to these negative values.

For the first third of his career Vonnegut suffered from obscurity and critical neglect. According to the *Book Review Index*, in the decade after he published *Player Piano* to appreciative reviews "no book of Vonnegut's is recorded as having appeared or been reviewed" until 1963 (Fiedler 9). Vonnegut laments that what some readers believe is his best book, *The Sirens of Titan* along with his first collection of stories, *Canary in a Cathouse* (1961), and the extraordinary *Mother Night* "were never reviewed" (*Bagombo* 9). In interviews he deplored his books' lack of initial popularity (see, for example, "Two Conversations" 200). One event proved particularly galling. *Esquire* magazine did a feature story on the American literary world. The article came complete with a list that purported to have on it every "living author of the slightest merit." To his considerable consternation, Vonnegut could not find his name on the list. "I wasn't on there," he bemoaned, "it . . . had made me feel subhuman" (*Wampeters, Foma & Granfalloons* 279–80). Martin Amis correctly suggests that "even by American standards, Vonnegut's career represents an extreme case of critical revisionism and double-think" (133). For within a few years, he would be hailed or denigrated as one of the most popular writers in America. He would then again suffer critical neglect but ironically this time due to his popularity, celebrity, and wealth. After the success of *Slaughterhouse-Five*, his novels were republished and repackaged in uniform editions that sold steadily and continuously for the rest of the century. Yet, many earnest critics then refused to take his work seriously—not because of his being a writer of science-fiction paperbacks—but because he had become a popular, successful writer. Almost twenty years after the publication of *Player Piano*, Max F. Schulz could argue with ample justification that "It is no exaggeration to say that his audience has been slow in learning how to read his stories," and go on to substantiate his case (7–8).

In contrast, by the end of the twentieth century Vonnegut's place among contemporary writers of fiction appeared more assured. No longer confined to the debilitating categories of black humorist, science-fiction writer, or cult figure, now many—though by no means all—critics even forgave him his popularity. Taken more seriously, he began to be hailed as an original American voice, what he once described as an "aggressively unconventional storyteller" (*Fates Worse Than Death* 55) who had devised a style modeled on Thoreau and his own early newspaper writing at Cornell and in Chicago. "I came up through journalism really," he remarked ("On Art" 35)—as did Whitman, Twain, Ernest Hemingway, and a host of other American writers.

Vonnegut's deceptively simple style has allowed him to reach a considerable audience and discuss with it what he sees as the major issues of the late twentieth century. "Vonnegut's lucidity is hard and brave work in a literary world where pure messiness is frequently thought to be a sign of some essential wrestling with the 'hard questions' " (Irving, "Vonnegut and His Critics" 214).[14] Vonnegut describes a reference book he considered writing for children to be called, "Welcome to Earth" (*Wampeters, Foma & Granfalloons* 276). Charles Berryman postulates that this book might well "be a contemporary version of Thoreau's *Walden*. Just as *Walden* often reads like a parody of a how-to-do-it book, Vonnegut's *Breakfast of Champions* with its absurd pen and ink [sic] drawings is a parody of an illustrated manual ("After the Fall" 102).

Peter Nichols, in his otherwise positive review of *Bluebeard*, commented not so much on the voice as on what he called Vonnegut's choppy style, which he connected to his penchant for self-caricature and identified as a source of his jocularity. He then went on to complain that it was also "disfigured by nervous tics." Thomas Disch's earlier review of *Galápagos* had already wittily anticipated and answered Nichols's objection in detail pointing to Vonnegut's serious purpose in introducing such "tics."

> To cavil at these monogrammed tics, as critics regularly do, is to fall into the trap of supposing that Vonnegut is being a lazy writer or that he is pretending to be a klutz in order to ingratiate himself with a world of klutzes. Neither is the case. The Vonnegut audience is in large part a generation younger than himself . . . and college-educated. His catch-phrases are not those his readers would use but belong to their parents' generation, and are *meant* to annoy them in just the way they annoy the critics, and also to establish an imaginary generation gap between the writer and his readers, the better to get on with the avuncular purpose of his comedy, which is moral instruction. (1267)

Circe Berman, a character in *Bluebeard*, similarly speaks for many such critics and reviewers when she asks Karabekian "How come you never use semicolons? . . . How come you chop it all up into little sections instead of letting it flow and flow?" (37). Karabekian does not deign to give a reason, nor does Vonnegut. The style of narration of any novel, whether by Vonnegut or someone else, intimately relates to the choice of narrator and point of view. Rank amateurs, single-book authors with no previous writing experience narrate all of Vonnegut's books, including *Bluebeard*. The unadorned "telegraphic . . . manner of [their] tales" proves as appropriate for them for reasons of simplicity as it was for the Tralfamadorians in *Slaughterhouse-Five* for reasons of dimensional orientation (see the *Slaughterhouse-Five* title page). As Vonnegut progresses through his novels the very physical means of writing them becomes part of their narration. Leon Trout writes *Galápagos* on air using only his finger. Karabekian uses a typewriter in *Bluebeard* to construct a series of small chunks of material spaced apart on the printed page, while imprisoned Hartke writes *Hocus Pocus* using whatever scraps of paper come to hand including tiny library slips.

Evolving over time and through the writing of many novels, Vonnegut's style allows him to communicate readily, as if he were telling the story in person with a kind of child-like innocence. He once said that "like Thoreau . . .[he wrote] in the voice of a child" ("Interview" with Allen and Smith 301). Hume finds that voice refreshing or, at least, honest. She accepts that Vonnegut "asks his questions with childish directness." But, she continues, "if the emperor parades in the nude and we ignore this, should we turn angrily on the naïf who wonders why in a penetrating voice? Vonnegut's naïveté and over-simplifications are real, but so are the issues he insists on raising" ("Heraclitean" 216)—even if most Americans choose to ignore them. "A man ought not to be ashamed of reading a good book because it is simple and popular," wrote the scholar and writer, C. S. Lewis ("High and Low Brows," quoted by Aldiss, "Was Zilla Right?" 9). He might have been addressing Nichols in his review as well as Berman in her snooping. Disch summed up "the interest of the Vonnegut voice" in the incisive review already mentioned:

the interest of the Vonnegut voice is not in what it reveals of the author but in the audience that it hypothesizes, an audience that must have the most basic facts of life explained to it in the simplest terms, an audience that will crack up at the sound of a fart, an audience that has the best of intentions even as it paves the road to hell, an audience of children who know they need to be scolded. (1267)

There has been, however, a noticeable reluctance among critics to take Vonnegut at his word that he is serious about how and what he is writing. Part of that reluctance may stem from his typical "public stance . . . not to take myself seriously" (quoted in Amis 134). Here's a representative instance from 1990: Answering the charge that he is somehow a disappointment for a promising writer, Vonnegut notes that people retire at his age whatever their position or whatever job they worked at. To find his fiction disappointing because he somehow is no longer a promising writer appears, therefore, "redundant (even silly). If they think I am a disappointment, they should see what the passage of time has done to Mozart, Shakespeare, and Hemingway" (*Fates Worse Than Death* 196). But in giving this kind of answer to the criticism that he is no longer a "promising writer," Vonnegut's cryptic self-deprecation leaves him open to still further criticism. Rampton speculated that Vonnegut's lack of critical acceptance may actually rest on his refusal "to take himself seriously [especially in interviews], and too many critics have dutifully followed suit. His self-deprecating irony questions the appropriateness of invoking any authority—the author, a source—and usually militates against solemn activities like source hunting and related speculations" (24). Comparing his career to that of the sculptor, Louise Nevelson, Vonnegut said that she once quipped to him, that it took years for the art world to realize that she was serious (letter to the author). Attracting critical and scholarly attention around the world as a serious writer and commentator on America,[15] translated into several languages, he became a spokesperson for America at home and abroad in much the same way, but with far better insight than American exported television or films. Finally, he used his fame to speak out on the important political, social, and environmental issues of our time.

A certain amount of misreading of Vonnegut's work also occurred when some critics wanted to find in it something that simply is not there. Vonnegut distinguishes himself from other writers—many of whom he admires—whose work he sees as part of an ongoing series of what he calls "literary experiments."

To me, there are some important writers—say, John Barth, Donald Barthelme and Jorge Luis Borges—who seem to be concentrating on what we could call "literary history," in the sense that they're responding to literary experiments in the past and are refining them. They're also responding to life, of course; I don't mean to imply they aren't. But they have a certain academic strain within their works, an awareness of being part of an evolutionary scheme, and I don't feel any such awareness. ("Two Conversations" 215)

Instead, his books reflect his involvement with life rather than literary history along with his exploration of the major issues of our time including genocide, the destruction of the environment, the various insane methods we have devised for exterminating the human race and all of life in the thin ecosphere; the importance of artistic integrity; the corrosive effects of corruption in government, drugs in society, and racism in the United States; the astonishing loneliness Americans experience as the other side of their mobility; the inexplicable nature of money and finance; the necessity of rejecting the collaboration with evil; the loss of imagination through mechanical reproduction of images; the obligation to love and, whenever love fails, to practice courtesy.

"Each story," he muses, "is an experiment at the frontier of my understanding" ("On Art" 36) and, as such, involves risk-taking that a less experimental, less self-assured novelist would not hazard. "In his fiction Vonnegut's most crucial imaginative habit is to gaze down at humanity as if from another world, fascinated by Earthling morés yet baffled by our convulsive quests for order, certainty and justice" (Amis 134). "This attitude," says Vonnegut, "was a result of my studies in biochemistry, before the war and anthropology after the war. I learned to see human culture as an artifact, which it is—vulnerable, precarious and probably futile" (quoted in Amis 134). From this vantage point, Vonnegut performs a public service for citizens of the United States through his speaking and occasional writing, but especially through his fiction in attempting to imagine being an American and pointing out how improbable and difficult that is. For Vonnegut, being an American also means being a citizen of planet Earth, one of those very people whose action and inaction will shortly make the planet unlivable for humans.

Hume concludes that "readers engage with Vonnegut's issues, but neither intellectually nor emotionally receive satisfaction. Vonnegut is too honest to produce false happy endings, and his bleak results challenge readers to consider whether or not happier philosophies are built upon strictly imaginary foundations" ("Melancholy" 231). Vonnegut's work will remain important—and often central—to those in our society who wrestle with the question of "What exactly are these United States of America and what could they, should they become?"; to those who believe with him in the process itself of trying to "imagine being an American" rather than simply accepting some received opinion of what an American is, or should be; to those who are aware of the country's and its citizens' shortcomings but who also appreciate hearing about such issues through humor, jokes, and satire rather than through sermons or lectures. Humorists, unlike the rest of us, experience a freedom to treat "life itself as a dirty joke," although they know full well that there is nothing and can be nothing beyond this life.

> *We do, doodily do, doodily do, doodily do*
> *What we must, muddily must, muddily must, muddily must:*
> *Muddily do, muddily must, muddily do, muddily must,*
> *Until we bust, bodily bust, bodily bust, bodily bust.*
> *(Fates Worse Than Death* 194, emphasis in the original)

Such sentiments place him in the good company of Robert Frost, who liked to end his public readings with this couplet:

> Forgive. O Lord, my many little jokes on Thee,
> And I'll forgive Thy great big one on me. (*Clearing* 39)

"The intensity of Vonnegut's comedy is directly proportional to the bleakness and agony of his material, a relationship which seems to lie at the heart of his own comedic awareness," writes Will Kaufman (22). To paraphrase Irving Howe: With Vonnegut "a new voice. . . . [t]hought and language, idea and image fold into a new being" as happens with the best of American writers ("American Voice" 1).[16] In his fiction, as in his essays, speeches, reviews, and occasional pieces, Vonnegut, like Emerson, challenges the reader to examine how he or she acts, thinks, and feels, which, as Richard Poirier reminds us, is the most important task of the writer. "We do not go to literature to become better citizens or even wiser persons, but to discover how to move, to act, to work in ways that are still and forever mysteriously creative" (44). Addressing the P.E.N. Conference in Stockholm in 1973, Vonnegut virtually restated Emerson's idea of the artist as society's "delegated intellect" ("The American Scholar" 54). "All Artists," said Vonnegut, "are specialized cells in a single, huge organism, mankind. . . . Our purpose is to make mankind aware of itself, in all its complexity, and to dream its dreams. We have no choice in the matter" (*Wampeters, Foma & Granfalloons* 228). In his writing, Vonnegut attempts to make people aware of themselves, their identity, dreams, choices, values. In several key aspects, he thereby exemplifies the creative artist Emerson described in his essay, "The Poet." As *the* representative American writer of his time Vonnegut, like Emerson's poet, has been "isolated among his contemporaries, by truth and by his art, but with this consolation in his pursuits, that they will draw all men sooner or later. For all men live by truth, and stand in need of expression. In love, in art, in avarice, in politics, in labor, in games, we study to utter our painful secret" (448).

In novel after novel, Vonnegut utters our painful secret but does so with good humor and a fine comic sense. "That healthful, liberating laughter has been the cause of Vonnegut's popularity as a writer. We admire him precisely because he can laugh at the irrationalities of our world. . . . Such laughter . . . is full of intelligence and common sense, in touch with ideals and realities at the same time" (Gill 81). In *Player Piano*, for example, the Shah visits a typical American family enjoying its freedom from dull daily chores now taken over by countless gadgets and automatic helpers from the radar range to ultrasonic dishwasher and washing machine. The visit parallels that of Richard Nixon who once took the Soviet Union's Chairman Nikolai Khrushchev to visit an Iowa farmer's kitchen which boasted many of the newest in laborsaving devices (see Reed, *Vonnegut* 42). Rather than parody Nixon—perhaps too easy a target—Vonnegut exposes the emptiness of his fictional family's life, its lack of meaning and value by having the Shah ask simple Thoreau-like questions such as: "What is it she has to do, that she mustn't waste any time?" and "And how is it you live and get so much fun out of life?" (142). The wife answers: " 'Oh, television,' she murmured. 'Watch that a lot. . . . And I spend a lot of time with the kids.' " The Shah counters: "Where are the children now?" to which comes the almost inevitable reply: "Over at the neighbors place . . . watching television, I expect" (142). Vonnegut allows the vacuity to sink in through the stark dialogue, then gives the punch line perfectly timed and without comment. Noticeably absent in this deadpanned dialogue—and absent throughout all his novels—is any special pleading, preaching, or "academic strain." Instead, his fiction is characterized by its comedy, considerable narrative skill, and, above all, by its "exuberance of invention" (Aldiss, *Spree* 328) as he goes about imagining being an American.

NOTES

1. The worst instance of using a dubious means to effect a good end in Vonnegut's novels has to be Winston Niles Rumfoord's design to "change the World for the better by means of the great and unforgettable [Martian] suicide" (*The Sirens of Titan* 174).

2. Because the version of this interview published in Reed and Leeds omits a crucial line and introduces numerous errors, the pagination will given of the original publication in *Hungarian English Studies* 22 (1991) now the *Hungarian Journal of English and American Studies*.

3. Peter J. Reed unaccountably describes this tragedy simply as "a train crash" not once but twice (Reed and Leeds xxii and 117). But surely much of the point of the absurdity and especially the meaninglessness of Vonnegut's brother-in-law's death lies in his being on "The Brokers' Special," the commuter train that uniquely "in American railroading history . . . hurl[ed] itself off an open drawbridge" (*Slapstick* 12). What

response can a person possibly make to such a nonsensical, *unique* yet deadly occurrence? "Think of that. This really happened," says Vonnegut in the prologue to *Slapstick*, as if trying to accept that such strange events could occur—let alone—actually did (12). After such an experience, perhaps not even a timequake would be much of a shock. For a detailed account of the Vonneguts' adopting the three children and the many resulting difficulties and joys, see Jane Vonnegut Yarmolinsky.

4. Far from reflecting what one critic calls Vonnegut's "aggrandizement of *his* 'problems' " (Meyer 100, his emphasis) such novels illustrate Vonnegut transmuting these problems into a tough-minded, often satiric examination of the fundamental American experience of loss. (For an in-depth refutation of Meyer, see "Poor Souls" and " 'Zang reepa dop. Faaaaaaaaaa!' " in chapter 5 "Under an Inexplicable Sentence of Death.")

5. See, for example, his lecture at the National Air and Space Museum on "The Legacy of Strategic Bombing" (*Fates Worse Than Death* 98–105) or his sermon preached at the Cathedral of St. John the Divine (139–49).

6. The best-known English translation remains that of Samuel Johnson, "On the Vanity of Human Wishes."

7. Klinkowitz emphasizes the important part played by Vonnegut's Indianapolis background in forming his beliefs: "his central beliefs can be seen as coming from . . . a humble source: the lessons of his parents and schoolteachers" ("Vonnegut in America" 11).

8. Many critics have remarked on Kilgore Trout as some kind of alter ego for Vonnegut. (His function will be explored further in later chapters of this book.) His name is also linked to Vonnegut's. *Vonnegut* derives from the German surname "Funnegut" meaning "the estate on the River Funne." A "Gut" in German is a significant property. When the Funneguts immigrated to the United States, they realized that their name "sounded too much like 'funny gut' in English" so changed it to Vonnegut (*Palm Sunday* 24). John Barthel points out that the last syllable of Vonne*gut* and that of Kil*gore* are similar. " 'Gore' also means 'gut' " (letter to the author 13 January 1999).

9. Lawrence Berkove argues convincingly that the whole of Twain's novel hinges on the series of impersonations that in turn leads to a loss of personal freedom (291–310).

10. Shriver's comment on suffering is part of his discussion of Dietrich Bonhoeffer, the martyred Lutheran German pastor executed for his part in the plot to assassinate Hitler.

11. Vanderbilt points out that "Kurt Vonnegut became the single major writer of the sixties in whom one could detect some discernible change. The moral miasma of the Nixon years was apparently good growing weather for Vonnegut" (138).

12. For example, as background for Sarah Wyatt and her family, Vonnegut attributes to the Wyatts one of the tragic stories from twentieth-century labor history (*Jailbird* 143–44). In the early 1900s, various watch factories recruited young women to paint watch dials with radium so the dials would glow in the dark. The workers—all women since the task was a delicate one—"painted about 250 dials a day for a cent and a half apiece, five and a half days a week. Within a few years, some of the young women became horribly ill from their exposure to radium, and some died" (Grady B14). No wonder Vonnegut remarks in *Jailbird* that "labor history was pornography of a sort in those days, and even more so in these days" (19).

13. Probably the best discussion of the appeal of such science fiction remains Hartwell's, especially in "The Golden Age of Science fiction Is Twelve" from *Age of Wonders* (3–24). For a lengthy contextualization of this discussion, see Tomas M. Disch, *The Dreams OurStuff Is Made Of*, especially 1-14 and 208-26.

14. David Andrews, in defending Vonnegut against the charge of being an anti-aesthete or anti-intellectual, comes to a similar conclusion. "The primary source of these pejoratives is his clear, concise prose style," says Andrews, but he adds: "verbal clarity entails neither compositional nor intellectual simplicity" (42n2).

15. For example, K. Satyanaryana Reddy writing in the Indian journal, *The Literary Endeavour: A Quarterly Journal Devoted to English Studies*, asserts that "Kurt Vonnegut, Jr., stands out among the contemporary American novelists as a great public writer whose work could serve as a measure for the achievement of American fiction during the past twenty years" (91).

16. Howe was speaking of American literature in general: "With America, a new idea comes into the world; with American literature a new voice. . . . Thought and language, idea and image fold into a new being, and we have the flowering of our literature" ("American Voice" 1).

3

No Reviews and Out of Print

"I was completely out of print . . . in 1965," Vonnegut ruefully remarked ("Foreword" ix). Then the huge success of *Slaughterhouse-Five* in 1969 changed everything. The critical acclaim and considerable sales of that novel spurred reconsideration of his five earlier novels *Player Piano, The Sirens of Titan, Mother Night, Cat's Cradle*, and *God Bless You, Mr. Rosewater, or Pearls Before Swine*. Slowly, each began to enjoy the critical success that previously had been elusive. Reading all five together in this new century, both their individual competence and their collective variety proves impressive. Utilizing a considerable range of modes and genres, they form an important chapter in Vonnegut's imagining being an American.

Vonnegut's first novel, *Player Piano*, for instance, falls within one of the longest and strongest suits in twentieth-century science fiction. "From H. G. Wells to Samuel Delany, science fiction is full of utopias, dystopias, ambiguous utopias, and 'heterotopias,' " claims Brian Attebery ("Anti-Utopian Mode" 5).[1] "*Player Piano* is astonishing for the richness of utopian and dystopian matter in this first major outing of the writer who would soon own the best utopian imagination in American literature since World War Two," asserts Kermit Vanderbilt (139–40).[2] It is also eerily prescient. In *Player Piano*, the world, having passed through the First Revolution where machines took over man's manual labor, and the Second Revolution where machines took over all human routine work, is now about to undergo a Third Revolution where machines will now do all the thinking. Vonnegut's model for this all-wise, all-powerful machine was the first digital computer, ENIAC or the "Electronic Numerical Integrator and Calculator." Developed at the University of Pennsylvania's Moore School of Electrical Engineering from a proposal by John Presper Eckert and John W. Mauchly and weighing in at thirty tons with 18,000 vacuum tubes, the first public demonstration of ENIAC occurred on February 14, 1946.[3] Half a dozen short years later, Vonnegut extrapolates from these events to create EPICAC XIV.[4] In *Player Piano* the president of the United States with not the slightest trace of irony refers to

EPICAC XIV as "the greatest individual in history." It sits smugly in the Carlsbad Caverns in New Mexico determining all of the country's needs from the number of refrigerators to be manufactured in any given month to the kinds of books people should read this year. It also decides which educational degrees any university may or may not offer. But this governing by computer results predictably in an increasingly sterile American society—a society with no real place or need for humans. The reality dominating this totally planned society is that it is run purely for corporate profit.[5] In such a world "the average human being of mediocre attainments or less has nothing to sell that it is worth anyone's money to buy" caustically observed Norbert Wiener—"the father of cybernetics"—in his popular book, *Cybernetics: Control and Communication in the Animal and the Machine* (quoted in Kenner 163).[6] A discerning visitor from another culture, the Shah of Bratbuhr, the spiritual leader of six million people, extends Wiener's comment by correctly identifying all the citizens of this new utopian United States as "Takaru" or slaves.

Juxtaposed to *Player Piano*'s corporate world lies Homestead, where ex-workers and those with minimal jobs live and where revolt may be incipient but life here is just as dead as it is at the top of the corporate organization chart.[7] There is no dignity in labor, no virtue in an honest day's wages, no reward for exceeding expectations. Instead, people realize that the corporate world wishes to use their labor as cheaply as possible and will, therefore, replace them with more reliable machines whenever and wherever possible, not stopping to count or even acknowledge the human cost of those dismissed, fired, or forced to quit. (One parallel in the twenty-first century would be the CEO, who has been obscenely rewarded for his mega-merger, while workers lose their jobs and retirement.) Early in the novel when Bud Calhoun invents a machine to replace himself, he is immediately fired (62–65). This theme of exploiting human workers and having machines take over their work—leaving behind a pile of human rubble with little or nothing to do—appears familiar from some nineteenth- and many twentieth-century British writers. For example, John Ruskin, D. H. Lawrence, E. M. Forster, Thomas Hardy, and J. R. R. Tolkien all inveighed against dehumanizing industrialization, while American writers from Mark Twain through the muckrakers and after attacked similar targets. Vonnegut's handling of the subject has a ring of truth as he describes the atmosphere of the corporation, its ethos and values that was based—at least in part—upon inside knowledge gleaned while working for the General Electric corporation. What he knew, he loathed. "It was a genuine concern that drove me to write my first book," he concedes ("Two Conversations" 200).

His second novel, *The Sirens of Titan*, has been alternately judged a great artistic success as well as an artistic failure. One critic, for example, who believes that "*The Sirens of Titan* was a worthwhile failure" (Allen, *Understanding* 41), contends that "the plot of the book suggests how far Vonnegut had traveled in the direction of pure fantasy from the relative realism of his first novel" (36). But this assessment ignores the genre of both novels. *Player Piano*, as an anti-utopian science-fiction novel, creates a fantastic setting in which realistic action takes place—action that Vonnegut extrapolates from the

1950s into the near future. *The Sirens of Titan*, on the other hand, makes no pretense of being remotely realistic in setting, action, or character. As far-future, satiric science fiction, this novel becomes a non-extrapolative exposé of human foibles, false beliefs, and hypocrisy, violating any and almost all the rules of realistic fiction. It may be plausible to describe *The Sirens of Titan* as more fantastic than *Player Piano* but that is a distinction without a difference.[8] More to the point is Klinkowitz's observation that "*The Sirens of Titan* is a considerable departure from the orderly use of science-fiction techniques in *Player Piano*. . . . Instead, Vonnegut provides space opera, enjoying the unsophisticated carnival of lurid and often self-indulgent pop devices which has made science fiction a true sub-genre" (*Kurt Vonnegut* 41).

In his third novel, *Mother Night*, Vonnegut moves away from science fiction to write a spy novel—one that examines questions of loyalty and integrity within the schizophrenic world of the double agent. That kind of conflicting loyalty experienced by every spy reflects tensions also shared by any immigrant. The new loyalties to the new country of emigration duel with those of the old country from which the person and/or the person's ancestors immigrated. German-Americans felt this tension acutely during the two twentieth-century world wars. As a second-generation German-American, Vonnegut experienced the prejudice against everything German that swept through the United States during and after World War I. (Good examples of both extreme and stupid prejudice were those radio stations that refused to allow orchestras to play Beethoven or Brahms over the air.) He also knew firsthand about some of those anti-German feelings aroused during World War II. But mostly he experienced that anti-German-American feeling as loss and absence in his life when his parents determined to bring him up in ignorance of any family history from Germany or of German literature, language, or music (*Palm Sunday* 21). Their omission resulted in what he describes as a kind of rootlessness but at the same time it also helped give him his clear—if bifurcated—vision on moral issues; a vision reflected especially clearly in *Mother Night*.

Published as an original paperback in 1962 but with a 1961 copyright date, *Mother Night* "was presented not as fiction but as fact, 'An American traitor's astonishing confession—mournfully macabre, diabolically funny—written with unusual candor in a foreign death cell,' according to the volume's cover" (Jamosky and Klinkowitz 216). In the original edition, Vonnegut was identified only as the editor in the now familiar "Editor's Note" (ix–xii), but otherwise the narrative was labeled, *The Confessions of Howard W. Campbell, Jr.* and dedicated to Mata Hari. It was not until the hardcover edition of 1966, some four years later, that Vonnegut added an introduction dated Iowa City, 1966, in which he pointed to the moral of the novel, and deliberately claimed it as his own.[9]

A brilliant study in "that simple and widespread boon to modern mankind— schizophrenia" (136), *Mother Night* endures as "an astonishing book, very gentle and funny and quiet and totally destructive. Nobody escapes without being shown, in a polite way, what an ass he is" (Crichton 110). Using war and espionage as basic metaphors, Vonnegut explores the nature of personality, values, and reality—all of which appear contingent upon having and maintaining a clear human identity. As Emerson remarked at the conclusion to "Self-Reliance," "Nothing can bring you peace but yourself. Nothing can bring you peace but the triumph of principles" (282). But pretense, rather than principles, rules the world of *Mother Night*, exactly as it rules the world of *Cat's Cradle*.

The plot of *Cat's Cradle* reflects the ultimate joke in which all life on Earth perishes thanks to the greed, stupidity, and shortsightedness of that part of life called "human beings"—a theme to which Vonnegut will return in *Galápagos*. As an American author writing in the 1950s, Vonnegut was hardly alone in thinking that all life on Earth was threatened. This fear of annihilation appeared so widespread because it appeared so justified. As the distinguished physicist Michio Kaku observed, "With the ability to master element 92 [uranium] comes the ability either to liberate our species from want, ignorance, and hunger or to consume the planet in nuclear fire" (288). A reputable journal of the period, *The Bulletin of Atomic Scientists*, featured on its cover a Doomsday clock with the hour hand set at midnight—the time a nuclear holocaust would end life on the planet. The minute hand would then be adjusted on each month's cover to accord with the current political prospects for such annihilation. For most of the 1950s that clock read—in Elmer Davis' memorable book title of the day—*Two Minutes till Midnight*. In other words, according to those scientists who should have known, life on the planet had very little time left before it would be consumed in nuclear fire—a very real and present danger that resurfaced in the twenty-first century. Similarly, a famous allegorical cartoon of the 1950s depicted a skeleton with its skull wreathed in a hideous grin as a bomb blew up its insides—the thumb of its bony right hand had just pushed the plunger activating the bomb. Eugene O'Neill's line in *The Iceman Cometh* could easily stand as a motto for the times: "All things are the same meaningless joke to me, for they grin at me from the skull of death" (128). In *Cat's Cradle*, the essential pessimism underlying this apocalyptic vision of the fifties was admirably caught in *The Fourteenth Book of Bokonon* entitled, "What Can a Thoughtful Man Hope for Mankind on Earth, Given the Experience of the Past Million Years?" As the narrator reports, *The Fourteenth Book* is a quick read: "It consists of one word and a period. This is it: 'Nothing' " (164).

American fiction of the period included a wealth of popular novels depicting either the end of the world or what life would be like for the remnants of humankind after an atomic holocaust.[10] Yet few of these other novels has proven as lasting as *Cat's Cradle*. Vonnegut's novel succeeds by melding a comic, satiric vision of modern society, its vacuity and lack of purpose, with a terrifying vision of human irresponsibility, and what John May calls "our insane pretensions, both technological and religious" (200). "As in nearly all of Vonnegut's fiction, the deadly serious and the comic are brought into dynamic tension" (Cooley 165). Moreover, *Cat's Cradle* belies Peter Freese's contention that this novel is an example of how "serious novelists of 'the end' never conjure it up for its own sake . . . [but] are interested in how to survive the end, that is, in the new beginning to be wrested from an all-embracing apocalypse"

("Surviving" 163). Freese's remarks would appear quite appropriate if they were directed either to *Slaughterhouse-Five*, which begins with the moment of apocalypse, or to *Galápagos* that pronounces the end benign. They do not, however, fit this earlier novel.[11] In *Cat's Cradle* there appears no new beginning for humans but only for a handful of ants. The three Hoenikker children, Frank, Angela, and Newt, placed in charge of the destinies of nations and, ultimately, of the whole human race, destroy all life on Earth because they do not or cannot love. Moreover, they do not see themselves as part of the human community and they fail utterly to acknowledge, care, or have respect for others. Instead, they sell their horrific legacy for the usual human price of "a mess of pottage," which in this instance is sex, money, and power. Frank buys a generalship, Angela buys a "tomcat husband," while Newt buys an ecstatic week on Cape Cod in the company of a Russian midget (163). The ensuing series of accidents leads to Earth's destruction, for which these three together with their father are ultimately responsible.[12] Vonnegut, so trenchantly critical in this novel of the ease with which the atomic bomb was accepted and readied for use, still never sermonizes or preaches. Instead, *Cat's Cradle* clearly illustrates Paul Boyer's contention that "the most affecting and durable of the . . . literary works to confront the atomic bomb are not the pontifical and didactic proclamations, but quieter and more tentative works" (252). "We may prefer to blame our nuclear predicament on an unbridled technology, but Vonnegut suggests that it is our failure to be fully human that especially endangers us," concludes Daniel L. Zins (68). Felix Hoenikker and his children vividly illustrate that failure. Hoenikker fails dismally as a husband (he is at least indirectly responsible for the death of his wife in childbirth), as father (he never relates to or plays with his children), and as colleague (he never interacts with anybody). After the cataclysm, Frank Hoenikker says to the others with no hint of irony that he has matured a lot. To which the narrator replies dryly "At a certain amount of expense to the world" (187).

These "babies full of rabies" (47) are also Vonnegut's comment on the world's incompetent, insensitive, shortsighted leaders, thinkers, and citizens who sacrifice ultimate good for short-term and, in the last analysis, trivial gain. Having the world's destiny in their hands, as their father did before them, the Hoenikker children drop it shattering the world and leaving each person frozen in isolation.[13] This is Vonnegut's trenchant warning on the urgent need to work for human community and human unity against the forces of destruction—a theme more fully developed in *Slapstick*. Opposed to this negative example of myopic greed and stupidity, United States ambassador Horlick Minton places himself within the larger context of history and views his country within the wider purview of the world. Minton in his speech commemorating the "Hundred Martyrs to Democracy" contrasts the patriotic dead with their fellow countrymen who still enjoy the precious gifts of life and consciousness. Those who die in wars are neither men nor martyrs, according to Ambassador Minton. Rather, they might more appropriately be described as "murdered children" (170). Rather than spending the holiday in celebrating their deaths, people should spend it in "despising what killed them," which—as the ambassador points out—is human "stupidity and viciousness" (170). (His speech anticipates Vonnegut's view of World War II depicted as a Children's Crusade in *Slaughterhouse-Five*.) The picture of the Mintons themselves disappearing into the Ice-9 bears out Vonnegut's notion that although scientifically Ice-9 was nonsense, it did enjoy "a certain moral validity" (*Wampeters, Foma & Granfalloons* 97).[14] The good, loving Mintons—who see themselves as an integral part of the human community—perish because of the greed, stupidity, and isolation of Hoenikker and his children that unleashed Ice-9 upon an unsuspecting world.

By contrast, *God Bless You, Mr. Rosewater* dangerously and successfully skirts sentimentality while focusing on the phenomenon of American philanthropy and its inability, ultimately, to stem the tide of evil. American philanthropy itself derives from contradictory impulses of generosity and greed. Greed is necessary for the accumulation of wealth without which there can be no philanthropy, while generosity is necessary for the dispersal of wealth that is the essence of philanthropy. The happy meeting ground of these twin impulses is the nonprofit foundation, such as the one found in *God Bless You, Mr. Rosewater*. The mid-twentieth-century Rosewater foundation proves typical. Modeled after the various foundations established by either the original nineteenth-century robber barons or their descendants, its ostensible purpose is to give away money while paying its officers handsome stipends and safely hiding the principle from the Internal Revenue Service. Twentieth-century American philanthropy owes its existence by-and-large to wealth accumulated in the nineteenth century. The Rosewater fortune is no exception: Noah Rosewater, "a humorless, constipated Christian farm boy," began the process of accumulating wealth during the American Civil War when President Abraham Lincoln decreed that "no amount of money was too much to pay" to restore the Union. Noah Rosewater "priced his merchandise in scale with the national tragedy" (11). Samuel, Noah's successor, in his turn "bought newspapers, and preachers" in order to spread the gospel of hard work for low pay as the American way (13). Thus the accumulated fortune comes down to Lister Rosewater, who, disdaining working for a living, used his fortune to ensure his election to the United States Senate where he could exercise his true vocation of "teaching morals" (14). As a way of saving the fortune from taxes and keeping it intact, the senator establishes the Rosewater Foundation. His son, Eliot Rosewater, a self-described "drunkard, . . . Utopian dreamer, . . . tinhorn saint, . . . aimless fool" (14) is then ensconced as president of the foundation able to draw an unlimited salary and do whatever he wants.[15] But instead, Eliot attempts to dispense uncritical love to those suffering from low self-esteem and a sense that they really do not belong anywhere, as he tries to alleviate human suffering. Unlike almost all of Vonnegut's other heroes, Eliot Rosewater survives and momentarily wins the battle even if he cannot win the war against greed, stupidity, and isolation.

Although these five early novels vary in form from utopian and science fiction through spy novel and apocalyptic vision to a more traditional work on philanthropy, they consistently confront the problems, affirm the values, and announce the themes that will remain constant throughout Vonnegut's career as a novelist. These problems, values, and themes are quintessentially American, echoing as they do from early American writers and thinkers. All become a vital part of Vonnegut's imagining being an American.

MARCHING TO UTOPIA

I like Utopian talk, speculation about what our planet should be, anger about what our planet is.

—Kurt Vonnegut

To imagine being an American at the end of the twentieth and beginning of the twenty-first century, means participating in the most powerful and one of the most wealthy countries on Earth. That power and wealth of the United States, which grew through the nineteenth and twentieth centuries in large measure thanks to an amazing outburst of creative technology and invention that, coupled with vast tracts of "unpopulated" land and seemingly limitless natural resources, remains almost synonymous with the machine. The most ubiquitous and most American machine, the car, provides America's famous personal freedom and mobility while contributing heavily to the feeling of American personal isolation. But the machine also may take the form of the telegraph/telephone or, more recently, the Internet, which tied the country together through instant communications. Or it may be the various electronic media machines (radio, movies, and television) that shifted the emphasis from reporting news to presenting instant events. Or it may be any of the vast array of technics that transformed agriculture into agribusiness, the company into the multinational corporation, or the sleepy stock market into a behemoth of arbitrage, leveraged buyout, and institutional investment.

Vonnegut remarks in the introduction to *Bagombo Snuff Box* (1999) that "*Player Piano* . . . predicted what has indeed come to pass, a day when machines, because they are so dependable and efficient and tireless, and getting cheaper all the time, are taking the halfway decent jobs from human beings" (7). While working at General Electric, Vonnegut saw a sample of the future upon which he based his extrapolation.[16] Wandering through a General Electric plant, he happened upon "an engineer who had developed a milling machine that could be run by punch cards." Operators of milling machines were very well paid at that time yet Vonnegut found himself facing a machine that could "do as good a job as most of the machinists ever could." Then came the real revelation: "I looked around . . . and found looms[,] . . . spinning machines and a number of textile devices all being run the same way and, well, the implications were sensational. ("Two Conversations" 199; compare *Wampeters, Foma & Granfalloons* 261.) These sensational implications are clear in *Player Piano*, where a future electronic society places the good of the corporation and the *full employment of machines* ahead of human needs and desires including the human necessity for meaningful work. "[T]he only safeguard of order and discipline in the modern world is a standardized worker with interchangeable parts. That would solve the entire problem of management," says The President in *The Madwoman of Chaillot* by Jean Giraudoux (17)—a sentiment echoed and reechoed throughout this novel. In *The Sirens of Titan* Vonnegut explores this issue further through an ultimate machine-run civilization on Tralfamadore, a planet whose people originally made machines in order to free human beings from work in order to contemplate and promote higher aims. Yet they remained dissatisfied with whatever new objective they found since, they thought, it never appeared exalted enough.

So machines were made to serve higher purposes, too.
      [They] . . . did everything so expertly that they were finally given the job of finding out . . . . the highest purpose of the creatures [humans] . . .
      The machines reported in all honesty that the creatures couldn't really be said to have any purpose. . . .
      The creatures thereupon began slaying each other, because they hated purposeless things. . . .
      And they discovered that they weren't even very good at slaying. So they turned that job over to the machines. . . . And [they] . . . finished up the job in less time than it takes to say, "Tralfamadore." (274–75, emphasis in the original)

As Zoltán Abádi-Nagy argues, "Tralfamadore turns out to be a dehumanized planet with a machine civilization: what they can teach man is that man should not learn from them" ("Ironic Historicism" 87).

Against nineteenth-century popular belief, Emerson vigorously and correctly maintained that "society never progressess" ("Self-Reliance" 279), yet there are always those, such as the twentieth-century behavioral psychologist, B. F. Skinner, who will promise societal advancement in return for merely surrendering unwanted human dignity and unneeded individual freedoms. As the Shah of Bratpuhr keenly observes in *Player Piano*, surrendering such freedoms in the name of progress or comfort or efficiency reduces people from their once-proud status as free citizens in a democracy to "takaru" or slaves. But those who follow Skinner or who believe in and belong to his Skinnerian utopia fully pictured in *Walden Two* (1948) "entertain no nonsense about democracy. . . . This is a totally planned society, structured so that a self-perpetuating elite shapes to their specifications the inhabitants of the world they control" (Elliott 150), and those inhabitants should be grateful. John Pierce invented an excellent term for this kind of thinking: "the hubris of altruism"; that is, the "blind pride in seemingly benevolent ideals," which must be imposed on humanity "for its own good" (168). From a wealth of historical examples of this kind of utopia, Pierce selects John Calvin's Geneva and Pol Pot's Democratic Kampuchea where "the practical consequences of the hubris of altruism" are so much in evidence. "It is important," Pierce adds, "to remember that both might still be regarded as noble ideas had they not succeeded so thoroughly" (168). In *Walden Two* the imposition of Skinnerian values and techniques happens to a population essentially not consulted either about the values themselves or about participating in such a noble experiment. Had they been so consulted, there might have appeared that lone individual or even a group who like Bartleby, in

Herman Melville's story, would "prefer not to" participate. It is against this kind of planned society dedicated to a certain set of values—however benign or well meaning—that anti-utopian literature, such as *Player Piano*, is written.[17] Vonnegut, in contrast to Skinner but much like Emerson, remains a nonbeliever when it comes to societal progress or the necessity for controlling society.

If Vonnegut continues very much aware of the almost absolute centrality of machines and of technology for late twentieth-century American society, he also insists on their right use. In his view, machines are both a proper and a necessary subject for the contemporary American writer. "Machinery is important. We must write about it," he said in one of many interviews ("Kurt Vonnegut, Jr." 157) and so he does throughout his career. His point in *Player Piano* so familiar from American history, philosophy, theology, politics, and literature is, however, that machines and technology are or should be *the means* by which humans gain—not lose—their freedom. They are not now nor should they ever become simply ends in themselves. Ralph Barton Perry argued that "even ideas and skills do not suffice unless they are linked with the purposes for which they are used, or the feelings which give them value." He continues, "It is necessary, furthermore, that these purposes and feelings should be shared, in order that they may afford a basis of reciprocal action. When thus socialized and charged with emotion, durable ideas constitute the essence of culture and of civilization" (27). Machines, therefore, do not need to be "preserved from dissolution"; only their "essential formulas and aptitudes should be remembered, in order to be re-embodied in new machines" (27). Not machines themselves but ideas, including the idea of the machine, are paramount. At the end of *Player Piano*, bitter irony resides in Bud Calhoun's immediate repairing of the orange soda machine. Those repairs, made as the revolution has barely concluded, become Vonnegut's sharply etched image of the failure of this individual and all like him to distinguish between the means and ends for which this machine and every machine was invented. He is about to do himself out of a job once more. Bud has become a true *takaru* or slave of the machine. As such, he exemplifies Mumford's contention that other cultures "had machines; but they did not develop 'the machine.' It remained for the peoples of Western Europe to carry the physical sciences and the exact arts to a point no other culture had reached, and to adapt the whole mode of life to the pace and capacities of the machine" (4). In Ilium this process has been completed.

The novel's title, *Player Piano*, derives appropriately from a machine invented in the nineteenth century and perfected in the twentieth. In an early chapter of the novel someone listening to a player piano observes that "watching them keys go up and down . . . [y]ou can almost see a ghost sitting there playing his heart out" (28). The late Tony Tanner most succinctly summarized the ominous quality of this symbol for the novel. "A piano player is a man consciously using a machine to produce aesthetically pleasing patterns of his own making. A player piano is a machine which has been programmed to produce music on its own, thus making the human presence redundant" (*City* 182–83). David Hughes, in developing the player piano as an ideal image and symbol for Vonnegut's satire, discovered that "the heart of a player piano, the perforated music sheet, was invented in 1842 . . .

and by about 1890 it was brought to perfection in the United States." He concludes that this image "affords Vonnegut the blend he wants of nostalgia, technical proficiency, and corporealization of the spiritual world" (114n20). This blend will reappear even more poignantly in *Galápagos*, when Zenji Hiroguchi programs Mandrax, the super computer, to reproduce the intricacies of ikebana, the Japanese art of flower arranging that Hisako, his wife, teaches. This results in her loss of pride, self-respect, and her very reason for existence. Then she discovers that not only could that black box "teach what she taught, but could do so in a thousand different tongues . . . ikebana [could be] . . . as easily codified as the practice of modern medicine" (68–69). In *Galápagos*, Vonnegut extends the argument and its consequences about the uselessness of human beings that he first outlined in *Player Piano*, made central to several short stories, and included as the pivotal question in *God Bless You, Mr. Rosewater*. The question, which the Shah in *Player Piano* wishes to pose to the giant computer, "What people are for?" (277) recurs in Kilgore Trout's novel, 2BRO2B, spoken by a customer to the hostess of the Ethical Suicide Parlor where he has gone to die, "What in hell are people *for*?" (*God Bless You, Mr. Rosewater* 21). What, indeed, are humans for if machines can duplicate not only their music and work, but also their arts and sports? (*Galápagos* 71). This question haunts all of Vonnegut's fiction from *Player Piano* to *Timequake*. But for Vonnegut there is no going back on technology, unless nature itself, deciding it has had enough of human destruction, should enter the picture as it does in *Galápagos*. In *Player Piano*, perhaps more acutely than elsewhere in Vonnegut's fiction, this issue of the right role of machines and their right relation to people illustrates the difficulty American society has often shown in clearly identifying right means to achieve good ends. *Player Piano*, as a mid-century anti-utopian novel, illustrates, albeit negatively, the right role of technology and machinery within the goals and values of human civilization while at the same time arguing passionately for the sacredness of human beings.

In his prophetic 1934 study, *Technics and Civilization*, Mumford maintained that:

Mechanization and regimentation are not new phenomena in history: what is new is the fact that these functions have been projected and embodied in organized forms which dominate every aspect of our existence. Other civilizations reached a high degree of technical proficiency without apparently, being profoundly influenced by methods and aims of technics. (4)

Mumford's description fits exactly the United States of *Player Piano* but especially Vonnegut's Ilium, where Paul Proteus tries but does not really succeed in becoming his own person remaining squarely within and controlled by a technically dominated society. The novel thus satirizes both the over-dependence on technology and the over-reliance on the expertise of technocrats. Sallye J. Sheppeard contends that "because technology is inextricable from twentieth-century man's life and has profoundly changed him, Vonnegut cannot reflect upon contemporary man's metaphysical anguish without also commenting upon his technology" ("Kurt Vonnegut" 15). But the reverse may be even truer in that Vonnegut cannot reflect upon the role of technology in the twentieth century without also reflecting on human metaphysical anguish, especially as exemplified in Paul Proteus.

Proteus's flailing about—trying to be at home in Homestead, buying a farm that he cannot run, or attempting to be the Messiah of the saboteurs—reflects his blind desire to become a truly conscious being, to become fully human. The corporation, on the other hand, wants him to be its ideal manager—bright, but with his identity derived wholly from his place in the corporate mold. His wife, in her turn, wants Paul to be her ideal husband—loving but totally dedicated to succeeding within the corporation. The revolutionary Ghost Shirts want him to be their ideal leader—famous, but selflessly dedicated to their cause. None of these—not the corporation, not his wife, not the Ghost Shirts—none of them wants him simply to be or to be for himself alone, and no one ever asks what he wants. The wonder is that he does not become like his fellow workers: alcoholics, dropouts, or flunkies—the hollow shells of wasted men. When the corporation or his wife is not using Paul, then the revolutionaries are using him. The latter write letters in his name, issue manifestoes he does not know if he agrees with or not, and act generally as if he were their Messiah—a role he definitely does not wish to play. If he does not really know what he wants to be or do, he at least knows that he wants to be neither a Messiah who leads the revolution nor a human manager who oversees machines.

Vonnegut's book is a plea for human beings to be what they are able to be best: human—which is, frail and strong, thickheaded and intelligent, cruel and kind, failing and succeeding, hating and loving. This belief in the humanness of human beings will become a constant in all of his later novels and stories. It is also his warning against that ancient human desire for perfection, especially perfection in society that all too often, as in this novel, leads simply to sterility. Aldous Huxley, similarly worried about what he saw as the dangerous belief in the perfection either of humanity or society, chose for the epigraph to *Brave New World* a telling quotation from Nicolas Berdiaeff's *Slavery and Freedom* that applies equally well to *Player Piano*: "*Les utopies apparaissent comme bien plus réalisables qu'on ne le croyait aurefois. Et nous nous trouvons actuellement devant une question bien autrement angoissante: Comment éviter leur réalisation définitive?*" (Huxley 5, emphasis in original). (Utopias appear far more realizable than we had formerly believed. And now we find ourselves facing a question equally painful in a new kind of way: How to avoid their actual realization? My translation.)

In *Player Piano,* the corporation, working to establish its notion of utopia here on Earth, actively opposes any belief in the importance of variety in humans or their experience—all in the name of making everything as easy as possible for everyone and granting everyone a far greater degree of certainty than would be possible in a nonplanned, unregulated, free society. The good life will be achieved in *Player Piano* thanks to the corporation responsible for running everything in Ilium. All it asks in return is complete, undivided loyalty and service. Such loyalty and service are, however, not just expected—they are required. Vonnegut satirizes the kind of husband-wife working relationships that may and, in the novel actually does result from meeting such expectations. Proteus plays the part of the upwardly mobile, aspiring young husband, while his wife, Anita—"Ilium's Lady of the

Manor" (14)—personifies the ideal corporate wife who dutifully spends all her time and energy plotting ways to boost her husband up the corporate ladder. Yet their daily conversations become meaningless, vacuous exercises. Much of Anita's energy goes into dressing Paul for success by buying him clothing identical with that of those who appear just a bit higher up in the corporation. She then coaches him on how to behave at meetings, how to deliver speeches effectively, and how to conduct himself on various social occasions.

"Men will quickly commit themselves to any cause that promises certainty in their existence," observed theologian, Paul Tillich (307). The all-knowing computer in *Player Piano* not only promises but delivers such certainty. But at a price, as seen clearly in Anita and Paul's juvenile relationship. That price lies both in what is present, and in what is absent. The Shah points to what is obviously present when he several times "equates American society with the noxious materialism suggested by the nephew's name . . . Khashdrahr ('cash drawer') Miasma" (Sheppeard, "Signposts" 18–19). What is absent in *Player Piano* and what is often overlooked in creating the good life in a perfect world has been succinctly described by the noted Irish writer, Francis Stuart: "Where everything is seen as making life easier for all, there is no room for grief, pain and doubt, in which are the roots of a thriving organic consciousness" (19).[18]

Robert C. Elliott argues that after World War II, the atom bomb, and the holocaust "we will never again be able to create imaginative utopias with the easy confidence of the nineteenth century; the terror to which the eschatological vision applied to human affairs has led in our time forecloses that possibility" (101). Yet at the beginning of the twenty-first century the American public and its leaders still fall prey to believing that society or its organization can be perfected. Many still believe naïvely in that recurring human delusion called progress. If, as Rampton reasoned, "the dystopia in *Player Piano* looks much more ominous to us in the 1990s than the ones in Huxley and Orwell" (24–25), how still much more ominous it appears in the twenty-first century with an American society dominated by the multinational corporation, "the only social unit of which our age is capable" (Giraudoux).

In imagining being an American in *Player Piano*, Vonnegut correctly identifies America's love affair with technics and the machine as a central problem for American society as well as a possible opportunity to create a better life for most people. *Player Piano* demonstrates superbly that above all, society must be run not by corporations or by machines but by and for free citizens.[19] The issues raised in this, his first, novel will emerge again and again in Vonnegut's later fiction and will preoccupy him for the rest of his writing career as he imagines being an American.

GIVING BIRTH TO A MOUSE

As a very young country, the United States has relatively little history. Yet, rather than treasure that history, many Americans choose to ignore or forget what little they have. Still, like all nations and all peoples, Americans do see themselves, however marginally, within the context of their history. In imagining being an American, Vonnegut in *The Sirens of Titan* examines and evaluates all human history, including that of the United States. What he finds in that history is neither purpose nor meaning—neither comfort nor consolation.

A brilliantly inventive novel, *The Sirens of Titan* reveals not only Vonnegut's realized potential as a comic writer of future fiction, but also his accomplishment in conceiving of and executing a dazzling, fast-paced tour of the solar system containing memorable incidents, characters, and language. As Gary K. Wolfe recognizes "*Sirens* is easily Vonnegut's most flamboyant novel, with its entire universe at the mercy of the 'outrageous fortune' that operates in varying degrees in all of Vonnegut's [early] novels" ("Metaphor" 968). Appropriately, the novel's style is equally flamboyant, employing multiple fictitious sources ranging from Dr. Cyril Hall's *A Child's Cyclopedia of Wonders and Things to Do*, through Waltham Kitteridge's *The American Philosopher Kings* and Howard W. Sams's *Winston Niles Rumfoord, Benjamin Franklin, and Leonardo da Vinci*, Lavina Water's *Too Wild a Dream?*, Crowther Gomburg's *Primordial Scales*, Beatrice Rumfoord's book of poetry, *Between Timid and Timbuktu*, *The Beatrice Rumfoord Galactic Cookbook*, Sarah Horne Canby's *Unk and Boaz in the Caves of Mercury*, Dr. Frank Minot's *Are Adults Harmoniums?*, Dr. Maurice Rosenau's *Pan-Galactic Humbug or Three Billion Dupes* to Winston Niles Rumfoord's *Pocket History of Mars* and *The Winston Niles Rumfoord Authorized Revised Bible*, all rummaged and quoted by an unnamed future narrator. Looking back warily to the previous century, this narrator writes "a true story from the Nightmare Ages, falling roughly . . . between the Second World War and the Third Great Depression" (8) or, in other words, the book of his not-so-distant past becomes the book of our not-so-distant future.

The narrator, himself a historian, pieces together—as historians must—published sources, statistics, especially war casualties (166–69), authoritative quotations (106), scraps of poetry (152), a famous sermon (251ff), fraudulent stories (49–50), letters (90–92, 124–32), an extra-galactic legend (274–75), a presidential speech (59–60), pop songs (149), and a prayer (215). Much of this received information he retells in a lively interesting way, yet by including with it such an incredible array of minute details he risks leading most readers to question his veracity. Clearly, no individual—historian or not—could know such a wealth of improbably precise detail no matter how thorough the research. But this future historian is, in fact, cast from the mold of Thucydides—whom he holds up as his model historian (165). Thucydides's great work, *The History of the Peloponnesian Wars*, records a time, much like that experienced in the United States during the Vietnam War, in fulsome detail replete with conversations, military strategy sessions, colorful local details, and so forth, most of which Thucydides himself never experienced. Nor could he have heard about them in person (compare Sigman 29). In a style similar to Thucydides's, the narrator of *The Sirens of Titan* retells the story of Chrono's good-luck piece (142–43) and recounts a conversation between Salo and Constant as the latter is set down on Earth to die (317–19). The tone of the first story, which takes place during a children's school tour of a flame-thrower factory on Mars (!), is wonderfully comic in its welter of implausible details about how that good luck piece came into being and how it got into Chrono's possession. As such, it serves to reinforce the novel's theme that accidents rather than planning shape all life and all lives, yet the story itself must be taken "with a grain of salt." Similarly, the last conversation between Salo and Constant simply told and emotionally charged becomes at first convincing reading through its details including a seemingly irrelevant person asleep in the background who makes indecipherable comments. Upon reflection, however, readers realize that the narrator could not possibly have known such details either about the school visit or about the reported conversation. Nor could those many details have been available to him from published or even archival sources and, therefore, as in the case of Thucydides's conversations, they must be of his own inventing.[20]

The flamboyancy, frenetic plot, and quick shifts from source to source in *The Sirens of Titan* may so overwhelm readers that they will become in danger of overlooking its other qualities. For the great tour of the solar system planets, the war between the worlds, the violent social changes necessitated by the nightmare of equality and irrelevance, are all only mechanisms Vonnegut uses to explore both human inner space and the question of essential human worth—a question that dominates much of his early writing through *Slaughterhouse-Five*. This does not mean, however, that Constant's adventures, far from being real within Vonnegut's fictive world, actually comprise some form of individual hallucination or fantasy. One critic, for example, in an unconvincing reading of the novel, ignores the historian-narrator in order to maintain that everything happens within Constant's "dreaming or hallucinating mind" (Broer, *Sanity Plea* 31):

The overriding truth of this novel is that nearly everything Malachi has done has been done "in his head," the product of that "drug-induced hallucination" by which he enters the "Alice-in-Wonderland door" to the Rumfoord estate, a microcosm of his own mind [sic]. . . . Malachi must battle the Rumfoord madness within himself. (Broer 43)

This battle within Malachi, according to this critic, takes place on various planets within the solar system. For example, the discussion of Constant's adventure in "the caves of Mars"[21] continually emphasizes Constant's striving to attain his identity:

Actually, Unk, the life-affirming voice of Malachi Constant, has been attempting to make his way up the spiral like prison walls of the caves of Mars [sic] for a long time; we read that soon after they had landed, he and Boaz moved in very different circles. The circles in which Boaz moves are small and at the bottom of the spiral; the circles in which Unk moves are vast and restless, suggestive of wider and higher consciousness. (Broer 41)

Perhaps. But for this reading to be even plausible the writer would need to account for the fact that Unk is moving *in the wrong direction*. Unk can never become free of the caves on Mercury no matter how high he goes or how much "wider [his] consciousness becomes" until he passes an intelligence test conveniently devised for him. This up-the-spiral metaphor becomes even muddier as we follow Unk's "progress." He realizes the answer to the test is identical with the means to effect his escape. He must first turn the rocket upside-down only *then* fire it since only under those conditions would the rockets be pointing toward "the bottomless, sideless pit of space eternal" (*The Sirens of Titan* 211). This is, indeed, a descent into the nothingness and meaninglessness and indifference of space but hardly into "higher consciousness" (Broer, *Sanity Plea* 41). Ellen Cronan Rose more creditably suggests that "what the Mercury episode does is to simplify some very complex problems of human relationships" (18). "The interlude on Mercury," she sees, as "a brief parable on the meaning of life. Through the harmoniums, the formerly wicked Boaz learns the meaning of love and friendship" (18)—a lesson Constant on Titan will also finally acknowledge learning.

Moreover, the focus on the possibility of a "drug hallucination" is patently antithetical to both the spirit and letter of *The Sirens of Titan* as well as to Lewis Carroll's Alice books, unless each is read under the influence of the 1960s. Joseph Sigman gives a far more plausible reading of Vonnegut's novel as he cautiously advances the possibility of seeing "the allusions to the Alice books in *Sirens* as natural expressions of a world-view deeply influenced by modern scientific thought" (38). *Alice's Adventures in Wonderland* and *Through the Looking Glass* Sigman recalls, "provided science writers with their favorite analogues to the world of the new physics. . . . The use of Carroll's work is a deeply entrenched tradition in scientific popularization that goes back to Sir Arthur Eddington" (37). In a substantive analysis of Vonnegut's novel and its use of twentieth-century theoretical physics, he enumerates the several theories present or hovering in the background of *The Sirens of Titan* (26–38). He also points to the various successful attempts in this century to popularize complex theories through the use of the Alice books including, for instance, those by Eddington and George Gamow (37–38). As a result he sees that Alice-in-Wonderland door not as a gateway to hallucination (Broer, *Sanity Plea* 43) but—far more creditably—as "a threshold imaging his [Constant's] entry into the intellectual space of the new science" (Sigman 38).

In order to maintain the thesis of hallucination, a reader would also have to ignore completely Vonnegut's use of the many conventions of science fiction. In this novel those conventions provide not literal representations but metaphors for human inner experience. Admittedly, the kind of science fiction Vonnegut writes in this novel differs greatly from, say, Isaac Asimov's *Foundation* series or Frank Herbert's *Dune* and its endless sequels where the conventions of realism are loosed within a fantastic world, usually of the future. Yet Vonnegut's novel remains science fiction—if of his own peculiar brand, but still most definitely science fiction. Vonnegut appears "at ease . . . with science fiction; finding in its conventions not a kind of restriction, but a way of releasing his own sentimental-ironic view of a meaningless universe redeemed by love; his own unrecognized need to write a New Gospel or at least to rewrite the Old," declared Leslie A. Fiedler (200, reprint 11).[22]

In her admirably detailed reading of *The Sirens of Titan*, Rose suggests that "Vonnegut is not making jokes *about* science fiction, but *with* it" and goes on to observe that "the science-fiction components of *The Sirens of Titan* are . . . wildly implausible" (15). Briefly, she argues that in Vonnegut's view not only is the universe not schemed in mercy but it is also utterly indifferent to humans and their predicament as seen in his use of science fiction:

It's all very bleak. We can tolerate it only because it's said jokingly. We can take the knowledge that the universe is indifferent to man because we learn it from Winston Niles Rumfoord aflame with St. Elmo's fire, his chrono-synclastic-infundibulated spiral on its way to another galaxy. The truth about the indifference of the universe is displaced onto science fiction. (21)

Like the clowns in Shakespeare—to which Vonnegut famously likened his use of science fiction (*Wampeters, Foma & Granfalloons* 262)—who "do not distract us from the truth, but relentlessly insist that we consider it" (Rose 22), the science-fiction conventions in *The Sirens of Titan* force the reader to consider what many might prefer to avoid. But "Vonnegut does not avoid or deny pain; by a tremendous act of creative energy, he turns it into pleasure" (Rose 23). Thus we have a novel that is wonderfully comic and bleak, as well as absurd, satiric, and serious by turns or all five at once. The novel also invents "a new form of religious consolation and the coming of a new messiah . . . [that is] associated with the utopian concerns of science fiction" and will become "a dominant theme in Vonnegut's novels," as David Ketterer points out (296).

At a graduation speech in 1978, Vonnegut claimed that he had written all of the "masterpieces . . . of science fiction" except for Arthur C. Clarke's *Childhood's End* (*Palm Sunday* 174). Clearly Vonnegut takes his science fiction seriously as should his readers and critics. Stanley Schatt did just that when he concluded:

In many ways this novel [*The Sirens of Titan*] is Vonnegut's most complex one since it functions simultaneously as a parody of "hard-core" pulp science fiction, a description of the mythic journey of a modern-day hero, and, perhaps most importantly, as a tongue-in-cheek exploration of the meaninglessness of the universe. (*Kurt Vonnegut* 30)

It is within this framework created by science fiction that Vonnegut introduces the motif of the quest, one of the oldest of all metaphors for human experience and one employed frequently in pulp science fiction. And as in so many of Vonnegut's novels, *The Sirens of Titan* records not one, but two distinctly different types of quests: the false quest for the meaning *of* life that is juxtaposed to the true quest for the meaning *in* life. In *Cat's Cradle* for example, Bokonon warns the faithful against the pitfall of the false quest through several sacred calypsos, especially this one:

> Tiger got to hunt,
> Bird got to fly;
> Man got to sit and wonder, "Why, why why?"
> Tiger got to sleep,
> Bird got to land;
> Man got to tell himself he understand. (124)

Vonnegut himself once told how, at the beginning of each writing class he taught, he would lay down one firm rule: students had to write only about "what happened" (*Palm Sunday* 189). Violating this rule, he warned, would, in itself, be sufficient grounds for tossing the student out of the class for the simple reason that no one knows why an event happened. "You do not know. You cannot know" (189). Characters in his novels, such as Malachi Constant, who violate this rule and attempt to discover why something happens pay dearly for it. Yet Vonnegut's characters remain continually, to use his word, "embarrassed" that they do not understand. Early in the novel, Constant, the richest man in the world, makes the mistake of believing he knows why he is so rich and powerful. It is because "somebody up there likes me" (20). This cliché, *somebody up there likes me*, gained currency a few years before Vonnegut's novel as the title of world heavyweight boxing champion, Rocky Graziano's autobiography published in 1955. Time teaches Constant a quite different lesson so that when he appears at last as the Space Wanderer wearing an improbable bright yellow suit decorated with huge "orange question marks a foot high," he proclaims: "I WAS A VICTIM OF A SERIES OF ACCIDENTS, AS ARE WE ALL" (229). In other words: "You do not know. You cannot know" why anything happened.

Perhaps what Kafka meant by his aphorism, "The world was made on one of God's bad days" is that the deity neglected to include a moral order in creation that human beings would be able to appreciate or at least perceive. Characters in Vonnegut's fiction who go on the false quest in search of such an order in the universe or the meaning of life, whether moral, political, or omnipotent, are doomed to fail. A more human, and, therefore, more appropriate stance for them would be to stop pretending to understand what cannot be understood and simply confess bemusement or bewilderment. When Vonnegut's children would ask him, "Why?" his standard rebuttal was "Shut up! I just got here myself. Who do you think I am? Methuselah?" (*Palm Sunday* 177).

An ancient story in Zen Buddhism illustrates Vonnegut's point. A master-teacher instructed his pupil "if you meet the Buddha on the road kill him!" Such advice, even from such an excellent source, shocked and mystified the pupil until, after giving it long thought, he understood. It is necessary that each individual discover the truth that life holds for him or her alone, and not take another's truth for his or her own, not even from the Buddha himself. Similarly, John Bunyan's *The Pilgrim's Progress* (1678), until quite recently the most read book in English after the bible, makes the point repeatedly that the nature and goal of any quest becomes apparent not in the beginning, but only during the journey, and then mostly at the very end. Bunyan's hero, Christian, before he sets out has little notion of where he is going. Nor are there any reliable maps of the territory. His guide, Evangelist, in attempting to give him directions to the Heavenly City of Salvation, asks him: " 'Do you see yonder Wicket-gate?' The man [Christian] said, 'No.' Then said the other, 'Do you see yonder shining light?' He said, 'I think I do.' Then said Evangelist, 'Keep that light in your eye, and go up directly thereto: so shalt thou see the Gate' " (11, punctuation modernized). (In *Slaughterhouse-Five* Vonnegut approvingly quotes Theodore Roethke in much the same vein.) When Malachi Constant in *The Sirens of Titan* believes that he knows exactly where he is going and what he is doing, then he is in the greatest danger of missing the meaning in life. As Vonnegut once quipped "thinking that the guy up ahead knows what he is doing is the most dangerous delusion there is."

Christine Brooke-Rose modifies this argument by labeling *The Sirens of Titan* as "an anti-quest," since

the hero, Constant Malachi [sic], has everything he wants . . . [h]is quest is not sought for, but forced upon him, and, thus denuded, all he will seek for, on Mars and later, is his friend Stony Stevenson and the love of the family he is told he has founded. He will only get a semblance of the latter, and a final illusion of the former, at the moment of death. (258)

But one could contend that most quests by most heroes are unsought for and many messengers, such as Constant, are, to say the least, reluctant Jonahs. Also, many of the most famous quests, such as Sir Gawain's in "Sir Gawain and the Green Knight," end either in disillusionment or in the acceptance of an illusion.

A better term to describe Constant's search might be ironic quest, since, although he succeeds in his acknowledged quest to be a messenger, that role proves completely unfulfilling. Constant wanted, in effect, to play Mercury, the messenger to the gods by finding "a single message that was sufficiently dignified and important to merit his carrying it humbly between two points" (17). His prayer appears answered when he gets to carry a message, but in the end that message proves neither important nor dignified and certainly not what he really wanted or needed, so he lands in despair. While this message— delivering the spare part needed to repair a Tralfamadorian broken-down spaceship—lies at the heart of *The Sirens of Titan* and is truly important for the Talfamadorian messenger, it is hardly "dignified" nor is it really Constant's message since the spare part holds no meaning and has no value for him. Rather than becoming a true messenger, he becomes merely an undignified errand boy. His errand is a fool's errand as he travels throughout the solar system in order to deliver the spare part to the Tralfamadorian messenger. That messenger, Salo, is, in turn, on his own fool's errand to deliver a contentless message from one side of the universe to the other. He has been waiting for this replacement part for his spaceship throughout all of human history. For him, this part represents "the culmination of all Earthling history. . . . [T]he mysterious something that every Earthling was trying . . . desperately, . . . earnestly, . . . gropingly, . . . exhaustingly to produce and deliver" (297). What Constant delivers proves to be his son's good luck piece, which almost all Earthlings living in the United States will recognize immediately as a "church key" or beer-can and bottle opener.[23]

All human history struggled to give birth to this "mouse"—this trivial gadget that, whatever else it may be and no matter how important it may be for the Tralfamadorians, hardly qualifies as the key to the "meaning of life" or as the "dignified" message Constant sought all his life to deliver. Nor does Constant gain anything by delivering it. "The further we go into outer space [in *The*

Sirens of Titan], the more trivial the universe becomes, until finally, beyond the rim from Tralfamadore, it all becomes a joke, a shaggy-dog story that tediously adds pointless afterthoughts" declares Richard Giannone (*Vonnegut* 37).

Only after Constant gives up on this false quest to deliver a "dignified and important" message—that is, after he gives up searching for the meaning *of* life, and only after he kills the Buddha who told him to be a messenger—does he discover the meaning *in* life or what life holds for him which is to love.[24] Such is the simple end of his complex quest for inner peace and the feeling of self-worth. On Titan, one of Saturn's moons, Constant has a purpose in life and feels truly at home, which he never did either as a fabulously wealthy Earthling playboy or as a derelict flitting about the solar system. Still, nothing he discovers remotely answers the question, "Why?" The narrator, mercifully ignoring Constant's original motivation, justifiably concludes: "It was all so sad. But it was all so beautiful, too" (305).

Yet the sadness and beauty of which the narrator appropriately speaks come at a high price. Few readers will overlook the myriad of contrasting cruel, horrifying, and ugly incidents in the book, such as the wanton slaughter of the Martian "invaders" or the gratuitous separation of Winston Niles Rumfoord and his dog, Kazak.[25] Rumfoord only appeared to have been in control, managing "human affairs by virtue of nothing more than his own sense of self-worth, . . . social Darwinism at its very worse," as Mustazza believes (*Genesis* 54). In reality he, too, is used mercilessly in order to bring the Grand Scheme of the Tralfamadorians to a successful conclusion. Dog and man, having then no more use, are blown apart by an explosion in the sun. "A Universe schemed in mercy would have kept man and dog together," but clearly the universe in which Winston Niles Rumfoord and Kazak find themselves appears schemed in anything but mercy. Blown apart, the great dog went his own way "on the great mission to nowhere and nothing" (295). Kazak, "the hound of space" (295), sent off into physical and philosophical nothingness contrasts with his prototype, "The Hound of Heaven" that in Francis Thompson's poem was sent to offer the sinner "refuge, salvation, reward, and fulfillment" (Cowan 280). Thus Vonnegut suggests, as G. K. Wolfe succinctly puts it, that "the harsh realities of meaningless cruelty and death, whether on Mars, Titan, Mercury, or Earth . . . will follow man wherever he goes, whatever he does . . . because, fortunately or unfortunately they are a part of what makes him human" ("Metaphor" 969). Similarly, any notion that things are getting better will be dispelled either by disastrous events or the bleak destiny of characters. Perhaps the best comment on the belief in progress lies in the bitterly ironic epigraph to *The Sirens of Titan* supplied by Ransom K. Ferm. "Every passing hour brings the Solar System forty-three thousand miles closer to Globular Cluster M13 in Hercules—and still there are some misfits who insist that there is no such thing as progress" (5). Yes, there is progress, if by "progress" we mean movement in some direction, in any direction. But in which direction does true progress lie? Ferm's statistic, "forty-three thousand miles per hour," holds little or no meaning for any human being, since such speeding across the firmament lies outside most humans' understanding and is also neither observable nor capable of being experienced by people living on Earth. Only when observed from an enormous inhuman distance and only when observing not the planet, Earth, but the entire solar system as well as the huge constellation of Hercules is this "progress" or movement of the solar system caused by the expansion of space discernible. The universe mirrored in *The Sirens of Titan* schemed not in mercy but in cruelty or, worse and more exact, schemed in indifference expands at an incredible rate. Each planet, star, galaxy races away from the others toward some unknown, if identifiable, destination, but this movement, this progress reflects nothing but the expanding nature of the universe itself. Some progress. Discovering that the universe is finally unknowable, indifferent, may be as unsettling epistemologically and metaphysically as discovering that the entire human history on planet Earth has been manipulated by aliens for truly trivial ends.[26] Thus rather than being a record of the human race's inevitable progress from caves to spaceships, as recorded in *2001*, history in *The Sirens of Titan* becomes manipulated for a trivial, nonhuman end. Human history itself becomes a kind of ultimate shaggy-dog story—a bad joke played on all humanity. Within this context, the novel explores what are essentially religious or theological issues but in ways appropriate to mid-twentieth-century secular belief and disbelief. The New or, perhaps, rewritten Old Gospel according to Vonnegut includes an uncompromising view of the random violence of the universe and the limitations of all human beings, that combined with flamboyant comedy, sadness and beauty, an original use of science-fiction conventions, and an ironic quest motif, results in the special quality of *The Sirens of Titan* as well as cementing in place an important block in Vonnegut's imagining being an American.

A CUCKOO CLOCK IN HELL

Another equally important piece consists of the ambiguity and complexity of decision-making, especially decisions that may appear clearly and morally justified to those people making them. What could be more justified than, for instance, a person donning a disguise in order to spy on an evil enemy? Vonnegut suggests that no instance—even one that appears so clearly right—is quite as obvious as it appears. *Mother Night*, subtitled *The Confessions of Howard W. Campbell, Jr.* after the only reliable American agent still operating in Nazi Germany and still alive at the end of the war, is a funny book but at the same time it is a serious study in the schizophrenic personality of whatever nationality or background. Vonnegut gives as his source of inspiration for *Mother Night* a cocktail party conversation he had with an ex-Intelligence officer who maintained that all spies "are schizophrenics. They have to be insane . . . because otherwise they would either blow their covers or simply die of fright. . . . someone ought to make a spy movie about what spies are really like." Then Vonnegut adds his usual self-deprecating understatement: "So I wrote a book about it" ("Two Conversations" 204).[27] In order to be a successful spy, the main character of *Mother Night*, Howard W. Campbell, Jr. had to become a thoroughly convincing Nazi, which he accomplished in part by becoming a larger-than-life Nazi—one who out-Nazied the Nazis.[28] But because of the inherently insane Nazi mental structure, all his actions, speeches, broadcasts, and proposals, which in another—more sane—setting would appear instantly absurd, were taken seriously, often adopted, and usually praised. No matter what suggestion Campbell makes to the Third Reich, the response is always the same: Wonderful! Let's do it! In 1941, for example, he drew what he thought was an absurdly grotesque racist cartoon character of "a cigar-smoking Jew" complete with money-bag, Soviet Union flag, and trampled crosses to be used in target practice (116). To ingratiate himself further with his superiors he wildly exaggerated every feature in the caricature. To his shock and amazement not only did he succeed in pleasing his superiors, but he also succeeded beyond his wildest imaginings. Both the SS and the Hitler Youth organizations immediately made his cartoon their official target-of-choice. Millions of copies were distributed for which he even received extra compensation in a form particularly valuable during wartime: "a ten-pound ham, thirty gallons of gasoline, and [an] all-expenses-paid vacation" (116).

Some sixteen or eighteen years after World War II, living in New York City, Campbell heard a recording of one of his wartime propaganda broadcasts. He simply could not believe that anyone would take such things seriously because they were so patently exaggerated. Yet his immediate and highly paranoid American audience did take them just as seriously as the wartime German hierarchy or his German father-in-law had earlier. It is as if the projector of Jonathan Swift's "A Modest Proposal," who ironically suggested that Ireland solve its problem of a starving, poor population by raising children to be butchered for meat at two years old, had his proposal accepted. But then, in addition, his notorious scheme succeeded so well that he was asked to propose another similar one! The highest, if most bitterly ironic, compliment Campbell received for his work came from his father-in-law. On the eve of the fall of Berlin, he mentioned that he once suspected Campbell of being a spy, but then quickly concluded that whether he really was or not did not matter, since however well he advanced the United States interests, he aided Germany far more effectively. For the source of "almost all the ideas . . . that make me unashamed of anything I may have felt or done as a Nazi," his father-in-law acknowledges, derived not from Himmler, Goebbels, or even from Hitler but from Campbell. "You alone," he confesses, "kept me from concluding that Germany had gone insane" (81).

In attempting to establish his trustworthiness with the Germans—so he can effectively spy on them for the Americans—Campbell actually furthered the Nazi cause by providing what it most needed and most lacked: an intellectual and logical underpinning that gave it the appearance of intellectual and moral respectability. Frank Wirtanen, who recruited Campbell as an American spy, maintains that Campbell was indeed a Nazi, for there was no other way he could have been so successful in convincing his superiors of his zeal. When Campbell vigorously protests against his characterization, Wirtanen, startled by his sharpness, answers by contending that "he was one of the most vicious sons of bitches who ever lived.' " When Campbell again protests that he had to do such things in order to survive as an effective spy, Wirtanen's answer leaves no room for argument. If the problem was his credibility as a Nazi, then "Very few men could have solved [that problem] . . . as thoroughly as you did." When Campbell asks if he believes he actually was a Nazi, Wirtanen reponds without hesitation: "How else could a responsible historian classify you?" (138).

At the end of the war, Campbell has nothing and no one to live for. Realizing the truth, what he has become disgusts him. "That part of me that wanted to tell the truth got turned into an expert liar! The lover in me . . . into a pornographer! The artist in me . . . into ugliness such as the world has rarely seen before. . . . [M]y most cherished memories . . . converted into catfood, glue and liverwurst!" (150).

Campbell took the advice given to Conrad's Lord Jim: "in the destructive element immerse," and found that he and his most cherished thoughts, feelings, possessions, and relationships became contaminated by that destructive element—nothing remained untouched. So he sits in his cell in an Israeli jail writing his memoirs and arguing with himself about history and his place in it, much as Adolph Eichmann had earlier. His recitation leads inevitably to the schizoid conclusion identical to that of the historian's: He was in word and deed a Nazi exactly as he was in word and deed the most reliable and only surviving American agent in the Berlin power structure. "[A]ny successful spy must be two things," said Vonnegut in an interview. "One, he must be a double agent— he must work for both sides or he's doomed—and, two, he is schizophrenic. He is not well. Only a sick person could do it" ("Serenity" 24, reprint 16).

Labeling the insanity that gripped the world for the better part of a decade, "schizophrenia," helps Vonnegut locate and dissect the disease in order to warn his readers against it. "Howard W. Campbell, Jr. was an authentically bad man," Vonnegut says elsewhere, and, as such, he becomes a clear warning against the power over humans that even the most ludicrous distortions about people and values can have ("Two Conversations" 222). In imagining being an American Vonnegut contends over and over again, that evil never appears pure and clear and easy to recognize. As Campbell says to O'Hare, "Where's evil? It's that large part of every man that wants to hate without limit, that wants to hate with God on its side" (*Mother Night* 181)—whether such hatred is directed against a people, country, cause, or religion.

The totalitarian mind . . . might be likened unto a system of gears whose teeth have been filed off at random. Such a snaggled-toothed thought machine, driven by a standard or even a sub-standard libido, whirls with the jerky, noisy, gaudy pointlessness of a cuckoo clock in Hell. (*Mother Night* 162)

"If I'd been born in Germany, I suppose I would have *been* a Nazi," muses Vonnegut on the limits of free will, all teeth intact in his gear system. Rather than hatred of the enemy without limits that easily converts people into inhuman monsters, his statement replaces such hatred with empathy. Empathy in the suggestion that had he been born in Germany and had he become a Nazi, then he, too, might have furthered the cause of genocide: "leaving boots sticking out of snowbanks, warming myself with my secretly virtuous insides" (*Mother Night* vii). Robert Merrill proposes that "*Mother Night* is enriched by

Vonnegut's painfully direct engagement of this philosophical and moral issue [of free will and determinism] as illustrated most vividly in time of war but also during its aftermath" ("German American" 78), while Martin Amis points out that Vonnegut's ethnic background becomes a source of the novel's strength. "In the superb early novel, *Mother Night*, this genetico-political accident [being born of German-American parents]—together with his peculiar charm and moral subtlety as a writer—empowered him to attempt the impossible: to write a funny book about Nazism. He succeeded" (134).

In 1966 Vonnegut wrote a new introduction for *Mother Night* in which he emphasizes that, except for this novel, his fiction does not have conventional messages or morals. On the other hand, *Mother Night* does have such a clear lesson that lies in the danger of believing that it is harmless to pretend to be something other than what we are. "We are what we pretend to be," he asserts (v) and therefore people need to take great care when pretending. Campbell, an American, pretended to be in the service of the Fascists, but in his pretending he became what he pretended to be. "Can one evaluate a lifetime by one single action?" asks a character in Jean-Paul Sartre's *No Exit*. The answer is a decisive, "Yes." Campbell learned to his sorrow that he could indeed serve two masters, but at the huge price of becoming split into two people. Judged by his own actions, he was both a superb German Nazi and a superb American spy. By dividing himself so violently, he robbed himself of integrity leaving no solid identity. But becoming the servant of the Nazis and the servant of the Americans left no room for himself as a human being. Knowing what he said and how he acted, Campbell survives "through that simple and widespread boon to modern mankind—schizophrenia" (136). But his case is hardly simple.

Campbell's is clearly a double personality. Probably the most famous explorations of the double personality in English literature are Mary Shelley's *Frankenstein*, Robert Louis Stevenson's *Dr. Jekyll and Mr. Hyde*, and Oscar Wilde's *The Picture of Dorian Gray*. Vonnegut has been interested enough in these works to turn two of them into plays. He wrote a musical comedy based on *Dr. Jekyll and Mr. Hyde* (*Palm Sunday* 260–90) and a dramatic skit, "Fortitude" based upon *Frankenstein* which features a modern-day Dr. Norbert Frankenstein and his enthusiastic assistant, the ebullient Dr. Tom Swift (*Wampeters, Foma & Granfalloons* 43–64). Rosemary Jackson, commenting on these and other works featuring doubles of various kinds, perceptively claims that "Dialogues of self and other are increasingly acknowledged as being colloquies with the self: any demonic presences are generated from within" (108), which is also a cogent description of the split or schizophrenic personality.

Frankenstein, Dr. Jekyll and Mr. Hyde, and *The Picture of Dorian Gray* all evoke the dangers in surrendering to the dark side of the personality. After acknowledging that a human being may be not one, but two distinct personalities, the hero in each of these novels destroys himself. By contrast, the psychologist Karl Jung contended that a healthy person, in order to become fully human, would acknowledge and accept what he called the "shadow" or dark side of the personality. Campbell in *Mother Night*, rather than acknowledging this dark side erroneously believes that he can simply pretend to be it, while maintaining his purity of character. "I've always known what I did," he boasts (136). He deluded himself into thinking that "[e]spionage relieved him of the necessity of operating with a conscience" (Leeds, "Pretending?" 84). He imagined he could merely play at being his dark double while all the time secretly he would nurture his good side, his true self. When what he pretends proves to be equally as real as what he thought he was, he commits suicide, having nothing left to live for. In effect, he discovers that he has no good self to which he can return.

Campbell's editor concludes that Campbell "served evil too openly and good too secretly, the crime of his times" (xii). But Campbell's case is not unique in *Mother Night*. Most of the other characters in the book have wildly conflicting double identities—and in each case one of those identities serves evil. Marc Leeds sees Campbell's split character as symptomatic of all the other characters in the novel. He contends: "Not only is Campbell incapable of distinguishing his core self in the face of his many parts, schizophrenia is presented as the predominant operational activity enabling all the characters to live in harmony with their many selves" ("Pretending?" 82). Thus George Kraft, a retired paint-and-wallpaper dealer from Indianapolis, turns out to be an unsuccessful Russian spy who will go to jail eventually and while there become an important modern painter. Resi Noth impersonates her dead older sister Helga, only to find that she has taken her place so completely that her new self leaves no room for her old identity. The Russian Stephan Bodovsky plagiarizes Campbell's literary works and—to get rich quickly—publishes those personal memories of love as *Memoirs of a Monogamous Casanova*, the illustrated edition of which sells for an extra forty rubles. Ironically, he later succumbs and becomes a writer himself but makes the costly error of writing satire against the Russian state—a crime for which he pays with his life.[29]

"Make love when you can," admonishes *Mother Night's* editor (vii). Campbell had spent a good part of the war making love to his precious wife, Helga. Together they formed a "Nation of Two" that also became the title of a play he wrote. As Mustazza contends, this world that Campbell creates, this "nation of two, is not so far-fetched that we cannot at least sympathize with the choice or even see it as quite desirable" (*Genesis* 64).[30] All True. Yet, while his dream of a nation of two may not be "far-fetched," it nevertheless rings false. Unlike the *duprass* of Ambassador Horlick Minton and his wife in *Cat's Cradle*—an ideal relationship maintained with integrity within a social and political world—Campbell and his wife relate to no one and nothing outside themselves. It is but a short step or two from their narcissism to Billy Pilgrim's quietism. Failing to become responsible human beings, and failing to acknowledge any ties to or responsibility for the human community, their island of love becomes not a Nation of Two but a No Man's Land for None. Helga ends up dead somewhere, while Howard commits suicide judging himself guilty of "crimes against himself" (192).

Although Campbell comes too late to self-realization, he does at long last painfully arrive there, unlike other characters, such as his self-righteous captor, Bernard V. O'Hare. O'Hare was on the right side in the war, the American side, and he appeared on the right magazine cover, *LIFE* magazine, and he does a good patriotic deed when he captures the notorious Campbell—not once, but twice. Yet, even with all those "good" acts, he demonstrates that time and again he is part of the hate, ugliness, and horror that bred the war itself. Vonnegut, through the character of O'Hare, warns that hatred without limits and the resulting mindless violence occur whenever the self-righteous are let loose, whether in Nazi Germany or contemporary America; and worse, such hatred will become sanctioned national policy when the zealously self-righteous seize control of a country—any country. For real self-righteousness involves a divorce from reality, and from the human, fallible self along with a complete failure of empathy for others. Campbell becomes, therefore, a perfect narrator for Vonnegut's theme, since the real enemy of humanity is a human being divorced from himself, a schizophrenic, an insane person, whether that person participates in the ludicrous Nazi beliefs or in the mindless hatred of things German and Japanese fostered in America during the war. When World War II ended, many people were puzzled by the United States's new international friends who were no longer pictured as inhuman monsters, but as human beings with families and plans and hopes just like those of Americans. In *Mother Night* a nameless policeman tells about his brother's recent visit to Japan where he found the people among the kindest and most likable he had ever met. Yet to his astonishment he recalls that these were the same people—or at least of the same nationality—as those who killed his father during the war.

In a conversation recorded at the University of Iowa, Vonnegut revealed that this novel was the most difficult for him to write of his first three because the material "was more personally disturbing to me" ("A Talk with America's Greatest" 29). He obviously did not mean that he had been tempted to become a spy, since spies have the chance to become crazy in a manner that itself becomes overpowering (*Mother Night* 140). Rather, he had to reconsider all aspects of the war, including the largest massacre of civilians in modern history, caused not by the evil side, *them*, but by the good side, *us*. Moreover, the enemy, far from conforming to his propaganda image, turns out to be a real human being with a human face and with human hopes and needs similar to our own, rather than a caricature of a human being whether Communist or Nazi, Gentile or Jew, Japanese, German, or American. Such thoughts do not "breed serenity"— Vonnegut's wry comment on novel writing ("Two Conversations" 221). But such thoughts apparently preoccupied him as early as 22 May 1941 when, in his column in the Cornell *Sun* for that day, he argued strongly against censorship of war reporting. He exclaimed "We must know the shortcomings of the British— and of ourselves—as well as of the Germans" (4 quoted in Reed, "Shaman" 54).

Lawrence Broer correctly asserts that "the tendency of Campbell's defeatist self to rationalize his guilt and to retreat from difficult moral issues postpones the process of awareness, atonement, and moral growth that might return him to a wholeness of spirit" (*Sanity Plea* 53). Mustazza concludes that Vonnegut denies Howard Campbell "even the solace of self-deception . . . it is Howard's very saneness that allows him to witness the uncreation of his world . . . and therein lies the horror" (*Genesis* 75). Without principles, there is nothing to prevent Chaos and Mother Night from invading and taking over Campbell's life. Vonnegut's novel shows clearly that he—both personally and as author—does not "succumb to this new and general feeling of helplessness" which led Doris Lessing to praise both his morality and his taking responsibility for his writing and speaking (46). This novel about the power of lies may help unmask some of the worst ones as well as help readers face some uncomfortable truths about themselves, the country they live in, and those values they hold to be "true" or "good." If Vonnegut is right, and "people *can* be instructed. People can take *lessons*, and so they can go *beyond* what they must be" (Short 306 quoted in Reed, "Shaman" 56); that is, they can learn to utilize free will within whatever limits of determinism they may find themselves, then *Mother Night* in all its moral complexity and ambiguity becomes an essential text in imagining being an American.

ALTERING THE NATURE OF THE WORLD

Ever since the first mushroom cloud appeared over the sands of Almagordo, New Mexico, the atom bomb has become—in J. Robert Oppenheimer's words— "a most terrible weapon, that has altered abruptly and profoundly the nature of the world" ("Atomic Weapons" 1945 quoted in Boyer 272). But more immediately, the atom bomb also altered abruptly and profoundly the nature of the United States, since it remains a prominent part of the United States's credibility as *the* superpower in the world. In his imagining being an American, Vonnegut focuses in *Cat's Cradle* on responsibility or the lack of it as exemplified in the American character and in American society. Of all his novels before *Slaughterhouse-Five*, the bitterest satire occurs in *Cat's Cradle*. If *Slaughterhouse-Five* reflects the fiery apocalypse of the firebombing of Dresden, then *Cat's Cradle* envisages an icy apocalypse of a post-holocaust world which, in Robert Frost's well-known words, "for destruction . . . would suffice."

> Some say the world will end in fire,
> Some say in ice.
> From what I've tasted of desire
> I hold with those who favor fire.
> But if it had to perish twice,
> I think I know enough of hate
> To say that for destruction ice
> Is also great
> And would suffice.
>   ("Fire and Ice")

In *Cat's Cradle* Vonnegut's mordant wit finds its appropriate subject in the end of the world with bitterly comic results. His first novel, *Player Piano*, also had many fine comic moments, such as the invention of the Shah's language that sounds vaguely obscene when spoken aloud. Other successful comic devices include recasting the patriotic slogan, "Eternal Vigilance Is the Price of Liberty" into "Eternal Vigilance Is the Price of Efficiency," parodying the General Electric Company morality play, and satirizing such staples as the corporate ethos and inflated bureaucratic language. Finally, there is Vonnegut's *tour de farce* in the *reductio ad absurdum* satire of the Cornell football program. There were not, however, many of those jokes that were to become the self-described hallmark of Vonnegut's early fiction. Those jokes began to appear and to proliferate in his second novel, *The Sirens of Titan*. They reach a kind of crescendo in *Cat's Cradle*. As Kenneth Cook points out "*Cat's Cradle*, a book of 127 chapters in 191 pages, is like a series of one-liners. Each chapter functions as a joke, and most end with a punch line. Beyond that, the typical humorous ploy of Vonnegut is the turn built up and communicated through short chapters, ironic titles, and quick juxtapositions" (51). John Leverence lists sixteen different traditional "aspects" of American humor in *Cat's Cradle*. (What he calls "aspects" Vonnegut would consider jokes.) Leverence's list includes "the tall tale; the unreliable narrator; the Negro minstrel; comedy in a grim situation; grotesque naturalism, [sic] incongruous language; narrative objectivity in a chaotic situation; satire; anecdote; the Westerner character; alazon-eiron relationship; the yarn spinner overwhelmed by his own tale; point counter point; avoidance or deprecation of extramarital sex; the humorless narrator; sentimentality" (955). The categories are neither hard nor fast. For example, here's an incident from *Cat's Cradle* that is clearly a joke but which could be labeled either "comedy in a grim situation" or "narrative objectivity in a chaotic situation." Whichever the category, the humor is wonderfully macabre and grotesque. During an outbreak of bubonic plague, Dr. Julian Castle, having worked frantically and hopelessly without sleep for many days, goes from bed to bed in his hospital searching in vain for a patient with enough life left to warrant medical treatment. But all the potential patients he finds are dead. When he finally cracks, he takes his flashlight and, while shining it on the stacks of corpses piled high outside the hospital, says to his son: "Son, . . . someday this will all be yours" (112). The joke depends upon our knowing and recognizing the father-to-son cliché about inheriting the family land and wealth, "Someday this will all be yours," and then putting it into the horrifying context of the piles of plague victims. Perhaps the best image for Vonnegut's jokes in *Cat's Cradle* would be that of the grin on the skull beneath the skin, for in this novel we are never far away from death. Whichever way we turn—politics, economics, religion, or sex—we head toward death. Even when the narrator uses a harmless cliché, "It's a small world," another character replies grimly *and* humorously, "When you put it in a cemetery, it is" (50).

Vonnegut's invented Caribbean language that contributes a variety of religious terms to the novel—all of which sound either vaguely or explicitly obscene—is an important second major source of humor. While *Player Piano* introduced a similarly made-up foreign language also with several comic terms, particularly *takaru* or "slave," *Cat's Cradle* refines and extends this joke with *wampeter*, *wrang wrang*, *karass*, *sin-wat*, *boko-maru*, *van-dit*, and so forth. Like Gulliver in Jonathan Swift's *Gulliver's Travels*, John, the narrator in his attempts to master his new language often generously translating sentences for the reader: " *'Dose, sore . . . yeeara lo hoon-yera mora-toorz tut zamoo-cratz-ya.'* 'Those, sir . . . are the Hundred Martyrs to Democracy' " (104).[31] Some terms may provide unintentional comic results as when the narrator titles a chapter, "What a *Wampeter* Is."

In addition to the multiple jokes and suggestive language, "*Cat's Cradle* illustrates almost every device, technique, attitude and subject we encounter in Vonnegut [through *Slaughterhouse-Five*]" as Reed observes in *Kurt Vonnegut, Jr.* (119). Vonnegut's invention works overtime as he combines a satire on modern "feel good" American religion with another on a banana republic's military dictatorship, then laces the brew with caricatures of what it means negatively to imagine being an American in his portraits of American greed, backslapping-good fellowship, and shortsightedness. The result is a truly fantastic satire—bittersweet and cutting. One critic, however, unable to accept what Mark Twain once characterized as the coincidences of life, declared that: "A weakness of *Cat's Cradle* is the shaky bridge that Vonnegut provides between the two major sections of the novel. In order to get John . . . to the island of San Lorenzo, Vonnegut treats himself to several unlikely coincidences" (Allen, *Understanding* 61). But this negative judgment blatantly ignores both Vonnegut's method and theme. In *Cat's Cradle every* event—not just one limited sequence of events—becomes part of an improbable series of coincidences. Lionel Boyd Johnson bounces from one corner of the world to another before being washed up on the shores of San Lorenzo to assume his rightful identity as the holy man, Bokonon. Another wildly improbable chain of coincidences propels John to write the book about the day the world ended, which he does indeed do, although as with most human endeavors, the results surprise even him. In the world of *Cat's Cradle*, all events *without exception*—and the more improbable, the more convincing—work toward one end, although exactly what that end may be remains hidden.[32] Also, verisimilitude will always be in short supply in a patently unrealistic, fantastic satire.[33]

As in all of Vonnegut's novels through *Slaughterhouse-Five*, *Cat's Cradle* wrestles with the quintessential American moral problem of means and ends; that is, does the good end ever justify employing an evil or even a questionable means? Could a good religion, for instance, be founded on harmless lies? Bokononism appears to give meaning, purpose, and value where none previously existed. Could a better society be created based upon a morality play that balanced good and evil? San Lorenzo appears to be just such a society. The utopia founded by Bokonon (Johnson) and McCabe features equilibrium between forces rather than the unbalanced schizophrenia of, for instance, *Mother Night*. The secret of their utopia lies in their successful adaptation of Charles Atlas's "Dynamic Tension" as a model for a viable society. Atlas's method of building muscles was simply to work one set of muscles against another set.[34] Similarly, Bokonon believed that a viable society would result if good were pitted against evil, and if then the tension between the two was kept at a continuously high level (74). Lionel Boyd Johnson brilliantly invents his Bokononist religion and brilliantly invents himself as Bokonon, both of which are good, while Eugene McCabe creates the bad military dictator who will rule the island and outlaw Bokonon and Bokononism. The novel incorporates "the Manichean dualism of good and evil, God and Satan, holy man and evil tyrant . . . country and city, corrupt civilization and pastoral nature" (Freese, "Invented Religions" 151). The results of this dynamic tension for the population generally appears benign since they see themselves appearing as actors and actresses in a readily understood morality play of the Good Bokonon in his jungle habitant opposed to the Evil McCabe in his urban setting. While the population remained contented with their roles, McCabe and Bokonon grew increasingly mad as they more and more assumed their respective roles (compare Howard W. Campbell, Jr. in *Mother Night*).

More generally, however, *Cat's Cradle* focuses on the potentially explosive conflict between the promise inherent in the creation of life and the threat inherent in humankind's destructive bent. Thanks to Bokonon's *foma*, or harmless lies, people are able to live with the ongoing contradictions.[35] Bokonon sums up the power of *foma* to overcome human despair in one of his sacred "Calypsos":

> I wanted all things
> To seem to make some sense,
> So we all could be happy, yes,
> Instead of tense.
> And I made up lies
> So that they all fit nice,
> And I made this sad world
> A par-a-dise. (90)

The resulting religion may on occasion appear comical, yet it remains ultimately serious. At a minimum Bokonon and his reasonable religion founded on *foma* illustrate the contemporary need for both religion and religious belief. Vonnegut, speaking at the Bennington College 1970 commencement, told the graduating class: "A great swindle of our time is the assumption that science has made religion obsolete" (*Wampeters, Foma & Granfalloons* 166). Moreover, religion remains important for Vonnegut because "all religions . . . provide the sense-making structures necessary for man's survival. . . . [T]hey serve as the essential antidote against the most dangerous 'religion' of all, the belief in unbridled technological progress with its alleged objectivity, which is nothing but amorality, and its built-in tendency toward ultimate self-destruction," contends Freese ("Invented Religions" 153). "By the end of *Cat's Cradle*, it is hard to remember that Bokonon is a fictional character—religions have been built around far less improbable creators before" (Brien 65). G. K. Wolfe argues that there is "a kind of structure for the reading of fantasy . . . which permits certain fantasy works to become analogues of inner experience virtually as valid as events of the 'real world,' and which expresses the author's own most fundamental convictions" ("Encounter" 12–13). Although he does not discuss *Cat's Cradle*, Wolfe's description admirably fits the Bokononist religion that appears to feature exactly such a structure. Bokononism is, therefore, comically serious, as the novel's plot is comically apocalyptic. "Like his author, Bokonon does not pretend to know the purpose of life, but he does devise artful, clever, and loving suggestions for living without the big answers" (Cooley 170). If there is no transcendent force, there is still the bedrock of humanity. "Bokononism, cutting religion and man down to size, is the contour of our hope. And if the hope is slender, it is nevertheless genuine," as John R. May persuasively argues (199).

On the other hand, John R. Cooley in *Savages and Naturals: Black Portraits by White Writers in Modern American Literature* discusses the significance of Bokonon not just as a religious figure but also as a black character. He finds that "Vonnegut's Bokonon is one of the rare examples of a basically successful black portrait by a white writer" (171). Cooley continues:

Although Bokonon does not become a public voice for his people, Vonnegut gives him an intellect as well as a sense of humor, thus producing one of the few white novels in which there is some sense of a black mind at work. Vonnegut upsets the apparent white assumption that blacks have bodies and soul but that they do not have the capacity for rational intelligence. (172)

Yet, such rational intelligence appears powerless to stop or delay the apocalypse. If within its intricate plot and counter-plot, *Cat's Cradle* provides memorable jokes, grotesque situations, witty repartee, and clever parodies they all contribute to making the serious point that human beings can and may very well choose to end life on planet Earth. As Henry Adams warned over 100 years before *Cat's Cradle*, "Some day science may have the existence of mankind in its power, and the human race commit suicide by blowing up the world" (quoted in Boyer 248). The narrator, Jonah-John, writing a book which he innocently believes will record the various activities of prominent Americans during the day when the first atomic bomb exploded over Hiroshima, chooses an ominously prophetic working title, "The Day the World Ended." The "sacred obligation" of a writer, he believes, lies in producing "beauty[,] . . . enlightenment and comfort at top speed" (*Cat's Cradle* 156)—a rather difficult assignment given his experience and the subject of the end of the world. *Cat's Cradle* itself, however, although also about the end of life on Earth, is definitely enlightening, and, as a work of imaginative literature, it has a certain beauty. But like all of Vonnegut's early novels, it does not contain much, if any, comfort. If anything, this novel appears written to afflict the comfortable, rather than bring comfort to the afflicted. This stance becomes especially clear in the ending where "Vonnegut . . . treats us to an imaginative view of the outcome of our insane pretensions, both technological and religious, asking us to thumb our noses at the image of ourselves we call progress and God" (May 200). While other commentators were enthusiastic about the possibilities of technology solving the great problems of war, waste, illness, and poverty, Vonnegut remained skeptical, and in *Cat's Cradle* downright fearful.[36] With the passing decades more and more thinkers, scientists, and social commentators have allied themselves with his view until, at the beginning of this new century, those who in the 1950s and 1960s announced that they believed in progress through technology, such as in the use of atomic energy for peaceful purposes, appear quaintly irrelevant to trying to solve the problems facing the world.

Cat's Cradle remains Vonnegut's comic masterpiece and, together with *Slaughterhouse-Five*, *Galápagos*, *Bluebeard*, and *Hocus Pocus*, his best work. This memorable story has worn well over the decades since its publication, and most readers will concur with Vonnegut's own evaluation of it as the best of the five early novels. Within the book Vonnegut's comedy spares no one: from the narrow military mind and values to the scientist's lack of morality and vision, the hypocrisy of religion, the dedicated American's will to get ahead, and the Hoosier *granfalloon*. The telegraphic style with its short punchy sentences and hilarious chapter titles (developed further from the earlier *The Sirens of Titan*) proves an exact match for his subject. The invented *Books of Bokonon* form a moral core for the novel that Vonnegut uses to comment on and/or to provide counterpoint to the action. In an otherwise mad whirling world, Bokonon—along with John, the naïve narrator—helps establish a positive set of values so necessary for the success of this apocalyptic normative satire. These positive values include a belief in the sanctity of human beings, the necessity for human love, the primacy of human community, and a vision of a world larger than a single person, family, or country. Unfortunately, like Shakespeare's "cloud-capp'd towers" all of these positive values perish in the frozen world of Ice-9:

> The cloud-capp'd towers, the gorgeous palaces,
> The solemn temples, the great globe itself,
> Yea, all which it inherit, shall dissolve
> And, like this insubstantial pageant faded,
> Leave not a wrack behind. (*The Tempest* 4)

That old nemesis in imagining being an American—the evil means used to achieve a good end—appears concretely in *Cat's Cradle* as the fictional Ice-9 and lurking just behind it lies the all-too-real atomic bomb guaranteed to overwhelm almost any end, however good. The notion of Ice-9 derives from the plot for a fantastic story that Dr. Irving Langmuir concocted to entertain H. G. Wells when he visited the General Electric Research Laboratory in Schenectady.[37] Wells never used the idea, so Vonnegut concluded "Finders, keepers—the idea is mine" (*Palm Sunday* 102). Thanks to Vonnegut's novel, Ice-9 has entered the popular imagination as a metaphor appearing even in a reputable medical research paper on deadly degenerative diseases.[38] This use also illustrates in a small way what N. Katherine Hayles means by her assertion that "culture circulates through science no less than science circulates through culture" (21).[39] Langmuir enjoyed the considerable distinction of being the first Nobel Prize winner in science employed in a private industrial research laboratory (*Palm Sunday* 102). Vonnegut used him as the model for Felix Hoenikker, inventor of Ice-9.[40] The portrait is not a flattering one. "Other civilizations were destroyed by barbarians from without. We breed our own. They have marvelous technical skill. They may even be very learned in specific disciplines. But they are barbarians," as Robert M. Hutchins once trenchantly observed (quoted in Boyer 269–70). He might have been speaking of Felix Hoenikker.

Although used for good ends—finishing World War II and eliminating mud for the marines—these means take on a life of their own escaping the leash of their creators. Boyer rightly asks

What was the appropriate aesthetic for the bomb? If an air raid on a small Spanish town could inspire one of Picasso's greatest canvases, or the individual brutalities of Napoleon's invasion of Spain Goya's most powerful work, how was one to respond imaginatively to Hiroshima and Nagasaki and, still more, to the prospect of world holocaust? (250)

Cat's Cradle is Vonnegut's enduring imaginative response. In mid-twentieth century, it was not only possible, but it was even necessary to imagine being an American in a world bereft of human beings—a world frozen in Ice-9.

THE APOTHEOSIS OF PHILANTHROPY

It strikes me as gruesome and comical that in our culture we have an expectation that a man can always solve his problems.
                                                    —Kurt Vonnegut

When the *Mayflower* set sail that original colonizing ship contained not only the Pilgrim Separatists with their dream of a New World where they could establish a New Jerusalem and practice their religion in peace and freedom, but also the "strangers," those in the majority who joined the company not for religious reasons but to seek their fortune on the new continent. The division between the two groups became so strong that it occasioned the colonists' first political document, the Mayflower Compact. The dreams of America held by each group—a land of peace with individual freedom of conscience and a land of plenty with individual accumulation of wealth—coexisted as uneasily on the *Mayflower* as they have throughout subsequent American history. For there are, and always have been, not one but two American Dreams. The first rooted in the dream of freedom and the second in the dream of riches. The collision of these conflicting dreams in imagining being an American becomes the matter out of which Vonnegut centuries later creates his satiric portrait of greed and uncritical love, inherited wealth and philanthropy in *God Bless You, Mr. Rosewater*.

Eliot Rosewater claims, quite correctly, that the Rosewater fortune accumulated because the Founding Fathers did not succeed in limiting the riches of each citizen (12). Yet Thomas Jefferson, for one, fought long and hard against what he called "an artificial aristocracy, founded on wealth and birth without either virtue or talents" (484). To Jefferson this was "a mischievous ingredient in government, and provision should be made to prevent its ascendancy" (484). Jefferson led the fight to pass legislation "abolishing entails . . . abolishing the privilege of primogeniture, and dividing the lands of intestates equally among all their children, or other representatives" (485). These laws by preventing the accumulation of wealth through the forced break-up of large estates, would, he believed, effectively abolish, or at least radically limit, inherited wealth as the basis for the pseudo-aristocracy of wealth and birth. Thanks to such laws, no individual or family would enjoy an unfair advantage through inheriting wealth in the form of land. Therefore, a new "natural aristocracy . . . [whose] grounds . . . are virtue and talents" would be free to emerge in each new generation (484).

Historically, things worked out quite differently from what Jefferson planned. The Rosewaters and their ilk circumvented the laws and/or made their fortunes not from land (which Jefferson's laws were designed to prevent) but from natural resources, inventions, slaves, technology, and so forth. As a result, such families could and did amass great wealth that they then secreted in foundations so that their heirs, regardless of their virtue or talents, could indeed become an aristocracy—an aristocracy founded upon greed.[41] Eliot inherits not only "a great deal of money but also . . . the family guilt" over how this money was accumulated (Godshalk 100). His ancestors and others like them, he realizes, had thwarted the promise that was America "which was meant to be a Utopia for all," replacing it with that pseudo-aristocracy of greed within an "entirely inappropriate and unnecessary and humorless American class system" (12) based upon inherited wealth. Eliot, in effect, exclaims *mea culpa* and sets out to atone for the loss of Utopia through giving away money—since "money is dehydrated Utopia" (121). Attempting to assuage his guilt through philanthropy, he spends huge sums buying paintings for museums, supporting starving artists and writers, staging operas, and so forth, but all with little success. He finds himself feeling much like Emerson's "foolish philanthropist" in "Self-Reliance," who gives money "to such men as do not belong to me and to whom I do not belong" (262). When Eliot abandons this unworkable philanthropy, he switches, instead, to what Emerson thought was a wise form of philanthropy, by giving personal service to "a class of persons to whom by all spiritual affinity I am bought and sold; for them I will go to prison, if need be" ("Self-Reliance" 262). Thus he visits the sick, comforts the lonely, feeds the hungry, gives drink to the thirsty, and even helps those in trouble by joining the Volunteer Fire Department. He becomes the one who listens to those who have no listener and who comforts society's outcasts. "I'm going to love these discarded Americans, even though they're useless and unattractive," he declares (36).[42] As Diana Moon Glampers tells him at the end of a telephone conversation in the middle of the night during which Eliot treats her like a human being, taking her fears seriously, with never a trace of sarcasm: "You gave up everything a man is supposed to want, just to help the little people, and the little people know it. God bless you, Mr. Rosewater" (61).

In addition, Eliot realizes that money's prime function in this form of philanthropy lies more in its symbolic value rather than in its immediate purchasing power. What people want is to know that someone cares so he "gave them love and trifling sums of money" (40).[43] But this form of philanthropy, to treasure human beings simply because they are human, requires huge quantities of emotional energy, as Eliot discovers. His beautiful wife divorces him not because she hates him or cannot stand what he does or because she does not approve or understand his actions, but because she simply does not have the emotional stamina to keep on doing it with him (53–54). A typical caller to the Rosewater Foundation, for example, will begin talking to Eliot by saying, "I'm nothing" (74) and believe it. Realizing that wealth will not help such folk, nor the arts and sciences, he offers them his time and a prescription against most minor physical and emotional aches and pains, "take an aspirin tablet . . . with a glass of wine" (78). Beyond this he also invents useful things for them to do. Some may appear as improbable as his fly hunts, yet their purpose becomes fulfilled when the participants feel they actually are needed, that they are rendering a useful service, rather than simply receiving a handout.

These so-called useless people Eliot Rosewater helps find themselves in circumstances similar to those people experienced in the 1930s, especially by Americans battered by the Great Depression. Brought up in the faith that God blesses those who truly believe and work hard, many Americans found themselves in the Great Depression with no work, without means to support their families, and, therefore, persons of no value. They were integers in a simple but harrowing equation: no job = no income = no worth. Tossed aside by society, like so many empty husks, people began wandering across the country—useless people with no job, no family, no one to care for, and no one to care for them. The legacy they left for Vonnegut's generation was devastating. Small wonder he concludes that people his age must leave behind that "envying, life-hating mood of the Great Depression at last" (*Wampeters, Foma & Granfalloons* 285). Near the end of the novel, Senator Rosewater contends that any person who is poor can "with gumption . . . elevate himself out of the mire . . . and that will continue to be true [in] a thousand years" (184). But Kilgore Trout rebuts his facile assertion by pointing out that, on the contrary, the feeling of uselessness, not the experience of poverty, is the major problem for such people. He maintains that "uselessness will kill strong and weak souls alike, and kill every time" (184). This statement is the closest any character in *God Bless You, Mr. Rosewater* or in any other of Vonnegut's early novels comes to preaching. The very character of the preacher himself, however, undercuts this sentiment, for the words are put into the mouth of the hack science-fiction writer who works at a green stamp redemption center. An amusing minor character, Kilgore Trout's science fiction exposes Eliot's considerable limitations as a reader since, he confesses, he reads only for plot. Rosewater says that writers such as Trout "couldn't write for sour apples" (18). Through his fiction, Trout does for readers what Eliot attempts to do with his money, which is to provide people with "fantasies of an impossibly hospitable world" (20). Finally, at the end of the novel, Trout is brought on stage to give his sermon on the dangers of soul-rot and the uselessness of human beings. Trout's own short story, "2BRO2B," which vividly highlights the uselessness of human beings, appears in plot outline form in *God Bless You, Mr. Rosewater*: As the Earth of the very near future becomes more and more crowded, and as work becomes more and more automated, more people frequently face the moral categorical imperative of committing suicide in order to provide room for others (20–21).

Although "people can use all the uncritical love they can get" (186), many have a vested interest in seeing that they do not receive it. The unscrupulous young lawyer, Norman Mushari, for instance, is determined to rid Eliot of his fortune and hopes in the process to siphon off a sizable portion of it into his own safekeeping. Mushari pictures himself as David doing battle against Goliath (10), but Eliot is anything but Goliath, being called by Mushari's own colleagues "The Nut," "The Saint," or "John the Baptist." Both David and Goliath are present in *God Bless You, Mr. Rosewater* but David is clearly Eliot Rosewater himself, while Goliath is the Rosewater fortune. Eliot responds to Mushari's attack by refusing to do battle—he retains no lawyers and he files no countersuit. Rather than making an opposing argument in court, he "turns the other cheek" and, in what may well be the ultimate philanthropic act, gives away all his fortune through inheriting the fifty-seven or more children of Rosewater County who fraudulently claim him as their father. Hence the Rosewater fortune, this leading character in the novel having proven impotent in alleviating pain and suffering, and revealed as "a force aligned with inhumanity" (Leff 31), leaves the Rosewater family forever, never to burden another with the responsibility of caring for it. Eliot feels only relief and happiness in practicing this third, and most sweeping, form of philanthropy as he watches the family fortune disappear.

All three forms of Rosewater's philanthropy—giving away large sums of money, giving away small sums along with uncritical love, and giving away the entire fortune—are linked through moral questions and the issue of personal guilt, to events in World War II. To citizens of the United States, World War II appeared to eliminate ambiguity from national and private morality, because the enemy was portrayed as terrible, inhuman, and evil. But moral ambiguity resurfaced when those who participated in the war, such as Eliot, found themselves in predicaments that forced them to ask difficult questions about their own or their country's actions. For Vonnegut, the ambiguity in these questions usually focuses on the Allies' bombing the open, undefended city of Dresden. Such actions led to the ethical dilemma familiar from *Cat's Cradle* of what happens when the supposedly good side uses inhuman, evil means (firestorms over Dresden or dropping the atomic bomb on Hiroshima and Nagasaki) in order to achieve a good end (the defeat of Germany or Japan). Is the result good or evil? Or is it perhaps morally neutral? These questions were part of what I described earlier as the worldwide moral hangover left by the war. In *God Bless You, Mr. Rosewater* the hangover is appallingly and personally present in Eliot Rosewater's memory of a tragedy, which occurred when he did his duty and obeyed what appeared to be legitimate orders, given under fire. As a soldier, he had been told to take an objective and hold it. Heroically, he led his troops in an assault on a building, and personally killed three of the enemy before someone realized that these enemy were unarmed. What proved especially—and bitterly—ironic, was that they were unarmed firemen (64). To make matters even worse, Eliot discovers that of his three unarmed victims the two he killed with a grenade were old men, while the one he bayoneted was a teen-age boy! It was, of course, no one's fault—mistakes are bound to happen in war.[44] But that is cold comfort, for Eliot now has to live the rest of his life with his vivid memory of killing three unarmed people who were acting selflessly to save the property and lives of others; hence his enthusiasm for volunteer fire departments and, in part, his engagement in philanthropy. Yet, like Dr. Schlichter von Koenigswald in *Cat's Cradle* who also works hard to overcome a moral deficit (126–27), his prospects of ever clearing his debt are doubtful, at best.[45]

If "Vonnegut goes well out of his way to show the validity of Eliot's viewpoint, making him perhaps one of the most endearing of his protagonists" (Mustazza, *Genesis* 99), he also assiduously avoids any sentimental treatment of either Eliot's ghastly mistake in killing three unarmed firemen or the many instances of his good deeds—always a danger in a novel with a good hero. Vonnegut accomplishes this, in part, by showing his main character's considerable limitations both in themselves and in contrast with those of other characters. For example, Eliot dramatically contrasts with the robust, healthy fisherman, Henry Pena. Pena with his sons works hard for a living, lives in constant danger of bankruptcy, and maintains a clear sense of what is real and what is unreal, fantasy, or phony whether it is a fish, woman, or man. Eliot enjoys none of these positive virtues, attributes, or abilities. Instead, he is alcoholic, fat, mentally disturbed, suffers from a bad conscience, and is enormously rich. Yet he does what he can to alleviate pain and suffering in the little town of Rosewater, Indiana, while his unknown nemesis, Mushari, plots to steal his inherited fortune by proving him mentally incompetent. His father also emphasizes his son's limits when without consulting him he hires a psychiatrist who claims that Eliot in bringing his sexual energies to his utopian project could thereby bring on a "samaritrophic collapse" (43). Eliot himself helps curb sanctimony by comically reducing the radical thrust of Christianity's New Commandment that "you love your enemies, bless them that curse you, do good to them that hate you, and pray for them which despitefully use you, and persecute you" (Matthew 5:44). His version is rather simpler: "'God damn it, you've got to be kind'" (93).

Eliot is clearly a good person unlike, say, the evil Howard W. Campbell, Jr. in *Mother Night*. "Vonnegut deliberately places his protagonist within a milieu where no one is morally superior to him, however troubled he might be," as Mustazza convincingly argues (*Genesis* 99). In many ways, Eliot is as naïve as Paul Proteus in *Player Piano*, as misguided as Malachi Constant in *The Sirens of Titan*, as mad as Howard W. Campbell in *Mother Night*, and as removed from life as Jonah-John in *Cat's Cradle*. His ultimate philanthropic gesture of giving away his fortune, while judged insane or at least highly eccentric by others in positions of power or responsibility, when looked at in light of either its limited but positive results or its larger ethical implications appears eminently sane and even highly commendable. Although Vonnegut as a rational atheist rejects all forms of institutional religion (see *Wampeters, Foma & Granfalloons* 240), in this novel he appears to advocate what might be loosely described as Christian ethics based upon the Sermon on the Mount in which Jesus admonished his listeners to follow a discipline of radical love, even to loving one's enemies and "doing good to them that hate you" (Matthew 5–6). In *God Bless You, Mr. Rosewater*, Eliot's life comes to reflect the Sermon on the Mount in that he becomes one of the "meek," who, Jesus says, will inherit not riches, such as the Rosewater fortune, but "the earth"—his true inheritance.

Vonnegut once claimed in a private conversation that "There's no better way to understand people than by looking at the stories that shaped their cultures" (quoted in Mustazza, *Genesis* 198n27). One of his own best stories about his early life in Indianapolis illustrates the power of New Testament texts as motives for philanthropic actions. At a luncheon with his father—the wealthy, successful architect whose fortune was wiped out in the Great Depression and who by this time found himself "in full retreat from life" (*Jailbird* 13)—and his Uncle Alex, Vonnegut was introduced to Powers Hapgood, the Harvard-educated labor organizer. Hapgood arrived straight from court where he had been on the witness stand to testify about a recent strike that involved picket line violence. The judge was enthralled. Addressing Hapgood directly he asked, " 'why would a man from such a distinguished family and with such a fine education choose to live as you do?' 'Why?' said Hapgood, . . . 'Because of the Sermon on the Mount, sir.' " Apparently unable to frame an appropriate reply, the judge declared a recess for lunch (*Jailbird* 18–19).

At the end of *God Bless You, Mr. Rosewater*, Eliot believes he has found a solution that will settle the whole case "instantly, beautifully, and fairly" (188) in what for him is the ultimate philanthropic act—giving away totally his inheritance to strangers. (The world in which he lives will view it as simply crazy.) His three criteria, "instantly, beautifully, and fairly," are naïvely utopian, although perfectly consistent with his life. Eliot's efforts may be doomed, because of "the confusions of money, power and love in a 'Free Enterprise System,' which provides a hostile environment for 'uncritical love' in mid-twentieth century America" (Mayo 37). Moreover, as Mustazza claims, he may well be "a man crying in the wilderness, crying against the tide of greed and hypocrisy that has swept over America, crying the only message he finds worth hearing: 'God damn it, you've got to be kind' " (*Genesis* 98). Yet giving away all he has to strangers, regardless of their worth or lack of it coupled with his use of formal, sacramental language, emphasize his uncritical, forgiving love for those dozens of unnamed children who will divide the Rosewater fortune. "Let their names be Rosewater. . . . And tell them that their father loves them, no matter what they may turn out to be" (190). A majestic figure in snowy tennis whites, he uses a tennis racket like a magic wand—as if it were Prospero's wand or perhaps God's hand—to add his blessing concluding with his paraphrasing of God's admonition to Adam and Eve to be "fruitful and multiply."[46]

Knowing that it is harder for a rich man to enter heaven than for a camel to pass through the eye of a needle, Eliot stops being a rich man and becomes poorer than the poor. Although earlier dissuaded by lawyers from selling all he has and giving it to the poor—as Jesus admonished the young rich man to do—in the end he does manage to distribute his fortune to innocent strangers. In another memorable sermon, Jesus divides people into those who do such good works and those who do not:

"for I was hungry and you gave me food, I was thirsty and you gave me drink, I was a stranger and you welcomed me, I was naked and you clothed me, I was sick and you visited me, I was in prison and you came to me." Then the righteous will answer him, "Lord, when did we see thee hungry and feed thee, or thirsty and give thee drink? And when did we see thee a stranger and welcome thee, or naked and clothed thee? And when did we see thee sick or in prison and visit thee?" And the King will answer them, "Truly, I say to you, as you did it to the least of these my brethren, you did it to me." (Matthew 25:35–40)[47]

Readers surely hope that having so quickly cut the Gordian Knot created by Mushari, Eliot will be able to return to peaceful Rosewater County, Indiana and take up his old life. But judging from earlier events, his prospects may not be that good. When the greedy lawyer forces him to leave Rosewater to defend his way of life in court, he becomes catatonic. Subsequently, he has a vision of the destruction of the Earth in a firestorm located directly over Indianapolis that appears several miles across and stretches up into the stratosphere—somewhat similar to the one which destroyed Dresden (176). In much the same way, his own world of Rosewater County at that moment appears about to be destroyed by lawyers, courts, and what the world calls "obligations." Eliot's efforts may, therefore, be doomed.

Other ambiguities and doubts also remain at the end of *God Bless You, Mr. Rosewater.* Eliot's imitating God in the Garden of Eden blessing His creation hardly guarantees by itself an increase in the amount of generosity or a decrease in the amount of greed in the world, although it may momentarily distract some of those bent on seizing all they can get while the getting is good. Clearly, Kilgore Trout's assessment, based on wishful thinking, results from viewing the world and people through rose-colored or perhaps deeply shaded glasses. He actually believes that because of what Rosewater has done that "millions upon millions of people may learn to love and help whomever they see" (187)—an extravagant pronouncement in its assurance of change and grandiose effect.[48] Eliot's example will affect, at most, a handful of people and those perhaps only momentarily. Enacted in an obscure corner of Indiana away from the keg lights of the media, the most that might happen will be a fleeting, momentary notice before the world moves on to another distraction somewhere else. Trout's millions will neither know nor care. Nor does Vonnegut believe it matters very much if they do. If all politics is local, so is all morality. Eliot does the right thing at the right time.

At the opposite extreme, some critics view Eliot's act as futile and empty:

in the face of American history his [Eliot's] gestures amount to nothing more than noble posturing. . . . [T]he tennis racket represents a concrete activity and serves as a historical reminder of Eliot's upper-class position; the magic wand is what Eliot would sincerely like to have, what millions of Americans in fact need, but what they will never get. (Uphaus 169)

But Eliot is not simply posturing since by this act he does actually and finally give away all of the Rosewater fortune. Moreover, the importance of his act lies not in any external changes that may or may not occur in others, or in the United States as a whole, or in American history. Nor does it lie in whether others acquire a "magic wand" or not. Rather its importance lies in the change in status of the Rosewater fortune and in the internal change within Eliot himself. After all, the only person any of us can actually change is our self. Nor is Eliot attempting to rectify any "damage" he may or may not have done to those he tried to help, as maintained by a few critics:

It is unclear whether Eliot is a saint replete with magic wand and Madonna's smile, a madman still recuperating in a hospital after a complete nervous breakdown, or a sane, repentent man who sees the damage [sic] he has done his "clients" and seeks to rectify it by one last, completely unselfish act. (Schatt, "World" 64)

In whatever way readers choose to view this act, the result itself remains indisputable: the Rosewater fortune has vanished never to be reconstituted, never to control another's life. David has indeed slain Goliath. Eliot's principle of uncritical love inherited from the Saints on the *Mayflower* has carried the day against the fortune-seeking Strangers and brought him peace without guilt at last.[49] As Emerson wisely said at the end of "Self-Reliance" "Nothing can bring you peace but yourself. Nothing can bring you peace but the triumph of principles" (282), which is exactly what occurs through Eliot Rosewater's gesture.

Thus, if the novel's conclusion is ambiguous about Eliot's ultimate success, it is not ambiguous about his immediate triumph. Rather than emphasize the "pageant of winners and losers" in American history (Uphaus 169), readers of *God Bless You, Mr. Rosewater* might more profitably reflect on the Saints and Strangers in the *Mayflower* and their very different conflicting dreams of the New World. No victory has been final for either side, nor has any defeat been lasting. Eliot Rosewater, through the medium of philanthropy based upon uncritical love, stands in the company of the saints having defeated—if only momentarily—the strangers. In that brief moment of victory he also joins the ranks of Thomas Jefferson's natural American aristocracy of virtue and talents so integral to Vonnegut's imagining being an American.

NOTES

1. Krishan Kumar maintains that utopias were in decline in the twentieth century, but as Barbara Goodwin points out "he does this only by discounting a healthy number of recent science-fiction and feminist utopias" (786). Vonnegut's book is one of the dozens within the science-fiction and/or fantastic mode. Vonnegut "borrowed" the familiar utopian plot from Aldous Huxley's *Brave New World* (1932), as Huxley, Vonnegut claims, had in his turn taken it from Eugene Samiatan's *We*. The publishing history of *Player Piano* reflects Vonnegut's fortunes as an author since of the original hardcover edition "less than a third of its first printing of 7,600 copies was purchased (and most of these, Vonnegut insists, in Schenectady where he was living at the time). The next year, however, the Doubleday Book Club prepared a cheap edition of 15,000 copies, which sold very quickly to its subscribers; a second printing of 5,000 was soon ordered. And in 1954 came the book's greatest success. .

.. Outfitted with a luridly futuristic cover and retitled *Utopia-14*, the Bantam paperback . . . hit the stands in numbers exceeding 248,000" (Klinkowitz, *Kurt Vonnegut* 40).

2. Vanderbilt lists the typical elements of a utopian novel—all, of which, he claims, are present in *Player Piano*. "The new post-industrial civilization will be, customarily, a socialistic commonwealth of rational men and women, with wisely planned urban communities, maximum individual freedom, socially oriented education, material abundance (with wise conservation of natural resources), non-alienating and non-competitive day labor and professional life, self-transcending leisure time for recreation and the arts, effortless virtue, dynamic social stability, permanent peace, and gratifying love" (140).

3. This demonstration by Presper and Mauchly was followed by a series of lectures at a conference in Philadelphia, summer of 1946, which led, in turn, to the widespread adoption of stored-program that eventuated in the modern electronic computer.

4. Vonnegut's giant computer's name, EPICAC, is awfully close to Ipecac, the children's medicine used to induce vomiting, as several commentators have noted.

5. Vonnegut's economics in *Player Piano* are intriguing. He postulates private socialism where the corporations, not needing to compete because of becoming monopolies, nevertheless are government regulated. Although there are no taxes on physical possessions, there is a heavy tax on machine labor.

6. Vonnegut was well aware of Wiener's work borrowing his first name for the boorish medical genius, Dr. Norbert Frankenstein in *Fortitude* (*Wampeters, Foma & Granfalloons* 43–64) and quoting from his work in interviews and in *Player Piano* (13). Hughes believes that "Vonnegut appears indebted not to Wiener's 1948 monograph *Cybernetics*, but to its popularization, *The Human Use of Human Beings* (Cambridge, Mass: Riverside Press, 1950). The latter was revised and toned down in the second edition (1954) after PP [*Player Piano*] was published. No mere catalog of borrowings can reveal Vonnegut's assimilation of the 1950 edition" (113n4). Wiener's revisions illustrate Hayles's contention that "culture circulates through science no less than science circulates through culture" (21).

7. Although there is no evidence Vonnegut is echoing Emily Dickinson in using "Homestead" ironically as the name for a lost Eden, his use of the word is strikingly similar to hers in the poem "The Bible is an antique Volume—," especially in lines 1–5:

> The Bible is an antique Volume—
> Written by faded Men
> At the suggestion of Holy Spectres—
> Subjects—Bethlehem—
> Eden—the ancient Homestead—
> (Johnson 1: 1065)

8. Of Vonnegut's five early novels, only *Cat's Cradle* in William Rodney Allen's words "travels [further] in the direction of pure fantasy" (*Understanding* 36) than *Player Piano*. Vonnegut's next three novels will be as varied as these first two: from the apocalyptic *Cat's Cradle* to pseudo-autobiographical *Mother Night* to the modestly mad *God Bless You, Mr. Rosewater*.

9. For a description of other introductions to other editions, particularly Polish editions see Jamosky and Klinkowitz.

10. For a discussion of some of the science fiction of the period that reflects this distopian view, see Boyer (257–65).

11. Freese also unaccountably describes *Galápagos* as "another fictional projection of mankind's dire future. Predictably, the midwestern atheist is not interested in the role of religion in man's fight to survival" ("Surviving" 167). One could argue that on the contrary Vonnegut is preoccupied with the role of religion in humanity's fight for

survival given the various forms religion takes in his several apocalyptic novels (see, for example, *The Sirens of Titan*, *Slapstick*, as well as *Cat's Cradle*, itself).

12. For a highly original, but unsubstantiated reading of *Cat's Cradle* as "the absurd fantasy of Jonah the apocalyptic" (61) in which the Hoenikkers are seen as heroic and fully human, see Dewey (53–86, especially 62, 69–71).

13. Josephine Hendin hastily misreads both the character and significance of the Hoenikkers in *Cat's Cradle* as she does Billy Pilgrim in *Slaughterhouse-Five*, and Salo in *The Sirens of Titan* (257–59). While such erroneous accounts usually would not merit comment, hers appears in the authoritative *Harvard Guide to Contemporary Writing*—a work destined for library shelves and multiple readers. Fortunately, Vonnegut's work enjoys a significantly wide and loyal readership mostly immune to such "authorities."

14. The successful search for other forms of water—ones that do not boil or freeze at the temperatures when ordinary water does—has often given rise to wild stories. *Time* reported on a Russian claim to have made "Unnatural Water" in December 1969, for instance. The first international conference on "polywater" was held at Lehigh University in June 1970 (Sullivan C 30). So far no one has succeeded in creating any substance remotely like Ice-9—that remains Vonnegut's invention. For a full discussion of the various speculations about Vonnegut's sources, see McGinnis ("Source" 40–41).

15. Vonnegut described how he once shared an office with the man who became his model for the philanthropist, Eliot Rosewater: "there really is a man who is that *kind*. Except he's poor, an accountant over a liquor store. We shared an office, and I could hear him comforting people who had very little income, calling everybody "dear" and giving love and understanding instead of money. . . . I took this very sweet man and in a book gave him millions and millions to play with" ("Interview" with Casey and Bellamy 160). Giannone suggests that "Rosewater seems modeled after his nineteenth-century namesake Frank Rosewater who in 1894 wrote '*96: A Romance of Utopia: Presenting a Solution of the Labor Problem, a New God and a New Religion*" ("Violence" 64), but offers no evidence other than the suggestive book title.

16. Besides extrapolating from the present to create his future utopian society, Vonnegut also adds a satiric, highly amused look at the morés of the corporate world as he had observed them while working for the General Electric Company. One of his prime satiric targets—on which he scored a direct hit—was the North Woods summer festival where General Electric executives had to go and play the silly games described in hilarious detail in *Player Piano*. "The island was shut down after the book came out," Vonnegut boasts in various interviews (see, for example, "A Talk" 113). "So, you can't say that my writing hasn't made any contribution to Western civilization" ("Two Conversations" 199). Paul Keating, *Lamps for a Brighter America* (New York: McGraw Hill, 1954) claims that General Electric's Association Island, the model for Vonnegut's The Meadows was used extensively between 1910 and 1930 but by the 1950s was no longer in use (see Hughes 110). Whatever the historical facts, Vonnegut's satire on corporate culture and its excesses as well as on the loss of "halfway decent jobs" succeeds admirably and continues to be timely in the twenty-first century. Vonnegut was chosen Man-of-the-Year on the 25th anniversary of the GE Alumni Association, an organization composed of people like himself who worked for GE then went on to other professions (Vonnegut, "Skull Session" 247).

17. Northrop Frye once characterized *Walden Two* as not "intended very seriously" and more specifically he noted that it "show[ed] the infantilism of specialists who see society merely as an extension of their own specialty. . . . [I]ts Phillistine vulgarity makes it a caricature of the pedantry of social science" (32).

18. What proves true for individuals also holds true for fiction, as Boon emphasizes: "Vonnegut's fiction [especially in *Player Piano*] points to the confluent boundary between

the morbid and the sublime where humor and grief are inevitably conflated" (*Chaos Theory* 111n86).

19. Yet, Vonnegut cannot be overly optimistic about the prospects for American society and culture as his introduction to *Slaughterhouse-Five* some fifteen years after *Player Piano* makes abundantly clear. There, he points to the contrast between the historic revolutionary events and the current corporate interpretations of them by Walt Disney and Ford Motor Company as seen at the New York World's Fair (18).

20. The narrator's style in *The Sirens of Titan* also proves a good match for his subject suggesting as it does that the anonymous author of this "true story" in the tradition of Lucian of Samosata hopes to be read widely by an audience who enjoys popularized history. For example, in describing the Rumfoord mansion on the Rumfoord estate at Newport, Rhode Island, the narrator concludes: "The density and permanence of the mansion were . . . at ironic variance with the fact that the quondam master of the house, except for one hour in every fifty-nine days, was no more substantial than a moonbeam' (18). The technical vocabulary of "density," "permanence," the use of formal words, such as "substantial," "variance" along with the Latinate "quondam" contrast vividly with the informal metaphor of the insubstantial "moonbeam." That metaphor coming at the end of the sentence serves, in turn, to deflate the earlier formal vocabulary as well as the status of the "quondam master" of the mansion. Thus the narrator endears himself to readers flattered by the formal vocabulary but reassured by the informal, "just folks," metaphor.

21. Broer insists that Constant is in caves on Mars (*Sanity Plea* 41) but in *The Sirens of Titan* (182–214) the caves are located on Mercury.

22. In 1970 Leslie Fielder evaluated Vonnegut's novels published up to that time in what became a well-known essay published in *Esquire*, "The Divine Stupidity of Kurt Vonnegut." He concluded that *The Sirens of Titan* was Vonnegut's "best book" (202, reprint 13). The essay was reprinted unrevised thirty years later in Leeds and Reed. Unfortunately, a few errors were introduced in the reprinting.

23. Ketterer's inventive reading of the meaning of the good luck piece or spare part as "spiral-shaped [which] might even be viewed as the mainspring of a watch" (326) proves untenable because of several crucial physical details. The spare part once cut from "a spiral of steel strapping," as Ketterer notes, no longer retains any spiral shape. Instead, it has been "stamped on . . . chopped . . . into four-inch lengths . . ." and two holes have been drilled in the end with a sharp point (Vonnegut, *The Sirens of Titan* 143). Later, that sharp point will rounded by shaping against a diamond-hard surface. Coincidentally, the sizes of the needed spare, Chrono's good luck piece, and the common beer-can opener or "church-key" found on Earth all match. But the shape of an Earthling beer-can opener, as millions of users will attest, is not remotely shaped like "the mainspring of a watch" as Ketterer claims (326).

24. While Constant cannot learn from Salo, the messenger from across the galaxy, readers can. As Peter J. Reed points out: "While often the source of comedy, Salso also brings sentiment, even pathos, to the novel. He is loyal, compassionate, and feeling, emotions stronger in him than in the humans around him and that brings him to self-destruct" ("Hurting" 21).

25. According to Vonnegut, his model for Rumfoord was President Franklin Delano Roosevelt. In response to a question about what analogies there might be "between what Rumfoord does in the novel and perhaps what Roosevelt did socially and politically?" Vonnegut replied. "They both have enormous hope for changing things . . . childish hopes, too. I don't think Roosevelt was an enormous success except as a personality" (ellipses in the original; Interview with Casey and Bellamy 160).

26. I view the exploding universe mirrored in Fern's epigraph as the central motif for *The Sirens of Titan* rather than Ketterer's universe governed by spiral movement.

Ketterer's reading of the novel in light of the spiral imagery is thorough and ingenious but, for me, ultimately unconvincing. As hard as he works at interpreting the spirals, they remain within the random indifferent universe of Vonnegut rather than within the coherent organic one of Yeats (see Ketterer 312–14, especially 313).

27. Vonnegut's account weakens somewhat Tanner's suggestion: "that the book may well have been inspired by the case of Ezra Pound. . . . [I]n 1960 Charles Norman's biography appeared. This contained the rather interesting bit of information that apparently the Italian Government 'mistrusted the broadcasts, even suspecting that they hid a code language'" (*City* 186–87).

28. Unaccountably, Sanford Pinsker refers continually to Harry [sic] Campbell rather than Howard W. Campbell, Jr. (90, 91, 98). Pinsker is a good illustration of Vonnegut's remark that *Mother Night* was the novel of his that academics liked best because they felt most at home with it. Pinsker has nothing good to say about any other Vonnegut novel he discusses, but does like *Mother Night*. The conclusion of his essay typifies its tenor and hollow content: "Vonnegut may *console*, but genuine exorcism must be made of sterner stuff. Tralfamadore, pleasant memories [sic] and all, hardly constitutes the right turf. Which is to say, critical love letters should be sent by air-mail. So it goes" (100). For an essay whose announced focus is the exposure and denunciation of Vonnegut's "radical cuteness," Pinsker's prose descends to clichés, such as "sterner stuff," odd and inexact metaphors, like "by air mail," wildly misapplied metaphors, including "so it goes"—has Pinsker read *Slaughterhouse-Five*?—, cosy slang, such as "right turf," unnecessary emphasis in italics, and includes misstatements, such as describing Tralfamadore as a pleasant memory. To whose memory does he refer? One hardly knows where to begin discounting such cuteness.

29. Compare my list of schizophrenic characters with Leeds's ("Pretending" 87).

30. Mustazza suggests that a nation of two has mythic significance. He claims that the phrase itself has echoes of both the Garden of Eden and Noah's Flood. Before the Fall, Adam and Eve were such an innocent nation, while immediately after the Flood in the ark perched on Mount Ararat "Noah and his wife knew for a few shining moments [such a nation of two] . . . before corruption started again" (*Genesis* 67).

31. Jonathan Swift in *Gulliver's Travels* delights in creating new languages for Gulliver to learn and then uses the process as a way of deflating Gulliver's pretensions. For instance, after only a few days study, Gulliver corrects words and phrases used by native speakers he regards as ill-informed or deficient in knowledge of their own language. While Vonnegut does not so deflate John, he does use the San Lorenzo dialect to point up his narrator's naiveté and disingenuousness.

32. Compare the role of history in *The Sirens of Titan*.

33. Somewhat similar to Allen's objection to Vonnegut's blatant use of coincidence in *The Sirens of Titan*, is another critic's finding one plot too many in *Player Piano*, seeing "the considerable number of major and minor characters" as a detriment, and experiencing the use of "two-dimensional characters if not outright stereotypes" as a disappointment (Segal 168). While such features often constitute a liability in naturalistic fiction, they often serve satire well as they clearly do in *Player Piano* and *Cat's Cradle*.

34. "Atlas" exploited "Dynamic Tension" as the basis for his mail-order bodybuilding program so familiar to most young American comic book readers of the forties. A callous high school coach gave Vonnegut a Charles Atlas body building kit ("Skull Session" 249). Klinkowitz asserts that Vonnegut's "Bokononism is based on the silliest of sacred texts: Charles Atlas's comic-book advertisements for muscle building through the exercise of 'dynamic tension' " (*Kurt Vonnegut* 54).

35. Zoltán Abádi-Nagy argues that Bokononism actually contributes to tipping the scales toward destruction by helping create "the social passivity of depoliticized San

Lorenzans" ("An Original Look" 89). Yet it is difficult to see what the undernourished, underpaid, uninformed citizens of that sad country could have done to protect either themselves or the world against the selfishness of the "babies full of rabies" that ultimately unleashed Ice-9. Frank may have indeed, as he claims, matured—although at the cost of the planet—yet who among the San Lorenzans could have prevented his totally irresponsible trading of that sliver of poison for his fancy uniform? Or who could have thwarted its acceptance by Papa Monzano?

36. Compare "Excelsior! We're Going to the Moon! Excelsior!" in *Wampeters, Foma & Granfalloons* (77–89).

37. The H. G. Wells story is eerily appropriate for *Cat's Cradle* since as early as 1914 "H. G. Wells had predicted an atomic bomb" (Boyer 257). Moreover, in his last book, *Mind at the End of Its Tether* "the dying Wells . . . concluded that neither science nor human reason could guarantee individual happiness or social progress" (Boyer 268)— themes that echo and re-echo throughout *Cat's Cradle*.

38. "In 1995, two medical researchers borrowed Mr. Vonnegut's scientific fantasy for the title of a paper about a deadly degenerative disease that turns the brains of sheep into something that looks like Swiss cheese. In 'The Chemistry of Scrapie Infection: Implications of the "Ice 9" [sic] Metaphor,' Dr. Byron Caughey and Dr. Peter Lansbury wrote about what many scientists had come to believe is a new kind of illness—one spread not by viruses or bacteria but by a protein crystal rather like Mr. Vonnegut's ice-nine [sic]" (Johnson 9).

39. *Player Piano*, as the text that may have led Norbert Weiner to revise his work on cybernetics, might be an even more powerful illustration of Hayles's contention (see discussion of *Player Piano*). Similarly, Loree Rackstraw reports that the inspiration for Fred Alan Wolf's discussion of the "new physics of time" in *Star Wave: Mind, Consciousness, and Quantum Physics* (1984) was "Billy Pilgrim's explanation of the Tralfamadorian view of time in . . . *Slaughterhouse-Five* ("Quantum Leaps" 50).

40. William S. Doxey speculates fairly unconvincingly on the significance of various proper names in the novel, "Felix," for example, "in Latin 'felix' means happy. 'Hoenikker' may be pronounced the same as 'Hanukkah,' which is a Jewish holiday . . . 'McCabe' . . . may . . . contain an ironic reference to the Judas Maccabeus who . . . caused the occasion for which the Hanukkah celebration was created" (6). All of which leads Doxey to venture that Felix gave Ice-9 as a Hanukkah gift to his children " 'Some Happy Hanukkah!' Vonnegut seems to be saying" (6). Maybe, but Doxey fails to make clear how all this punning relates to the actual language of Vonnegut's novel as opposed to Doxey's strained reading of it. Far more to the point is Sallye Sheppeard's more modest suggestion that "as the name Felix implies, Hoenikker's happiness derives from his childlike fascination of discovery-for-discovery's sake; uncovering nature's secrets is a game whose end product for him is sheer joy. As Vonnegut may suggest by the scientist's Germanic surname, however, Hoenikker's childlike 'innocence' is offset by a cruel indifference to the destructive potential of his discoveries" (20). Yet, we also need to recall that as a German-American, Vonnegut was acutely aware of his position vis-à-vis American patriotic excesses against all things German during World War II (see Merrill, "Kurt Vonnegut as a German American," especially 77–82).

41. A few critics of *God Bless You, Mr. Rosewater*, such as Robert W. Uphaus, emphasize this negative phenomenon: "the United States was founded on a highly imaginative (if not utopian) ideal of 'life, liberty, and the pursuit of happiness.' This ideal, regrettably, is easily transformed into a pageant of winners and losers, for without money an American is only 'free' to lose . . . Eliot is thus a winner who wishes to share his wealth with losers, but the drama of his efforts is played against the resistant backdrop

of American history—a history which says that 'all men are equal' but which also implies that 'some men are more equal than others' " (169).

42. This phrase may reflect Vonnegut's reading of Wiener's *The Human Use of Human Beings*, the popularization of *Cybernetics*. (See n6.)

43. Broer's description of these acts appears particularly ill-founded and actually imitates Senator Rosewater's teaching of morality. "In truth, Eliot's cajoling and bribes can be seen as a form of moral prostitution, trading money for peace of mind" (*Sanity Plea* 76). Mustazza's description also needs some qualification: "An artist whose tools are uncritical love and vast wealth, Eliot comes to effect change, to undo the damage done by his forebears' greed and pride, as well as to set time moving again and thus provide hope to the hopeless" (95). But the one thing Eliot does not do at this point in the novel is to give away vast sums of money. In fact, he gives away such insignificant sums that Senator Rosewater complains about the pitiful small amount Eliot does give away each year he lives in Rosewater, Indiana while practicing uncritical love.

44. The current, twenty-first-century term for such mistakes is the Pentagon's infamous "collateral damage."

45. Eliot's belief that he was responsible, at least in part, for the death by drowning of his beloved mother during a boating accident reinforces his feeling of guilt.

46. Uphaus unaccountably substitutes Christ for God, the Creator, when he describes Eliot's blessing as "his last Christ-like words to be fruitful and multiply" (166). Nowhere in the bible does Jesus ask anyone to "multiply" only God gives this command to his new creation in Genesis.

47. And compare Eugene Debs's epitaph given in *Hocus Pocus* (ix).

48. Some critics of Vonnegut become so preoccupied with Kilgore Trout that they attach more importance to him than his actual place in this particular novel deserves. He will, however, later become a major character in *Slaughterhouse-Five*, *Breakfast of Champions*, *Jailbird*, and *Timequake*, while making a brief appearance in *Galápagos*.

49. By attributing all Eliot's problems, guilt, and "insanity" to his "lifelong unwillingness to deal with the more painful and immediate hostilities between himself and his father," Broer severely oversimplifies the novel (*Sanity Plea* 78).

4

Breaking the Silence

Art can only manage so much repair against annihilation.
—Arthur M. Saltzman (98)

Vonnegut wrote *Slaughterhouse-Five*—the crucial novel in his imagining being an American—against the background of the moral confusion occasioned by World War II's brutal, excessive destruction done in the name of goodness, justice, and Mom's apple pie. Like Lot's wife, whom he applauds for daring to witness the fiery destruction of Sodom and Gomorrah at the price of being turned into a pillar of salt, Vonnegut, too, "because it was so human" looked back at the conflagration of Dresden (*Slaughterhouse-Five* 22). And he did so in light of Hiroshima, Nagasaki, and Vietnam. Unlike God's destruction of "the cities of the plain," Vonnegut insists that the ferocious devastation of Dresden in all its horror resulted not from God's eradicating Evil, as occurred with Sodom and Gomorrah, but from human beings slaughtering other human beings. Moreover, the moral poison caused by viewing the wartime enemy as absolutely evil, rather than as ambiguously human, persisted long after the war was over: "If for years you fancy that you are engaged in fighting utter evil, if every element and impulse of society is busy eradicating wickedness, before long you will come to believe that therefore you yourself must incarnate pure goodness," insists Paul Fussell ("Writing" 76).

The devastation wrecked on Dresden from the air corresponds in kind but not in scale to the arrest, trial, and senseless execution of Edgar Derby in *Slaughterhouse-Five*.[1] To ensure that readers keep this juxtaposition in mind, Vonnegut mentions continually the cause and event of Derby's death beginning as early as the novel's fifteenth word. Within the first few pages he expatiates on Derby's fate regaling his old wartime buddy, Bernard V. O'Hare with his plans for the novel's climax, which will be Derby's death. Vonnegut focuses on the blatant irony of a famous, major city being incinerated with tens of thousands dead in the rubble, while an American soldier picks up a teapot out of the ruins, is placed under arrest, put on trial, sentenced, and executed on the spot. "Derby's crime is so miniscule in comparison with the larger crime of destroying an undefended city that if death is the proper punishment for his actions, what punishment should be given to those responsible for burning Dresden?" rightly asks Tom Hearron (190). This event thus raises acute moral questions about the justice both of Derby's execution and the leveling of Dresden.

Looking back at these events, Vonnegut raises anew Job's questions: "Why do the innocent suffer?" "Why do the evil prosper?" and "Where is justice to be found?" But he hears no answers. The answers Job himself finally heard from out of the whirlwind puzzled him for they explained nothing. God's words implied that a person's goodness does not guarantee that he or she will escape evil nor that he or she is incapable of doing evil and—most important of all— that if there exists an ultimate justice in the universe then it lies beyond human comprehension. Job's expectation, that evil would not be visited upon a good or an innocent person, was as ill-founded as the widely held American belief that the end justifies the means and, therefore, no evil will be committed in a good cause—such as the good cause of defeating Hitler and Japan in World War II. Vonnegut demurs suggesting that the destruction of the innocent was as common during that war as it was when Job bewailed his fate.

For much of his career as a writer and for half his career as a novelist, Vonnegut wrestled with the attendant Joban issue of why he personally survived while 135,000 people died during the Dresden firestorm in which "[t]he city appeared to boil" (*Palm Sunday* 302). "Surviving the annihilation of 135,000 civilians not only sharpened awareness of his own death but also brought home his relationship to collective death on a nearly unimaginative scale" (Greiner 41). Returning home after being repatriated as a Prisoner of War (POW), he discovered although he could share interesting stories about the war and the comradery he experienced, that he failed again and again to find the right words with which to describe the massacre, its aftermath, and its meaning—if any. Unable to accept passively such destruction, he asked the survivor's questions, "Why was I allowed to survive when so many innocent, good people perished?" "How could this terrible destruction have been allowed to happen?" "How could human beings do such awful things to one another?"

In novel after novel Vonnegut tried to deal with these difficult questions either directly or indirectly. In *The Sirens of Titan*, for example, he probed into human history for the answers, but found nothing there but absurdity. In *Mother Night* he examined the possibility of good collaborating with the forces of evil in order to subvert and ultimately destroy such forces, but concluded that this kind of naïveté was no match for a truly powerful evil force, such as Fascism. In *Cat's Cradle*, he explored stoic cynicism as a possible answer to the moral dilemma through his splendid creation of Bokonon and Bokononism. If human beings are so hell-bent on their own destruction, then, suggests *Cat's Cradle*, no one or nothing can stop them, and all the novelist can do is warn against the impending disaster by becoming the proverbial canary in a coal mine.

In *God Bless You, Mr. Rosewater*, Vonnegut took the opposite tack from *Cat's Cradle*, examining the possibility of doing good works as a way of stopping or at least retarding the forces of evil. "Sell all you have and give it to the poor," Jesus admonished his followers in the first century, and in the twentieth Eliot Rosewater uses his foundation to give money away in the hope that money might solace those who call for help. But good works ultimately do not appear to slow evil down. Instead, they actually may encourage it to greater extravagances of connivance and fraud. Evil itself worms its way into the very heart of Rosewater's good works and threatens to destroy the Rosewater Foundation until Eliot thwarts it by giving away all he has.

When Vonnegut finally came in *Slaughterhouse-Five* to write directly about surviving the Dresden massacre he discovered that dwelling on such massive destruction had a profound impact on the novel's style, especially on its most famous or, for some, most notorious phrase "So it goes." Vonnegut confesses that he felt compelled to repeat "So it goes" after any death mentioned in the novel whether of a person, animal, plant, or thing (such as champagne). "It was a clumsy way of saying . . . '[d]eath and suffering can't matter nearly as much as I think they do. Since they are so common, my taking them so seriously must mean that I am insane. I must try to be saner' " (*Palm Sunday* 296). The significant achievement of *Slaughterhouse-Five* lies then in Vonnegut's discovering artistically (in the novel's form and style) and personally (with his feelings and thoughts) how to deal with commonplace death and suffering on a horrific scale.[2] And scale is crucial here where a distinction in size does prove a distinction with a difference.

In American literature, probably the best-known confrontation of an individual with commonplace death on the battlescape occurs in Stephen Crane's *The Red Badge of Courage* (1895). Henry Fleming running away from battle races headlong into "a dead man who was seated with his back against a columnlike tree. . . . The dead man and the living man exchanged a long look" (36).[3] Returning to the battlescape, Fleming encounters other dead men and meets the maimed whose "torn bodies expressed the awful machinery in which the men had been entangled" (39). Vonnegut in *Slaughterhouse-Five* attempts to capture Fleming's experience of confronting individual death and his confronting aggregate or mass death in battle to which he then adds the hideous distortion caused by the sheer scale of obliterating a city of 135,000 in two nights.[4] The result is a duty dance with omnipresent death.

By introducing the Tralfamadorians—those now-famous visitors from another galaxy—Vonnegut shifts the novel's perspective from a human one, such as found in *The Red Badge of Courage* or in most of the Book of Job, to a godlike one, such as found in the conclusion of the Book of Job. For instance, when Billy Pilgrim discovers himself in a Tralfamadorian zoo, he asks the obvious human question: "Why me?" (76). The Tralfamadorian answer he receives both puzzles and instructs him:

"That is a very *Earthling* question . . . Mr. Pilgrim. Why *you?* Why *us* for that matter? Why *anything?* Because this moment simply *is*. Have you ever seen bugs trapped in amber? . . .

"Well, here we are, Mr. Pilgrim, trapped in the amber of this moment. There is no *why*."
(76–77)

Hundreds of years before Billy Pilgrim, Job asked the same question, "Why
me?" in the prologue to the Book of Job (chapters 1 and 2). A series of
messengers arrived bringing him news not of family members being captured by
strange beings in a flying saucer, but of appalling destruction. The first
messenger reveals that all of Job's servants have been killed; the second that his
sheep have been destroyed by fire from heaven; the third that nomads have
carried off his camels and slaughtered his herdsmen; and the fourth brings the
worst news of all, that a hurricane has suddenly killed all his sons and daughters.
Naturally Job is heart-stricken. He rends his clothes and goes and sits on the
village dunghill in deep mourning.

Job's tragedy consists in being a good man who, although he has done no evil,
nevertheless experiences great loss. Similarly, Dresden was a good city—that is,
an open, undefended civilian city whose architectural beauty was legendary. "I
am one of the few persons on Earth who saw an Atlantis before it disappeared
forever beneath the waves," Vonnegut wrote several decades after the event
(*Bagombo* [1999] 3). Dresden, the "Florence of the Elbe" was "reduced . . . to a
jagged moonscape" (*Bagombo* 2), destroyed for a good purpose says the
conventional wisdom, which Vonnegut satirically quotes without comment in
Slaughterhouse-Five. The purpose behind all this carnage was "to hasten the end
of the war" (180). One of Job's most complacent friends likewise maintains that
Job's innocent sons and daughters were destroyed to "teach Job a lesson." (Both
Vonnegut and Job suggest that the price paid in innocent deaths for such
instruction is far too high.) One of most unsympathetically treated characters in
Slaughterhouse-Five, Harvard history professor Bertram Copeland Rumfoord,
believes that destroying Dresden was absolutely necessary and, therefore, it is
pointless to expend emotion over it because "That's war" (198). Rumfoord may
gain authority from his writing a one-volume history of the United States Army
Air Force in World War II, but he remains justly despised by doctors and nurses
who themselves prove to be the novel's most sympathetic characters (193).
"Bertram Copeland Rumfoord . . . becomes the fictitious caricature of official
historiography which is less interested in the human dimension of an historic
event than in construing versions of the world 'according to the Ford Motor Car
Company and Walt Disney' " argues Joseph C. Schöpp (339). Robert Merrill
and Peter Scholl, after reviewing dozens of incomplete readings and/or
misreading of *Slaughterhouse-Five*, conclude:

The scene involving Rumfoord and Billy Pilgrim is positioned at the end of
Slaughterhouse-Five because it is the real climax to Vonnegut's complex protest novel.
The object of satiric attack turns out to be a complacent response to the horrors of the
age. The horror of Dresden is not just that it *could* happen here, in an enlightened
twentieth century. The real horror is that events such as Dresden continue to occur and no
one seems appalled. (148–49)

By the end of the Book of Job, still dismayed by the loss of life and material possessions, Job nonetheless accepts the imperfection of the world and his inability to account for the evil present in it. As a man of faith, he also comes to accept the goodness of his Creator, although that goodness may not always be apparent in the less than perfect world in which he must live. In effect, he says "I believe—help Thou mine unbelief." Vonnegut, as a rational atheist, derives no such consolation from the answers of traditional faith.[5] He can and does, however, find some consolation in accepting an imperfect world where the power to destroy is real and often terrifying, whether the agent be human beings in wars, assassinations, riots, or natural forces such as hurricanes, tornadoes, mud slides, or earthquakes.

Occasionally the power of human reason and goodness does, however, momentarily prevail over evil. So Eliot Rosewater in *God Bless You, Mr. Rosewater* gives all he has away to frustrate the unscrupulous young lawyer, Norman Mushari, and Malachi Constant in *The Sirens of Titan* at long last learns to love. In *Slaughterhouse-Five*, there may well be such a momentary triumph of goodness, but if so it is fleeting and fairly complex. Billy Pilgrim and Montana Wildhack are put on exhibit as interesting specimens of an endangered species in an extra-galactic Tralfamadorian zoo. Although their captors have long ago concluded, based upon thousands of years of observation, that the most prominent characteristic of human beings appears to be their ability to self-destruct, these two humans copulate and produce an offspring. Their action illustrates humanity's drive to continue the race that may somewhat counterbalance that same humanity's drive to destroy it.[6]

This modest hopefulness is a far cry from the near-total despair of *Cat's Cradle*'s conclusion, when Mona, the phenomenally beautiful woman of the Sunday supplements, refuses to make love to Jonah-John as the world ends, because "that's the way little babies are made" (178). After all, no sane person would want to have a child under such hopeless circumstances. But Montana Wildhack and Billy Pilgrim, less worldly-wise and far more childlike, under much less favorable conditions in the Tralfamadorian zoo amidst their Sears Roebuck furnishings, reproduce to the delight and glee of their audience. Perhaps they represent humanity's ultimate function in the universe: to puzzle and delight extra-terrestrial on-lookers by presenting them with the paradox of beings who both reproduce and destroy themselves at one and the same time.

Pointing to this human penchant for self-destruction through war and brutality becomes part of Vonnegut's role as a latter-day Joban messenger who brings the news of the commonness of death. "The Dresden experience forced home to Vonnegut the truth that appropriate responses to death do not exist," claims Donald J. Greiner (48). To help account—at least in part—for unmerited human suffering he examines the accidental nature of life. Some of this reasoning is already familiar from *The Sirens of Titan*, where the Space Traveler proclaims "I WAS A VICTIM OF A SERIES OF ACCIDENTS, AS ARE WE ALL" (229). There is an important difference between the novels, however. In *The Sirens of Titan* the accidents are caused by visitors from Tralfamadore who manipulate all human history for their own ends. Worse, as Salo their messenger points out, these visitors are not even human beings or sentient creatures, but machines. In *Slaughterhouse-Five*, on the other hand, there appears no purpose whatsoever in human history nor is anything or anyone in control. Like Voltaire, who wrote *Candide* at least in part as a reaction to the Lisbon earthquake's shocking toll in human life, Vonnegut writes *Slaughterhouse-Five* in reaction to the massacre of Dresden. Like Voltaire, Vonnegut also invents a character who simply accepts everything for the best. "*Everything* is all right" becomes Billy Pilgrim's refrain (198) as "Everything is for the best in the best of all possible worlds" became that of Dr. Pangloss in *Candide*.[7]

In replacing the question, "Why me?" with its twin "Why not you?"—to which there can be no reply—Vonnegut echoes the conclusion of the Book of Job where first Elihu then God pose exactly the same pair of questions. Each asks Job in turn: Why did you expect that your goodness would give you immunity from the effects of evil or from accidents of nature? Human beings do not enjoy such immunity. Good people suffer and bad people suffer—"the rain falls on the just and the unjust." Suffering, by itself, is no measure either of a person's evil—as Job's three friends mistakenly maintain—or of a person's goodness—as Job had assumed. Suffering simply happens irrespective of person. It is simply a part of all human experience. As Vonnegut suggests through his epigraph from Martin Luther's Christmas carol, "Away in a Manger," suffering is part of the human but not part of the divine condition and no divine force will intervene in human history to modify much less to stop it:

> The cattle are lowing,
> The Baby awakes.
> But the little Lord Jesus
> No crying He makes.

Vonnegut says he chose these four lines from Luther's carol because Billy rarely cried "though he often saw things worth crying about, and in *that* respect, at least, he resembled the Christ of the carol" (197). (The only time Billy cries in the novel is over the sorrowful plight of some horses [197].) Vonnegut carefully limits his comparison of Billy with Christ unlike some of his critics who favor a full and complete identification, such as "Billy, the new Christ, preaches that human beings *do* have eternal life—even if there is no life after death" (Allen, *Understanding* 88). One critic even reads the novel as a rewriting of the New Testament! (see Allen, especially 85–88). But doing so ignores the obvious falsehood of Billy's "*Everything* is all right." Whatever truth such an expression may hold for Tralfamadorians, it remains for humans at best a harmless lie. While Billy's beliefs may console him, they bring small comfort to others and hardly qualify as the New Gospel.[8] Moreover, Billy's response to Rumfoord's assertion "That's war" is far removed from either Christ's values or Vonnegut's. "I know. I'm not complaining" is all Billy has to say (198).[9] His lack of tears, his inability to weep over human tragedy contrasts with Vonnegut's shedding tears as, like Lot's wife, he finds much to weep over both in *Slaughterhouse-Five* and in life generally.[10]

Informing *Slaughterhouse-Five*, therefore, is what might be called a fairly orthodox form of Judeo-Christian theology that nevertheless has often proven too challenging for some narrow-minded Americans, especially those who serve on school boards and other official bodies. Like Job's three friends, such people hold a simpler, safer view of human beings and their relation to the deity. They have many times attempted to ban, censor, or otherwise destroy the novel.[11] In a "Dear Friend" letter written to solicit funds for the ACLU (the American Civil Liberties Union), Vonnegut reveals that *Slaughterhouse-Five* is among the ten "most frequently censored [and banned] books" in American public schools and libraries. (Others in the top ten include John Steinbeck, *The Grapes of Wrath* and *Of Mice and Men*, Judy Blume, *Forever*, and Mark Twain, *Huckleberry Finn* [2–3].)

Much of the book's perceived threat stems from its morality, which challenges orthodoxy by asserting that terms, such as "punishment" and "reward" along with the values they embody do not make a lot of sense from a human, but only from a divine or at least a godlike perspective. The unnerving implications of such a position are clear. If human beings cannot perceive, much less receive rewards or punishments, then why should anyone do good rather than do evil? According to the Book of Job and much of Judeo-Christian belief, a good person is a person who does good for its own sake rather than out of hope of reward or from fear of punishment. Good people are good rather than evil because that is who and what good people are. When people do good that becomes their reward. Someone who does evil, on the other hand, is simply someone who does evil and that in turn becomes its own punishment.[12]

None of Vonnegut's characters, including those in *Slaughterhouse-Five* is fundamentally evil and some, such as the nurses and doctors do much good. Most are innocent. Vonnegut's father once shrewdly observed that there was a marked absence of villains in his son's stories and novels, but then his son had survived the worst civilian massacre in modern European history. "Surviving an apocalyptic experience diminishes the need to affix blame or to divide the victims into allies and enemies" (Greiner 42). Billy Pilgrim is neither John Wayne, riding into town to save Western civilization from the Fascists, nor Jesus preaching the necessity of "doing good to those who do evil to you." He is instead an unremarkable, passive individual. C. S. Lewis, discussing characters such as Billy Pilgrim, argues that "[e]very good writer knows that the more unusual the scenes and events of his story are, the slighter, the more ordinary, the more typical his persons should be. Hence Gulliver is a commonplace little man and Alice a commonplace little girl. If they had been more remarkable they would have wrecked their books" (60). Similarly, Billy Pilgrim is a most ordinary, commonplace person and no Christ figure—unless he is seen as an ironic Christ figure preaching his "complacent gospel" (Louis 173). Additionally, there are, as the narrator of *Slaughterhouse-Five* affirms, "almost no characters in this story, and almost no dramatic confrontations, because most of the people in it are so sick and so much the listless playthings of enormous forces. One of the main effects of war . . . [is to discourage people] from being characters" (164).

Unlike Billy Pilgrim, Kurt Vonnegut himself is anyone but "a commonplace little man" as exemplified by his war experiences. On 29 May, 1945 just three days after being repatriated, Pfc. K. Vonnegut, Jr. wrote home catching his family up on how "our division was cut to ribbons . . . [by] seven fanatical Panzer Divisions" ("50 Years Later" 44). He went on to describe how he became a prisoner of war subjected to brutal inhuman conditions that killed many fellow prisoners. How he and his fellow prisoners were "bombed and strafed" by the Royal Air Force which "killed about one-hundred-and-fifty of us." Of the remaining hundred and fifty privates "shipped to a Dresden work camp . . . I was their leader by virtue of the little German I spoke," he writes (44). But the conditions were so bad, the guards so sadistic and fanatical, the food ration so miserable that Vonnegut, "after desperately trying to improve our situation for two months," told off the guards, was beaten for his trouble, and "fired as group leader" (44). There is nothing in this letter to his family describing his plight as soldier and prisoner of war that remotely corresponds to Billy Pilgrim's activities, actions, inaction, or personality. Clearly, Billy is not Vonnegut's "alter ego" as several critics have claimed[13]—such an identification is simply too easy and fails to fit the facts. Nor is Billy by any stretch of the imagination "a modern Everyman" (McNelly 193) or a "contemporary Everyman confronted with and overwhelmed by the cruelties of war" (Freese, "Invented Religions" 155). Billy accommodates to his Dresden experience and accepts without qualm the ubiquity of death. Vonnegut emphasizes that Billy's reactions are *negative* and juxtaposed to those of the hospital staff who believed that "weak people should be helped as much as possible, that nobody should die" (193). Throughout the novel, and explicitly in its introduction, Vonnegut rejects Billy's quietism (19). Dolores K. Gros Louis perceptively notes that Vonnegut rejects Billy's complacency:

his writing of this novel with its overt pacificism show[s] that for him everything is *not* all right. Unlike the Tralfamadorians, Vonnegut the narrator looks back at many *horrible* moments: the destruction of Sodom and Gomorrah, the drowning or enslavement of the thousands of children in the Children's Crusade, the 1760 devastation of Dresden by the Prussians, the extermination of millions of Jews by the Nazis, the firebombing of Dresden, the atomic bombing of Hiroshima, the bombing of North Vietnam, the napalm burning of the Vietnamese, the assassination of Robert Kennedy, the assassination of Martin Luther King [, Jr.], the daily body count from Vietnam. (173–74)[14]

In that same May 1945 letter home to his parents from Le Havre POW (Prisoner of War) Repatriation Camp, he recounts how tens, hundreds, and hundreds of thousands of people died in his vicinity from British, American, and Russian planes, "but not me" (44). The tone of the letter is that of the survivor's understated wonder at being alive. The contents of the letter reflect a soldier who actively takes charge of whatever possibilities come his way—something Billy could never do. When it is necessary to surrender, Vonnegut surrenders; when it is necessary to challenge the all-powerful labor camp guards, he does so. When he must hide and avoid bombs and bullets, he hides. When he must risk beatings or death to steal that vitamin-rich malt extract intended for the mothers of the Master Race, he takes the risk and so survives. In *Fates Worse Than Death* Vonnegut discloses that rather than using himself as the model for Billy Pilgrim he chose instead a hapless young man, Joe Crone, who was never able to catch on to how to become a soldier. Nor did Joe Crone make it to the Tralfamadorian zoo to be with Ms. Wildhack. Instead, he committed the ultimate passive act in committing suicide by starvation before the Dresden conflagration occurred. Joe remained buried there in Dresden but Vonnegut brought him back home where he became a successful, wealthy optometrist in *Slaughterhouse-Five.*

As a young soldier in war and a child in peace Billy Pilgrim illustrates Céline's observation—quoted with approval by Vonnegut—that "When not actually busy killing, your soldier's a child" (Céline 118). Vonnegut incorporates Céline's identification of soldiers as children through the novel's alternate title *The Children's Crusade* that also alludes to General Dwight D. Eisenhower's best-selling account of World War II, *Crusade in Europe.* Vonnegut's subtitle, in turn, links the great war to end all wars with one of the most futile, exploitive, cynical events in all of Western European history—the thirteenth-century Children's Crusade—a crusade that never went anywhere and never accomplished anything, except to provide ample prey for all kinds of human vultures to feed upon. In *Slaughterhouse-Five*, the soldiers in World War II, like the children on their crusade and unlike General Eisenhower, have little or no idea what they are doing and often do not know even where they are. The child is, of course, not morally responsible, as an adult would be. Someone else besides the child-soldier must be in charge and that person or persons can be held morally accountable for what happens. It was the generals acting as adults who planned such glorious operations as the destruction of Dresden (*Slaughterhouse-Five* 186–88).

The reduction of a monument of human civilization, such as the lovely city on the Elbe, to a pile of rubble overnight or the metamorphosis of over 100,000 unarmed people into a corpse factory can, and, indeed, has happened in a world where everything is permitted. In such a world, says Ivan Karamazov in *The Brothers Karamazov*, the issue is not whether or not to believe in God, because the sheer overwhelming horror of the power of evil makes such a question irrelevant. Eliot Rosewater, also suffering from discovering the meaninglessness of life, in part because of his war experiences, assures Billy Pilgrim that "everything there was to know about life was in *The Brothers Karamazov* . . . But that isn't *enough* any more' " (101). Perhaps all anyone can do under such circumstances is to follow Theodore Roethke's advice, which Vonnegut quotes with approval, to "learn by going where I have to go" ("The Waking" line 3). But what of the child-soldiers and others who somehow survived the massacre? Next noontime after the Dresden firestorm, the American POWs together with their German guards appeared above ground: "the sky was black with smoke. The sun was an angry little pinhead. Dresden was like the moon now, nothing but minerals. The stones were hot. Everybody else in the neighborhood was dead" (178). What do you say about a massacre? "[T]here is nothing intelligent to say about a massacre" (19). Massacres simply cannot be comprehended and there are no words to express what lies beyond human comprehension. "Everybody is supposed to be dead . . . Everything is supposed to be very quiet after a massacre . . . except for the birds. . . . . . . [W]hat do the birds say? All there is to say about a massacre, things like "*Poo-tee-weet?*" (19)

"The belated publication of *Slaughterhouse-Five* seems . . . to indicate that all is not well with writing in our time, that there is hardly an adequate way of responding to the atrocities which defy description. The activity of the mind seems to fail 'before the incommunicability of man's suffering,' " Lionel Trilling concluded eloquently, if somewhat hyperbolically (*The Liberal Imagination* 265 quoted in Schöpp 335). But other critics have badly erred in misreading the bleakness of the end of *Slaughterhouse-Five*. One maintains, for instance, that "the final statement of *Slaughterhouse-Five* is not one of death and its concomitant 'So it goes.' Rather it is a statement of rebirth, the cyclic return of springtime and singing birds that tell Billy Pilgrim 'Poo-tee-weet'" (McNelly 198). But such sentimentality proves at marked variance with the bleak moonscape of Dresden after the firestorm (*Slaughterhouse-Five* 179–80) and with the narrator's (215) and Vonnegut's (19) inability to find anything coherent or intelligent to say in the face of humanity's brutal inhumanity. Placed in the context of the end of the novel, that bird song—if it can be described as song— becomes a meaningless cry testifying to the indifference of nature over the worst human massacre in modern European history.

Like the writer of the Book of Job—who affirms the goodness of creation as an article of faith made possible only by believing in the goodness of the Creator—Vonnegut affirms the essential goodness of *all* creation but ironically and most importantly also from a *nonhuman*; that is, from a Tralfamadorian perspective. "Everything was beautiful, and nothing hurt" is an appropriate Tralfamadorian epitaph for Billy Pilgrim or anyone else *able* fantastically to "come unstuck in time." Paul Davies in *About Time* describes Billy Pilgrim's fantastic situation as a "sort of immortality . . . restricted to a fixed set of events" (41). Davies recounts a childhood fantasy he had where he pressed a series of imagined buttons to jump forward into the future or backward into the past. His fantasy is remarkably similar to Billy's reality:

With these buttons, gone would be the orderly precession of events that apparently constitutes my life. I could simply jump hither and thither at random, back and forth in time, rapidly moving on from any unpleasant episodes, frequently repeating the good times, always avoiding death, of course, and continuing *ad infinitum*. . . . It is but a small step from this wild fantasy to the suspicion that maybe someone else . . . is pressing those buttons on my behalf, and I, poor fool, am totally oblivious to the trickery. On the other hand, so long as the mysterious button-pusher keeps at it, it seems as if I will enjoy some sort of immortality, though one restricted to a fixed set of events. (40–41)

Still there are a few readers who either ignore or argue away this fantastic premise of the novel—a premise that becomes essential if Billy is to experience then adopt his inhuman Tralfamadorian view of time. One critic, for example, rather than accepting Billy's ability to move within time into the future, asserts that: "Billy Pilgrim . . . takes refuge in an intense fantasy life, which involves his being captured and sent to a remote planet. . . . He also comes 'unstuck in time' and present moments during the war may either give way to an intense re-experiencing of moments from the past or unexpected hallucinations of life in the future" (Tanner, *City* 195; see also McGinnis 115).[15] But this description appears closer to Paul Davies's childhood fantasy than to Billy Pilgrim's reality. From beginning to end *Slaughterhouse-Five* establishes and maintains that "Billy Pilgrim has come unstuck in time" (23)—one might as well suggest that Gregor Samsa only hallucinates being a cockroach in Franz Kafka's "The Metamorphosis." Neither Kafka's story nor Vonnegut's novel makes much sense either as an intense personal fantasy or an hallucination (see Morse, "Gaudi"). Yet this view typifies those who read *Slaughterhouse-Five* as a realistic novel with a hero who fantasizes.[16] Such readers deny the fantastic premise of Vonnegut's novel that Billy Pilgrim does come unstuck, that he does indeed move forward and backward in time.

One of the more aggressive readings of *Slaughterhouse-Five* as a realistic novel, belongs to a critic who, after accusing others of "not understand[ing] the narrative viewpoint" and having a "simplistic concept of narrative viewpoint" (Blackford, "Physics" 38), proceeds to construct his own reading of the novel as the product of Billy Pilgrim's brain damage suffered when "Roland Weary shakes him and hits his head against a tree. Earlier in the novel, the narrator tells us that this was the very moment when Billy first came unstuck in time" (Blackford 40). Unfortunately for this reading, neither assumption proves correct. First, this incident of the supposed head bashing is clearly downplayed in *Slaughterhouse-Five* as not terribly significant. The narrator reports that "Weary . . . banged Billy against a tree, then pulled him away from it, flung him in the direction he was supposed to . . . [go]" (*Slaughterhouse-Five* 47; compare 156 where Weary's actions are also described). No serious consequences result from this incident. Later, after the war, Billy will fracture his skull in an airplane crash in New Hampshire (156). Apparently, this critic conflated the two events because they are interleaved in the story through Billy's time-tripping (156–57). Second, and more important, Billy's first time traveling described in extensive detail (43–47) occurs *before* the occasion where Weary shakes him (41). The shaking incident brings Billy *back* to the forest and back to Roland Weary from time-tripping rather than the other way around (compare *Slaughterhouse-Five* 47 and Blackford 40). Billy does not hallucinate; instead, as Vonnegut tells us repeatedly, he simply, if fantastically, comes "unstuck in time" and is, therefore, able to move in time forward as well as backward. As a result, Billy enjoys the nonhuman consolation of seeing time and events as God sees them or as—the equally nonhuman—Tralfamadorians see them; that is, all at once. "Tralfamadore . . . by abolishing time, abolishes hope and change, development and free will," as Joseph C. Schöpp shrewdly observes (345). Similarly, Billy's ability to escape suffering by viewing only those good moments in his life where "nothing hurt" becomes appropriate if—ultimately—self-defeating for this utterly passive victim of other people and events.

As an alternative to Billy's adopted nonhuman perspective, Vonnegut offers a more human, less Godlike one through the many references to Reinhold

Neibuhr's famous prayer that Montana Wildhack carries in a locket about her neck and that Billy keeps framed on his office wall for the benefit of his patients. "God grant me the serenity to accept the things I cannot change, courage to change the things I can, and wisdom always to tell the difference." The prayer asks for divine help in viewing the human situation in light of each person's individual abilities to cope with suffering and loss. Familiar to many Americans as the prayer of Alcoholics Anonymous, Neibuhr's words describe the end point of Vonnegut's moral odyssey through his first six novels. [17] Like Job, he moves from anger through disbelief to rebellion before finally coming to accept what is and what must be—all of which must include the omnipresent fact of human suffering and death.

Such a change comes about through Vonnegut's acceptance in *Slaughterhouse-Five* of the central place of suffering in human experience whether that suffering is caused by the firebombing of Dresden or by natural or human-made disasters. Along with accepting the mystery of human suffering, Vonnegut also recognizes the presence of evil in the world for which there is not now and can never be a fully satisfactory human explanation. *Slaughterhouse-Five* thus raises acutely the profound moral issues with which Vonnegut has had to wrestle as an adult human being and as a writer. "Vonnegut's fiction," Marc Leeds contends, "demands all his protagonists relive the central moment of his life: the entombment within the slaughterhouse meatlocker during the firebombing of Dresden" ("Reading" 91–92). Vonnegut himself believes that *Slaughterhouse-Five* results at least in part from what Céline calls his "duty dance with death" without which, he believed, no art is possible. Perhaps the rigors of this duty dance help account for the difficulties that he encountered in writing the novel as well as the relief that he experienced in concluding it. Having at last completed *Slaughterhouse-Five* Vonnegut felt that he "didn't have to write at all anymore" that he had reached the end of "some sort of career" (*Wampeters, Foma & Granfalloons* 280). After wrestling with some of the most profound and some of the most difficult human questions in *Slaughterhouse-Five*, Vonnegut promised himself that his next book would "be fun" (*Slaughterhouse-Five* 22), which proved true in the comedy of *Breakfast of Champions*.

It would be almost twenty years after the completion of *Slaughterhouse-Five* before Vonnegut would return in *Bluebeard* to the war's end in Europe. In that later novel, the end is pictured as a field crowded with people (268, 270–76, 282–85 compare *Slaughterhouse-Five* 5–6)—the lunatics, refugees, prisoners of war, victims of the concentration camps—all the ragged remnants of an exhausted world and—most important—all survivors. These are living human beings, rather than the stacked corpses of the Hospital of Hope and Mercy in *Cat's Cradle* or the bodies found in the "corpse mine" of the desolate Dresden landscape. But *Bluebeard* with its happy ending in praise of human creativity and community will appear only four decades after the end of World War II and almost twenty years after *Slaughterhouse-Five*.

Several hundred years after the Book of Job's composition, an editor, unable to accept the work's stark vision of the power of evil and the central role of unmerited suffering in human life, added a happy ending. In the amended story, Job received back everything he had lost and more—except, of course, his dead children. Vonnegut, like Job's editor, also tacks on an equally fantastic, equally happy ending in Billy Pilgrim's epitaph: "Everything was beautiful, and nothing hurt." This Tralfamadorian expression far from being a "stoical, hopeful acceptance" (McNelly 198) is quite simply *foma*. Such harmless untruths that fill *The Books of Bokonon* in *Cat's Cradle* enable Billy and others like him, who have no hope of ever escaping from the miseries of this life, to nevertheless be "brave and kind and healthy and happy" (epigraph to *Cat's Cradle* from *The Books of Bokonon* 4). As Merrill and Scholl persuasively conclude "the Billy Pilgrims of this world *are* better off saying that everything is beautiful and nothing hurts, for they truly cannot change the past, the present, or the future. All they can do is survive" (146).

Not so Vonnegut. Although he appears, like Billy, a messenger who "alone . . . escaped to tell you," the message he brings through his fiction, especially through the narrator-persona in *Slaughterhouse-Five*, proves far different from Billy's message of quietism and reassurance. Instead, the emphasis falls on the necessity of accepting suffering with neither the comfort that "everything is beautiful" nor the dream that "nothing hurt" but with the attendant obligation to attempt courageously to change the present and thereby change the future. So Vonnegut reports that he has admonished his sons never to participate in, rejoice over, or feel satisfied by reports that enemies have been massacred. "I have also told them not to work for companies which make massacre machinery, . . . [while expressing] contempt for people who think we need [such] machinery" (*Slaughterhouse-Five* 19).

If a major difference between mature and immature adults lies in the immature letting "other people clean up the mess they had made," as Daisy and Tom Buchanan most conspicuously did in *The Great Gatsby* (170), then mature adults will assume responsibility for mistakes, accidents, crimes, evil acts, and so forth. Billy Pilgrim remains the immature child who refuses to take responsibility for anything—after all he's only an exhibit in a zoo! But as Doris Lessing pointed out in her review of *Mother Night*: "What Vonnegut deals with, always, is responsibility: Whose fault was it all—the gas chambers, the camps, the degradations and the debasements of all our standards? Whose? Well, *ours* as much as *theirs*" (46). As the faithful messenger, Vonnegut in *Slaughterhouse-Five* delivers his crucial, if unwelcome, message: "We have met the enemy and he is us."[18]

The slaughterhouse from which the novel takes its title was once a house of death. It became, paradoxically during the inferno of the Dresden firebombing, a house of salvation when it gave oxygen to its occupants rather than to the firestorm. Vonnegut's novel is, in part, an account of a house of death—of the massacre of unarmed civilians—but it itself becomes also a house of salvation through its plea for a change in values and attitudes that would make other such massacres impossible. Vonnegut accomplishes his dual purpose in breaking the silence by making the massacre itself public knowledge. The novel thus thrust back into living memory, in a way that could not be ignored, a portion of

American history which had never officially been acknowledged, and which had been either inadvertently or deliberately concealed. According to Vonnegut, in the whole twenty-seven volumes of the *Official History of the Army Air Force in World War Two*, for instance, little had been reported about the Dresden raid and ensuing fire-storm despite the fact that it had been judged a "howling success." But the huge size of that success remained hidden from the American public (*Slaughterhouse-Five* 191).

Having looked into the depths of the physical and moral firestorm, Vonnegut brings news of disaster. But he also insists on the necessity of examining the profound moral, social, and theological issues raised by the disaster—issues such as the power of evil, the awareness of inhuman destruction, the omnipresence of suffering, and the issue of responsibility. In some cultures when a messenger brought such an unwelcome message he was quickly killed—preferably before he could officially deliver the message. In the United States—somewhat more cynically, but perhaps equally effectively—the messenger may become transformed into a celebrity and grow fabulously rich, thus distracting people's attention away from his message—a message that no one really wanted to hear anyway.

NOTES

1. "Like *Slaughterhouse-Five*, Vonnegut's *Deadeye Dick* counterpoints a massive catastrophe, the destruction of Midland City, for which no one is punished, with a smaller event that is punished severely: Rudy Waltz's accidental shooting of Eloise Metzger" (Hearron 190).

2. Martin Amis favorably appraises Vonnegut's achievement in *Slaughterhouse-Five*, if in a somewhat patronizing manner, as "a cunning novella, synthesizing all the elements of Vonnegut's earlier work: fact, fantasy, ironic realism, and comic SF. In my view, *Slaughterhouse-Five* will retain its status as a dazzling minor classic," but he remains puzzled by its wide readership since, according to Amis, "quality alone can hardly explain its spectacular popularity" (135). Donald J. Greiner, on the other hand, speaks for many readers in believing that the book's distinctive accomplishment derives from Vonnegut's "successful expression of . . . deeply felt personal emotion without sentimentality" (43). Amis suggests that "[p]erhaps the answer is, in some sense, demographic," and postulates an American audience reading from *Slaughterhouse-Five* to Vietnam by way of World War II (135). (Amis found the plot for his own novella, *Time's Arrow or The Nature of the Offense* [1991] while reading *Slaughterhouse-Five*.) The most extravagant praise of *Slaughterhouse-Five* may well have been Stanley Schatt's, when he claimed that "*Slaughterhouse-Five* is a vision, a dream, Vonnegut's version of James Joyce's *Finnegans Wake* in which he and the reader both learn by 'going where I have to go' " (84). Such a claim would be difficult to substantiate.

3. Compare Edgar Derby reading *The Red Badge of Courage* while Billy enters his morphine heaven (99).

4. Schöpp suggests a clear qualification for the parallel between *The Red Badge of Courage* and *Slaughterhouse-Five*. He claims persuasively that Crane's novel "fails as a model. Dresden rules out maturation" of the kind that Fleming experiences as he confronts death and returns to the battlescape (339).

5. Vonnegut in *Timequake* describes his faith as that of a Humanist. "Humanists try to behave decently and honorably without any expectation of rewards or punishments in an

afterlife. The creator of the Universe has been to us unknowable so far. We serve as well as we can the highest abstraction of which we have some understanding, which is our community" (72).

6. The film of *Slaughterhouse-Five* ignored the darker side of this pairing of destruction and procreation by emphasizing Billy, Montana Wildhack, and their new baby in its happy ending. Compare such sentimentality to *Deadeye Dick*'s hard-edged realism where Rudy considers "having the voice of God from the back of the theater" announce that the purpose of humanity is "to reproduce. Nothing else really interests Me. All the rest is frippery" (185).

7. James J. Napier may have been one of the first to recognize this parallel.

8. See Allen, *Understanding* 85–88. Allen also appears to be rewriting Stephen Hawking's *A Brief History of Time* when claiming that Hawking was "becoming more convinced that there is no reason why under some circumstances the 'arrow of time' might point from future to past rather than from past to future" (81). But, all of Hawking's book resists this thought (see especially, Chapter 9, "The Arrow of Time" [143–53]). Paul Davies submits that "[I]n the 1980s, Stephen Hawking also toyed with the idea of a time-reversing universe for a while, only to drop it with the admission that it was his 'greatest mistake' " (*Last Three Minutes* 147).

9. Maurice J. O'Sullivan, Jr. puts it well: "Billy Pilgrim represents a standard—an essentially negative although often sympathetic standard—against which the persona [which O'Sullivan defines as "the authorial persona who dominates the first chapter and appears periodically thereafter"] measures himself" (245).

10. When Vonnegut draws his self-portrait in *Breakfast of Champions*, for instance, he includes tears streaming from his eye (296). The epigraph of *Breakfast of Champions* is taken from the Book of Job: "*When he hath tried me, / I shall come forth as gold*" (emphasis in the original).

11. At least once in Drake, North Dakota the local school board ordered a school janitor to burn a copy of *Slaughterhouse-Five* in the school furnace (*Palm Sunday* 4, see also 3–17). Clearly the members of that school committee were attempting to protect the young from the contents of this novel, which they believed threatens their view of the world and the sterility of their religion. Vonnegut's book thereby takes its place in an honorable company of disturbing texts that includes the Book of Job, the Old Testament Prophets, and Jesus's Sermon on the Mount—all of which have at various times threatened the calcified beliefs of those in authority. See the prologue to Vonnegut's *Jailbird*, especially 18–20.

12. Compare Emerson's equally disquieting notion of evil as "merely privative" in his "Divinity School Address."

13. See, for example, McGinnis (114). But the only alter ego Vonnegut acknowledges in his fiction is the character of Kilgore Trout (*Timequake* xiii).

14. See also Greiner (49) and Merrill and Scholl (149–50).

15. Tanner gives a similar misreading of Mark Twain's *Huckleberry Finn* when he declares that Huck's "compassion . . . takes in not only Jim, but a drunk at a circus (while others laugh)" (*Reign of Wonder* 169). But the others laugh because, unlike Huck, they are "in" on the joke that the "drunk" is actually a clever clown performing his "act." Twain's point is not Huck's compassion but his literal-mindedness about people and events, unless he is producing the "stretchers."

16. For example, "Billy imagines himself on a Trafamadorian space ship" (Burhans 180), "*Slaughterhouse-Five* with its mad [sic] protagonist" (Godshallk 105), "the Tralfamadorians, those mythical creatures who live on a distant planet in Billy Pilgrim's mind" (McGinnis 115), "one must sympathize with Billy need to create Tralfamadore" (Merrill and Scholl 146), "Billy . . . forg[ing] his illusory trip into outer space. . . . His

hallucinations must . . . become his reality, making him a permanent dreamer" (Mustazza, *Genesis* 103), and "every element of Billy's 'sci-fi fantasy' can be explained in realistic, psychological terms" (Edelstein 129).

17. Vonnegut says, "In the Soviet Union they imagine that I've made up that prayer" ("Serenity" 23, reprint 15). Sanford Pinsker unaccountably attributes the prayer to St. Francis (97).

18. The phrasing is Walt Kelley's from his comic strip, *Pogo*, but the sentiment is pure Vonnegut. For a diametrically opposite reading, see Edelstein, especially 135–39.

5

Under an Inexplicable Sentence of Death

"We all live slapstick lives, under an inexplicable sentence of death," wrote Martin Gardner in his introduction to *The Annotated Alice* but he might have been speaking equally appropriately of Kurt Vonnegut's novels. Peopled with slapstick lives, Vonnegut's America is bereft of belief in gods, progress, revolution, political wisdom, and justice as mirrored in *Breakfast of Champions*, *Slapstick; Or, Lonesome No More, Jailbird*, and *Deadeye Dick*. Substituting wishful thinking for responsible action leads to calamity as seen in the ubiquitous pollution in *Breakfast of Champions*, in the brutal child rearing in *Slapstick*, in Richard Nixon's multiple failures in *Jailbird*, and, most trenchantly, in the false belief in progress in *Deadeye Dick*.

Before he was fifty, Vonnegut appeared to have fulfilled the American dream of worldly success. Financially well off thanks to the success of *Slaughterhouse-Five*—his great work—accomplished to huge acclaim, he enjoyed a lifetime marriage, a loving family, and a comfortable home in a beautiful location. Yet somehow his life appeared to be coming apart at the seams. Chaos loomed. He began to experience what Karl Jung calls "the mid-life crisis." According to Jung, whether a person succeeds, fails, or simply survives the early years, he or she must at mid-life still decide what to do for whatever remains of his or her active working life. As Vonnegut entered his fifties, what had proven most comfortable and familiar in his life disappeared. The dream of a lifetime marriage proved illusionary, his children left home no longer needing—and, perhaps, even resenting—a parent nearby. Like many Americans his age, he found himself in a time of waiting—waiting for whatever would happen next while experiencing the bleakness of separation from family and friends. His family tale now centered on "an American father's departure from his hearth . . . [his] cold sober flight into unpopulated nothingness" (*Palm Sunday* 304). In a small apartment in New York City he found truth in a Statler Brothers song, "Flowers on the Wall." A song short on hope or success but long on a man's lack of value (*Palm Sunday* 307).

Hitting bottom in deep depression, he pondered his mother's example of suicide but came to reject it, as he testifies in *Breakfast of Champions*. Later, in an interview he would claim that that novel itself "isn't a threat to commit suicide. . . . It's my promise that I'm beyond that now. Which is something for me" (*Wampeters, Foma & Granfalloons* 283).[1] *Breakfast of Champions* also suggests that Vonnegut overcame the temptation of a writer's metaphoric suicide where he would despair over ever writing again. He returned to writing as "a very pleasant endeavor" (Vonnegut, "Two Conversations" 12) having dealt with the extreme pain occasioned by his children leaving home and by his separation and subsequent divorce from his first wife. "It is hard to adapt to chaos," says the narrator of *Breakfast of Champions*, "but it can be done. I am living proof" (210).[2] That statement hardly applies to the bumbling narrator of *Breakfast of Champions*, although it could truthfully be said of Vonnegut himself. Having successfully faced and overcome the question of suicide, he gives himself a fiftieth birthday gift of *Breakfast of Champions* (4).

A marvelous melange of familiar characters, plots, and jokes, *Breakfast of Champions* is narrated in a short punchy style by a fictional version of Vonnegut, himself. Unlike the actual writer Kurt Vonnegut, this narrator describes becoming fifty years old as if it suddenly demarcated a line of great significance—one that would divide the years behind from those ahead. He also parodies his own earlier announcements that he would stop writing fiction to concentrate on drama (for example, "About This Play" vii) and that he would create only new characters, rather than continue to bring back the old ones. Both decisions were later recanted. The finished novel itself reflects a secure as well as a mature writer, one who feels free to experiment with narration and, even more surprisingly, with magic marker drawings. It also reflects a highly successful writer whose publisher willingly indulges him by agreeing to publish whatever he writes.[3] But neither maturity nor success appears to characterize the narrator of *Breakfast of Champions*.

In response to a question in a televised interview, Vonnegut said: "If you make things move fast enough, you can say anything . . . and I am trying to be a good citizen" ("Interview with Kurt Vonnegut," Writer's Workshop). In *Breakfast of Champions*, he successfully mixes serious social and political commentary with antic action. The novel proves an entertaining, yet serious warning against the effects of pollution, commercial exploitation, advertising, war, racism, and, above all, drug dependency and addiction. For example, Vonnegut savagely, satirically attacks both pollution and white racism through the gruesome story Dwayne Hoover's father tells of a lynch mob sawing in two an innocent man using "the top strand of a barbed-wire fence" (240). As he recounts this incident to his son with evident approval, they work together dumping garbage and trash into Sugar Creek, thus adding ecological contamination to their emotional and verbal pollution.

Part of the bleakness of Vonnegut's material lies not in such social or ecological problems, however—though they are often bleak enough— but instead lies in the omnipresent loneliness that he finds at the heart of the American experience as well as in his own. This is especially clear in *Slapstick*,

Jailbird, and *Deadeye Dick*. If imagining being an American usually involves either achieving the American Dream of riches and success or involves fulfilling the other American Dream of living in freedom and democracy, then Vonnegut's is a rare case. For Vonnegut, both of these American Dreams must accommodate loneliness and the necessity of waiting. Loneliness, like the experience of loss so eloquently documented in *Timequake*, is, if not central, then for this writer an extremely important component of American experience. The sheer size of the United States breeds isolation, as does extreme American mobility, compared with almost any other country. That mobility yields exhilaration derived from affirming individual freedom, but often comes at the steep price of lonesomeness and individual isolation. It is what Vonnegut calls the "Great American Experiment . . . with liberty . . . [,] rootlessness, mobility, and impossibly tough-minded loneliness" (*Fates Worse Than Death* 35). Rather than the "easier footing" in ordinary relations of everyday social or political life in America described by de Tocqueville, Vonnegut focuses on the weak attachments between people, especially in those difficult times when a person needs the kind of strong attachment that offers understanding, warmth, and comfort.

Vonnegut enjoys telling of his meeting Sargent Shriver, the substitute Democratic candidate for vice president of the United States on the hopelessly doomed George McGovern ticket running against Ronald Reagan and George Bush. Vonnegut "proposed to Shriver . . . [that] a candidate who ran on the promise of 'Lonesome No More' would win an awful lot of votes. It was my thought that the people of this country would be well served by a project in which we could re-form ourselves into artificially extended families" ("Two Conversations" 224). When asked to submit ideas for the Democratic presidential campaign, Vonnegut reiterated his idea and then added "a war cry for the American people 'Lonesome No More!' " (*Playboy* 103). But neither Shriver nor the campaign staff listened and the result is history.

Dr. Wilbur Swain, the grotesque hero of *Slapstick*, unlike the hapless Sargent Shriver, takes such advice seriously and runs for president of the United States on just such a platform and with just such a slogan—"Lonesome No More!" As Vonnegut predicted of Shriver and McGovern *if* they had taken his advice, Swain wins overwhelmingly. Becoming president, he immediately goes about the business of creating hundreds of artificial extended families. These families are inclusive rather than exclusive with all members accepted unconditionally no matter what they may do or say—the same unconditional blessing that Eliot Rosewater conferred upon all his adopted children at the end of *God Bless You, Mr. Rosewater*. All those friendless, bereft folks who had "had to believe all their lives that they were perhaps sent to the wrong Universe" (*Slapstick* 176)— now were all made welcome in their new family with hundreds of siblings, and thousands of cousins. All Americans in *Slapstick* become "Lonesome No More!" while the United States becomes the site for a series of huge ongoing family reunions. For a while at least, Swain succeeds in "reversing the way the politics of power have infiltrated the intimacies of experience" (Giannone, *Vonnegut* 124).

But balanced against Swain's successful stamping out of American loneliness is the air of defeat so much in evidence in *Jailbird* and *Deadeye Dick*.[4] Walter Starbuck in *Jailbird* lives life only in a minor key, experiences almost everything secondhand, never gets very deeply involved in life or with other people, and as a recidivist leaves jail at the beginning of the novel only to return to jail at the end. Rudy Waltz in *Deadeye Dick* effectively stops living at age twelve when he commits a double murder.[5]

Although the United States at the beginning of the twenty-first century is without question the most powerful nation on Earth, the central event in its history—the one most remembered and the one most studied—remains its civil war. All of American history leads to or away from the American Civil War—a war that the United States won by defeating itself. This victory/defeat figures, if not centrally, then at least peripherally, in virtually every study of the United States whether in literature, history, politics, religion, anthropology, psychology, or sociology. In the twentieth century, the United States again experienced both victory and defeat. The country participated in the victory of World War I and received great credit for winning World War II on both the European and Asian fronts. Yet the image with which America ended that century became not one of the glorious photographs from World War II, such as the marines raising the flag over Iwo Jima, but a television tape of an ignominious defeat broadcast around the world. Images appeared and reappeared of the last American helicopter leaving the United States Embassy in Saigon with a desperate Vietnamese clinging to, then falling from, its skids—an image Vonnegut indirectly exploits in *Hocus Pocus*.

This air of defeat, so prominent in all of Vonnegut's novels but especially so in *Jailbird* and *Deadeye Dick*, relates as well to his own personal experience of loss—yet another way in which he is *the* representative writer of his time. In contrast, one critic concludes that "Vonnegut's power [as a writer] must be shown to depend upon his elevation of America, not his aggrandizement of *his* 'problems' " (Meyer, "Kurt Vonnegut" 100, his emphasis).[6] But America and "his problems" cannot be so easily separated, since Vonnegut's so-called "problems" have proven to be identical with those of a majority of Americans, from the 1930s through the 1990s. As a nation, these problems include the loss of will and belief in self brought about by the Great Depression; the loss of moral certainty originating in America's being implicated in the massacre of Dresden and in the destruction of Hiroshima *and* Nagasaki; the loss of certainty in America's invincibility occasioned by the defeat in Vietnam; and the loss of belief in a safe society caused by the breakdown in law and order and the parallel breakup of the nuclear family. On an individual level, Vonnegut's so-called "problems" mirror those of millions of his fellow Americans including the loss of a belief in immortality or permanence occasioned by the death of parents, siblings, or the serious illness of children; the loss of identity as parent after the rearing of children occasioned by their leaving home known popularly as the "empty nest syndrome"; the loss of partnership, security, and comfort occasioned by the end of a long-term marriage; and the loss of self-worth reflected in thoughts of suicide. Vonnegut has often discussed many of the traumatic effects of such events in interviews, essays, and the prefaces to his novels. If these problems are the stuff out of which " 'Midwestern' novelists" are made (Meyer's condescending label 104), then they do not in and of themselves lead to what this critic glibly identifies as "purely 'middle class' inanities" (104). They may equally well lead to the fictional confrontation with significant loss that, I would contend, lies at the heart of most Vonnegut novels. What Kaufman says of *Breakfast of Champions, Jailbird*, and *Deadeye Dick* also demonstrates with great clarity: "The book represents both private and public anguish, showing how in Vonnegut the two are mutually inclusive, feeding on each other; the characters . . . are stranded in a stagnant, indifferent American present with no promise of a viable future" (24).

Out of "*his* problems" Vonnegut makes *his* fiction. Major events in his and his family's life, such as his mother's insanity and eventual suicide and his father's withdrawal from life, become important in relation to that fiction as they illuminate the air of defeat that is omnipresent in the novels. Hume astutely relates the uncertainty found in his characters to feelings aroused in him by the suicide of his mother, which "because of its timing . . . appears to have been a gesture directed at her son" ("Myths and Symbols" 204).[7] But there are other extensive losses as well, such as his separation and divorce, which, as noted earlier, his family refused to accept (*Palm Sunday* 186). Far from reflecting what this critic calls his "aggrandizement" of his problems, such novels show Vonnegut transmuting these problems into a tough-minded, though often satiric, examination of the fundamental American experience of loss. The nature and meaning of loss, like that of loneliness and defeat, becomes for Vonnegut a dominant part of what it means to imagine being an American in the twentieth century.

KURT VONNEGUT'S LITERARY OFFENSES

Of all Kurt Vonnegut's novels to date, none has provoked such strong and diverse reactions as *Breakfast of Champions* (1973). A novel some critics love to hate—so much that a few of them devote a disproportionate amount of space to denigrating it while pointing to what they believe are its weaknesses. "To read *Breakfast of Champions* a decade after its publication," writes one with qualified disdain, "is to be somewhat put off by the author's crabbiness, effrontery, self-indulgence, and admissions of mental instability" (Cowart 173). Others remain comfortable discussing the novel using critical clichés, such as "no matter how assertively or repetitiously the claim is made, there is no 'I' that means an author outside the text" (Greer 317).[8] Still others appear content to belabor the obvious as a result of believing that "Vonnegut has taken a fictional cul-de-sac" (Messent 113–14), while an unwary few take *Breakfast of Champions*' narrator's assessments at face value as those of Vonnegut himself with unfortunate critical results. "Vonnegut describes himself [sic] as 'programmed at fifty to perform childishly.' The style of the novel with its drawings of a light switch, a cow, and a hamburger is so apparently childish that perhaps Vonnegut should be taken at his word. . . . *Breakfast of Champions*' . . . mixed critical reception is therefore no surprise" (Berryman, "After the Fall" 101).[9] But it is. As Peter J. Reed rightly argues, *Breakfast of Champions* "is perhaps the most obviously experimental of all of his novels, forthrightly downgrading traditional novelistic preoccupations such as character motivation and plot development. The author appears—as author and as character—in the fiction and notes the fictionality of the other characters" ("Kurt Vonnegut, [1922–]" 534). Other novelists have downgraded one or another of fiction's many techniques. Some have eliminated the narrator, for example, or made the narrator almost completely unreliable, while still others have included drawings, diagrams, pictures, or even more outrageously left a page blank for readers to fill in with their own description of the ideal heroine. Yet when Vonnegut innovates in such or similar ways and with considerable skill and art as in *Breakfast of Champions*, critics pounce. What are Vonnegut's literary offenses in this wonderfully self-reflexive, postmodern, fantastic comic novel that so infuriated critics and reviewers? A historical parallel may help clarify the problem.

Vonnegut's literary progenitor in American literature, Mark Twain, also had a predilection for offending the literary establishment of his day. His most memorable offense may have been his famous December 1877 after-dinner speech given as part of John Greenleaf Whittier's seventieth birthday celebration. The event was hosted by the publishers of the *Atlantic Monthly* on the twentieth anniversary of the founding of that distinguished magazine. In the audience were a host of contributors to the *Atlantic*, plus dignitaries such as Henry Wadsworth Longfellow, Ralph Waldo Emerson, and Oliver Wendell Holmes—each of whom Twain parodied in his talk. The parodies involved satiric versions of these famous poets' verse, including misattribution, comic speech, comic action, and even physical comedy. The setting for them was a miner's cabin in the far West. The piece concludes with Twain assuring the poor beleaguered miner that "*these* were not the gracious singers to whom we and the world pay loving reverence and homage; these were impostors." To which the miner replies: "Ah—impostors, were they?—are *you?*" (114). This speech, including its postmodern conclusion, was entirely satiric and meant to be wildly comic. Instead, it produced a prolonged silence and what Twain later described as "a sort of black frost."

Almost 100 years later—and, I believe, for quite the same reasons—Vonnegut's *Breakfast of Champions* met with a similar black frost reception. Twain and Vonnegut both gore some sacred cows and pay for it with poor reviews. Twain's herd belonged, of course, to the Boston Brahmins, the literary establishment of his day, while Vonnegut's sacred cows are the darlings of some of the most fashionable literary critics who form the literary establishment of his day. *Breakfast of Champions'* offense lies first and foremost in Vonnegut's parodying the postmodern novel. His novel successfully laughs at several postmodern fictional devices, especially that of the self-reflexive author who trespasses the boundaries of his own work. Charles Berryman correctly concludes that "if the author becomes a naive character, bewildered and lost in his own novel, the result is comedy and satire. No one has presented this aspect of postmodern fiction with more comic delight than Kurt Vonnegut in *Breakfast of Champions*" ("Comic Persona" 162). Vonnegut's bungling and inept author loses control of his fiction, not only "performing childishly," but also foolishly and often ineptly. When Flann O'Brien in *At Swim-Two-Birds* (1939) had the characters of his fictional author revolt against him, because he, as author, insisted on writing inappropriate, childish, and often immoral actions for them as characters to perform, the result was a clear parody of the convention of the omniscient author. O'Brien's author, modeled on James Joyce, having established his fictional world, then attempts unsuccessfully to remove himself from it in order to pare his fingernails. Then his characters revolt. Rather than stage a character revolt like O'Brien's, Vonnegut focuses instead on his fictional author's complete inability to perform as an omniscient, omnipotent narrator. Not only can he not control his characters, but he also has difficulties with elements of the setting and even with some of his own actions within the story. "Vonnegut's narrator has very limited power to create or destroy. He is trapped and victimized in the world of his own characters. Any attempt to assume godlike power leads quickly to a pratfall," as Charles Berryman argues ("Comic Persona" 167).

Perhaps to compensate for such limitations, the narrator of *Breakfast of Champions* adopts a pose of innocent, uninvolved objectivity—"I just got here myself," might sum up his attitude—and uses it to point out the lunacy of much of what he sees. In the most obvious example, that of people manufacturing poisons or taking other similarly suicidal actions that will destroy the Earth, the narrator expatiates without comment on America's willingness to despoil the planet in order to produce waste from "Kleenex tissues, . . . newspapers[,] . . . soot[,] . . . wash day products, catfood, pop" (83–84). The results are clear in the polluted New Jersey meadows and marshes. Apparently having only a rudimentary comprehension of English, the narrator speaks as if deciphering activities and feelings for a visitor from another galaxy.

The narrator's disingenuously naïve style also proves well matched to his indiscriminate interest in everything on this peculiar planet. Nothing escapes his comment from the Architectonic Plate Theory of the earth (143), the identity, and biography of St. Anthony (211–12), the diagram of a plastic molecule (227), to the famous Nelson Rockefeller greeting and handshake. He is so impressed with "a Mexican beetle which could make a blank-cartridge gun out of its rear end . . . and knock over other bugs with shock waves" (160) that he includes a felt-tip pen drawing of a beetle. This deadpan, always-willing-to-explain-even-the-obvious pose reflects the narrator's objectivity, while also emphasizing how he attempts to remove himself from the novel's action. Yet these same remarks may also lead to social criticism. For example, the narrator describes Kilgore Trout's hitching a ride on that destructive truck going from New York City to Midland City, Ohio:

He crossed the island of Manhattan from east to west in the company of Kleenex tissues and newspapers and soot.

He got a ride in a truck. It was hauling seventy-eight thousand pounds of Spanish olives. It picked him up at the mouth of the Lincoln Tunnel, which was named in honor of a man [with] . . . the courage and imagination to make human slavery against the law. . . . This was a recent innovation.

The slaves were simply turned loose without any property. They were easily recognizable. They were black. They were suddenly free to go exploring. (83)

Of the nine sentences quoted, eight are simple declarative sentences: subject, verb, object; and very few of the words have more than two syllables. It is as if the narrator were explaining something to a child. Ostensibly, he clarifies the tunnel's name, but more subtly his digression describes the origins and continuation of America's racism. The United States ended slavery but conspicuously failed to provide economically for the newly freed slaves.

This flat naïve style has a secondary effect as well. Although some critics have argued that Vonnegut's "stylistic approach basically fails and comes close at times to mere childishness' (Messent 113–14), a closer analysis of the text of *Breakfast of Champions* reveals that this naïve style, this so-called "mere childishness," actually helps defamiliarize what we have come to accept as ordinary everyday truth. For example, there is often an inherent, if rarely remarked upon, contradiction in phrases and name brands, such as Pyramid Trucking Company whose fleet of trucks is ironically named for buildings immobile for over 2,000 years (*Breakfast of Champions* 109, Hume's example in "Heraclitean" 210). Vonnegut's technique of "digging the literal out of what have become dead metaphors" (Hume 210) often startles the reader. Moreover, the overall satiric effect of this childishness, naïveté, and simplicity arises from the increasing comic dislocation. Addressing his apparently extra-terrestrial audience, for instance, the narrator patiently explains—all too simply—the logic behind the Vietnam War. The United States, he says, was attempting to halt the spread of communism in that country "by dropping things on . . . [the Vietnamese] from airplanes" (86). The notion of changing a people's political beliefs by dropping things on them from airplanes is worthy of Jonathan Swift or Mark Twain. People who are being bombed rarely regard those who bomb them as friends nor do they see the bombing as part of an educative or persuasive process, but rather as one designed solely to achieve their own destruction. Here, logic has gone haywire since the means used (bombs) almost guarantee that the end they were designed to achieve (ending communism in Vietnam) can not, will not be achieved. The satire and comedy work by taking the political and moral justification for the Vietnam War—saving that part of the world from communism—and juxtaposing it to the method employed to save it—bombs and, worse, napalm and defoliants. This becomes yet another example of what Hume calls "the interrelating of disparities" (211).

Finally, the narrator of *Breakfast of Champions* becomes himself the butt of satire and parody. Nowhere in Vonnegut's fiction is there precedent, except as parody or satire, for this narrator's pretentious assertion that "I was on a par with the Creator of the Universe" (200). As creator, the narrator is not personally remarkable. If the comic book hero Superman could "leap over tall buildings in a single bound," this narrator can imitate him on a lesser scale by jumping over a car in a single bound, but meanwhile, as he narrates this eventful scene, his toe is broken by one of his own characters. Later, a dog from another version of the novel almost bites him! Not exactly an outstanding record. Yes, he can foretell the future, but whenever he does so what he says is truly trivial and ultimately not very revealing. Seemingly unable to really manipulate his characters, this narrator discovers that once he creates them they have a life of their own that he is not free to violate.

If "pride goeth before a fall," then this narrator is headed for a very big pratfall indeed. Berryman succinctly and correctly advises: "We should laugh at the vanity of the narrator" ("Comic Persona" 168).

> Once the narrator of *Breakfast of Champions* is viewed as a naive story-teller, the many conversations in the novel about the very process of writing are understandable in a new context. When the narrator says to himself, "this is a very bad book you're writing," we should hear the comic despair of Philboyd Studge unable to live up to the standards of the Houynhnms. If the dissatisfaction were Vonnegut's, there would be no excuse for publishing the book. ("Comic Persona" 167)

Still, several critics insist on equating the author with his persona or narrator in ways somewhat similar to those of readers, such as Queen Anne of England who famously misread Swift's "An Argument Against Abolishing Christianity." But the Vonnegut who narrates *Breakfast of Champions*—this fictitious character with all his "crabbiness, effrontery, self-indulgence, and admissions of mental instability" (Cowart 173)—clearly bears little or no relation to Kurt Vonnegut, the author of numerous novels, stories, and plays.[10]

The narrator does not merely narrate the book; he also cannot resist playing a substantial role in it. He often comes perilously close to what Kaufman has described as "oily, devious, flattering, and two-faced as Mephistopheles or Tartuffe—and cruel as well. . . . By calling attention to his own confidence game as an artist and comedian, he warns that escapism into art may assist adaptation, but it may also amount to self-deception with dangerous consequences" (32). Vonnegut, as author, meanwhile continuously undercuts such perilous consequences by holding the narrator also named "Vonnegut" up to ridicule whenever he boasts of his omniscience or omnipotence.

> Anticipating an audience now ready to chip away at his new fame and fortune [after the critical and commercial success of *Slaughterhouse-Five*], Vonnegut presents a comic image of the author dissatisfied with his own work and then attacked by a ravenous dog at the end of the book. The writer appears as a character in his own novel, not merely to conduct a dialogue with himself about the relationship of art and life, but also to deflect the charges of his audience. (Berryman, "Comic Persona" 164)

Both as narrator and as character this "Vonnegut" simply fails to accomplish much, if anything. Perhaps the best, clearest example of his ineffectiveness occurs close to the novel's end when the narrator as all-powerful author in pursuit of his character Kilgore Trout attempts to turn on the dome light of his rented car and instead turns on the windshield wipers. While this error is a common enough, if mildly embarrassing experience of anyone who's rented an unfamiliar car, it becomes devastating for this particular narrator. For this narrator claims to be not just anyone, but Someone who is both Omnipotent and Omniscient. Similarly, when this narrator issues his pompous, god-like, pronouncement, "Arise, Mr. Trout, you are free" (294), he is immediately confronted not by a grateful Trout, but by the image of Vonnegut's father. Like the vicious dog that bites the fumbling narrator, his father is yet another rejected character from another unfinished novel (*Jailbird* 13–15).[11]

Although the narrator of *Breakfast of Champions* appears far removed from Vonnegut, the successful, accomplished author, he is perilously close to the unsuccessful, hack, Kilgore Trout. Trout emerges in *Breakfast of Champions* not only as a central character but also as *the* exemplary failed author. As character, Trout spins improbable and half-thought-out plots that allow Vonnegut to introduce ideas, motifs, characters, and situations without committing to them fictionally or having them become an integral part of the story. As the failed author *primer inter pares* Trout fails in *every* sense, not just in one or two. He fails commercially, being published in sleazy porn magazines as filler between the lurid, graphic pictures. He fails critically, having never been reviewed or acknowledged by any reader, reviewer, or critic, except Eliot Rosewater who has enough money to make Trout famous. He fails artistically, producing only hackwork, trivia, and ill-considered potboilers. (All of that makes him a perfect foil for Vonnegut's own carefully formed and crafted work.) Trout as failure plays a key role in the climax of *Breakfast of Champions*, where the pompous narrator makes his long-awaited announcement about setting his characters free. Confronting Trout as his creator, he announces: "I am going to set at liberty . . . the literary characters who have served me so loyally during my writing career" (293).[12] "The paradox, of course, is that by setting him free, Vonnegut reveals his character's *un*freedom. This is a paradigmatic postmodernist moment of ontological short-circuit," as Brian McHale observes (214). And Trout, who as the novel progresses has come more and more to resemble Vonnegut's father, answers in a voice that is also that of Vonnegut's father, "Make me young, make me young, make me young!" (295). Trout dreams of returning to his youth, dreams of magically receiving a second chance from his creator—as do many people, but with the difference that this creator, as novelist, can make such fantasies come true by simply typing a new page. Yet even here, Vonnegut makes an ironic joke at Trout's expense, for, like the famous sibyl of Cumae, Trout makes the mistake of asking for youth and no more.[13] If the fumbling narrator of *Breakfast of Champions* is powerless to grant his wish since he is, like all of Vonnegut's narrators, a single-book author, Vonnegut himself, the author and creator of Kilgore Trout, can and does willingly oblige him. In *Jailbird* he does make Trout young again, but puts him in jail serving a life sentence. As the Latin satirist wryly remarked, "When the gods want to punish us, they answer our prayers!"

Breakfast of Champions itself proves to be much like Trout's wish for youth—a fantasy of returning to lost innocence. Set first in the bleak landscape of New York City, then in the psychotically disturbed one of Midland City, the book projects an air of innocence throughout—even when discussing pornography, pollution, and crime. In part, this viewpoint reflects the narrator treating everything and everyone equally, so that nothing surprises and nothing stands out—not even himself as creator. There may also be echoes of *Slaughterhouse-Five*'s duty dance with death in the discussion of suicide (192) and in the certain knowledge of mortality shared by all the characters including the narrator. The narrator at the beginning of the novel describes himself as feeling like he has climbed up a steeply pitched roof and now finds himself "crossing the spine" (4). But unlike in *Slaughterhouse-Five*, all such considerations of the duty dance with death in *Breakfast of Champions* become linked with the book's antic comedy and playfulness. Resisting the temptation of fatalism, Vonnegut suggests that if "we cannot make ourselves young again, . . . we can make ourselves more humane" (Merrill 160).

Besides the dream of personal eternal youth externalized in Trout's *cri de coeur*—"Make me young, make me young, make me young!" (295)—there lies behind *Breakfast of Champions* a second, similar all-encompassing dream of regaining the lost innocence of the United States. Once a green and pleasant land, America is now in great danger of being destroyed by greed, lust, and stupidity. Once there was the promise of America, "the last and greatest of all human dreams," as F. Scott Fitzgerald phrased it in *The Great Gatsby*. As *Breakfast of Champions* demonstrates, that promise disappeared on the anonymous interstate, in the drab motel, in the polluting washing powder and tissues and waste, and in the omnipresent advertising for these and other ephemeral products. "What passes for a culture in my head is really a bunch of commercials, and this is intolerable," lamented Vonnegut in *Wampeters, Foma & Granfalloons* (281) and so wrote this satiric novel about the lack of a true culture in the United States. The false culture is evident in the book's title, *Breakfast of Champions* and subtitle, *Goodbye Blue Monday* which represent two of the over 5,000–6,000 ads that an average American sees every single day. What then becomes of the parallel, equally naïve dream of the young child staring at the cereal box with its advertising slogan liberally dipped in hope—"Breakfast of Champions?" That motto promised the child that she, too, could be a winner, a champion. But even that dream disappeared, trivialized, turned into the consumerism of American sports. In its place there appears the pornographic dream of male dominance parodied in *Breakfast of Champions* by the significantly large dimensions of the narrator's penis (284). (Of course, even his sizable organ fades to insignificance when compared to that of the blue whale! [147].)

Moreover, all the characters in *Breakfast of Champions* together with the gauche narrator "are stranded in a stagnant, indifferent American present with no promise of a viable future. . . . Death is pitted against the life of America itself, a nation deceived by the impression of its own glory and moral supremacy, slowly suffering from the crumbling of its very foundation, the spirit of its people" (Kaufman 24, 25). Some critics misinterpret this picture of "a stagnant, indifferent American present" as "signs of tiredness" in the author rather than as a satiric, critical portrait. Some go so far as to patronize Vonnegut by citing *Breakfast of Champions* as clear evidence that the efforts required to write *Slaughterhouse-Five* mentally and emotionally drained him (Messent

104). Still others view Vonnegut's fiction after *Slaughterhouse-Five*, beginning with *Breakfast of Champions*, as a descent from the peak of Billy Pilgrim's story. Such vistas and views are, however, more likely to be in the eye of the reader than in the fiction itself. In the exuberant comic dislocation of *Breakfast of Champions*, Vonnegut plays in a serious way with the nature of narrative and with his role as a writer. "It appears to me [that] I'm wildly experimental," he once remarked and this novel proves him right.

These innovations in narrative and point of view also enable Vonnegut to discuss large social issues, such as ecocide, racism, drug addiction, and economic inequality. Having dealt in his first six novels with such imponderable questions as why evil appears universal and how there can be such unmerited human suffering in the world, writing the antic comedy of *Breakfast of Champions* must have come as a kind of relief. In *Breakfast of Champions*, he shares with his reader the exhilaration that comes with "crossing the spine" of the roof—including the attendant danger of being so far above the ground—and the speculation possible when viewing the human comedy from such a height. The flux of human life must be accepted as permanent, suggests *Breakfast of Champions*, as *Slaughterhouse-Five* stresses the necessity of accepting the inevitability of suffering in human experience. Vonnegut "has explored this flux as madness, as the product of evil, as the result of man's consuming greed, and as the result of natural forces," writes Hume.

He has looked anthropologically at man's defenses against the instability, and he has explored man's ways of keeping the tides of change at bay. More important, Vonnegut has found his own way of anchoring his perceptions amidst the flow. What he can accept as fixed may be very limited, but he has found some stabilities—human consciousness, helpfulness, decency—and from these he is beginning to build further fictions. ("Heraclitean" 224)

Such stabilities form the normative base from which Vonnegut launches his elaborate satire of the postmodern, self-reflexive novel in *Breakfast of Champions*. Hume once asked: "how can a novel convey a sense of affirmation without relying on traditional symbols or becoming preachy?" ("Myths and Symbols" 429). Vonnegut offers one solution in *Breakfast of Champions*. While the affirmation it offers might be limited, it is nonetheless real. The novel acknowledges the human propensity for suicide, both individually and collectively, while pillorying the contemporary inability to treat serious problems seriously from rampant racism to ecocide. Suicide is not the answer, nor is ecocide inevitable. They may appear all but inescapable, given humanity's, and especially Americans' refusal to face and deal with such problems. Yet Vonnegut holds out that slight hope, through his satirizing of pretensions, that people could begin by simply acknowledging their humanity along with the planet's fragility. They could begin to talk thoughtfully about taking meaningful action in the present and paying the price for past folly. If humanity is to survive, Vonnegut believes, then it must cleanse the planet of pollution and its death-dealing effects, purge human society of racism and drug dependency, and wash the human mind of its superciliousness and hypocrisy.

Breakfast of Champions suggests all this with antic humor, satire, and a large helping of vulgarity. Like Twain and countless American writers before him, Vonnegut, in imagining being an American, "engages and absorbs the common and the vulgar" (Spiegelman 148). Also like Twain, Vonnegut's "creative genius transforms [the common and the vulgar] into the new and the strange" which, as Willard Spiegelman—among many commentators and critics—cogently observes, is characteristic of most American writers (148). It is Vonnegut's humor, especially as employed in deflating the pretensions of the author-narrator in *Breakfast of Champions*, that affirms what is possible and what is necessary. While this most experimental of all Vonnegut's novels may have produced a black frost of critical reception, it has also proven in its postmodern comic self-reflexivity one of his most complex, most accomplished of fantastic fictions.

ACCOMMODATING TO LIFE OR BARGAINING IN GOOD FAITH

Only fiction appears capable of sustaining a utopian vision. One value of such fiction is its definition of an ideal or goal worth striving for, even if that goal remains always out of reach. *Slapstick* presents such a utopian fantasy where Vonnegut imagines an ideal United States or, more precisely, an ideal portion of the United States since the breaking up of this vast country into smaller, more humanly manageable autonomous sections forms an essential part of that vision.

The novel involves not one but three distinct, interrelated fantastic stories that in turn appear as part of a daydream Vonnegut has on the way to his uncle's funeral—the ostensible occasion for the novel. The first story reverses the European colonists' attempt to create a utopia in the New World. In 1620, the Pilgrims, upon first viewing the shore of the New World, saw not Fitzgerald's green and pleasant land but only wilderness and savages. They quickly set about destroying both, thanks to their vastly superior technology, and replaced them with their more familiar "civilization." In *Slapstick*, Vonnegut inverts that historical movement from nature to city, from savage to civilized by creating an Eden in the wilderness—or in as much wilderness as modern Vermont allows—and peopling it with a primitive-appearing, simian-like, monstrously tall Adam and Eve. In these innocent great apes, Wilbur and Eliza Swain who are distinctly superior to ordinary humans, Vonnegut challenges a popular cliché in the evolutionary stereotype of humans progressing up and away from apes toward angels. Armed only with astronomically high intelligence quotients (IQs), the zygotes thrive in their idyllic setting and together make up one supra-human person. When together, they wrote a work critical of Darwin's theory of evolution and another critical of the United States Constitution, learned ancient and modern languages, and mastered calculus. Apart, each becomes "stupid and insecure" as each feels as though his or her "head were turning to wood" (87). Progress in the person of an embittered psychologist proves the modern snake in this paradise condemning Wilbur and Eliza to separation and exile. Thus they are expelled forever from their Garden of Eden. Worse, they are separated. If a genius should appear, suggests *Slapstick*, humanity would treat her or him not as a potential means to genuine social, political, or cultural advancement, but as a pariah. Collective wisdom would conspire to throw such a person or persons not just out of Eden but out of the human community by confining her or him to a mental ward.

Slapstick's second fantastic story is the familiar one of a blighted land placed under a curse by a wicked witch that is at last rescued by an innocent hero who, after reforming the society, dies leaving a scrap of verse behind:

> And how did we then face the odds,
> Of man's rude slapstick, yes, and God's?
> Quite at home and unafraid,
> Thank you,
> In a game our dreams remade. (230)

And finally, the novel includes the tale of Melody, the King of Candlesticks' granddaughter, who successfully accomplishes her amazing journey on foot all the way from Michigan to New York encountering helpful relatives as she goes who give her food and directions as well as gifts such as a compass, raincoat, gold thimble, and needle and thread. One relative even braved the dangerous Harlem River by rowing her across to Manhattan, the island popularly known as the Island of Death. In this account of Melody's trip, Good wins out over Evil because Good remains innocent—the pure in heart survives various ordeals. In this improbable happy ending borrowed from fairy tales, Melody, facing an impossible task, is rescued through the intervention of the good fairy that makes everything all right again.[14] Her grandfather celebrates his one-hundredth birthday with a thousand lit candles that becomes the novel's final vision: "Standing among all those tiny, wavering lights, I felt as though I were God, up to my knees in the Milky Way" (228).

Slapstick remains Vonnegut's only novel where he even partially accepts what Brian Attebery defines as the "American tradition of fantasy": "a long-range attempt at . . . creating an American fairyland. . . . The American writer must find some way of re-entering the ancient storytelling guild . . . he must find an archetypal analog for his own land—an American fairyland—to which . . . old world magical motifs may be drawn" (*Fantasy Tradition* vii). Vonnegut earlier in *Breakfast of Champions* had rejected outright any such notion. There, fairyland turns out to be a dangerous delusion rather than a fantastic reality. Wayne Hoobler, astonished by the sudden appearance of the Will Fairchild Memorial Airport runway lights, compares them to miles of magically appearing stunning jewelry. He also innocently mistakes this commonplace technological marvel for that ideal world of his dreams. Moreover, that fairyland so beautiful and inviting, his experience fails utterly to verify. What is worse, his experience demonstrates that such American fairylands appear forever closed off to blacks, such as himself, whose very birth looks like a terrible mistake or bad joke. Other fairylands in Vonnegut's fiction prove equally dangerous illusions. In *The Sirens of Titan*, Boaz believes he's being addressed by the Harmoniums who invite him to remain in what appears to be a fairyland complete with magical motifs where he will become the sole, central, necessary person there. The reality is far more mundane—even sordid—for in truth Winston Niles Rumfoord cynically controls

Boaz, his environment, and the Harmoniums. In *Deadeye Dick*, the fairyland of Shangri La lives up to its name as it turns out to be an unattainable, never-to-be-realized chimera opposed by the all-too-real radioactive "shitboxes" where people actually live and from which they are powerless to escape. In *Cat's Cradle*, the utopian society constructed by Lionel Boyd Johnson and Eugene McCabe, which briefly functions as a fairyland, proves impotent against human stupidity and greed that brings about the end of the world including their ideal society. In *Galápagos*, humans almost systematically destroy not only themselves but also this beautiful planet which potentially could be fairyland for all creatures great and small if it were not for "the only real villain in my story: the oversize human brain" (270). What actually materializes in *Galápagos* is not so much an American fairyland as—what Klinkowitz calls—"a better reality" ("Review of *Slapstick*" 188).[15] But this alternative reality is achieved only *at the expense of destroying the Earth, as we know it* and radically altering human beings, as we know them. Sending humanity back to the sea with flippers to fish does save planet Earth, but at a certain expense of human population. Similarly, instituting the utopian scheme of extended families in *Slapstick* does indeed take care of society's problems from welfare and health care to old age and warfare but also comes at a high price—the destruction of almost all of the modern world, especially its technology though fluctuating gravity. Along side the vision of a better reality, lies the knowledge of how impossible it would be to realize that reality. Thus Vonnegut returns in *Slapstick* to a theme already familiar from *Player Piano* in proposing that people turn away from their love of gadgets, machinery, and modern technology in general, and focus instead on maintaining human relationships. This chimera of a world without machines, without modern technology, will be further explored even more imaginatively in *Galápagos*, where human beings will reduce, or have reduced for them by evolution, their needs to the basic ones of food, safety, and reproduction without giving much thought to community. By way of contrast in *Slapstick*, human beings, while also decreasing their needs to survival ones, achieve this sense of community where they value human life, treat one another with respect and decency, and, despite a few madmen who wage war, manage to live a relatively peaceful, ordered life.

In Swain's scheme of large American folk families, community replaces rugged individualism. People who belong to such arbitrary, randomly selected groups learn that they can rely upon one another, unlike in the former but now defunct United States of America in which "nobody . . . [had] a right to rely on anybody else—where everybody [had] . . . to make his or her own way" (*Slapstick* 93). "We must wear old shoes and have aunts and cousins," as Emerson wrote in his journal (126), but for Vonnegut, as for most twentieth-century Americans, there are no available aunts and few cousins live within easy reach. This necessity for belonging to a viable human community coupled with the contemporary failure to create such communities in the United States becomes central to Vonnegut's experience of imagining being an American.[16]

In *Slapstick*, Americans discover and practice mutual respect for one another. Blackford maintains that "Common decency as Vonnegut conceives it is clearly a more beneficent quality than those kinds of love which allow for intolerance, possessiveness, or neglect. It is also more important than love conceived of as mere physical affection. The concept acts as a paradigm not of what love is, but of what it should be" ("Definition" 201). But his terms need refining. For Vonnegut, the social value of respect far outweighs the social value of love since successful social values must rest upon limited, defined obligations, such as respect, rather than on more open-ended ones, such as love. The most equitable societies are, therefore, those built upon justice rather than love. Justice clarifies social relations and values by imposing boundaries, whereas love muddies them by providing no limits. Vonnegut also prefers respect, because respect demands honesty and decency—values anyone can practice in any relationship, whereas love demands unconditional acceptance—a value most people find difficult to practice in most relationships. Like the novelist James Morrow, Vonnegut would wish to "rid ourselves of those grand absolutes, those terrible transcendent truths, in whose name human beings have routinely menaced one another" (34).[17] Such an absence of absolutes would leave no basis for a crusade against the infidel nor would there remain any litmus test for belonging.

Besides this utopian goal of giving respect to all human beings and being respectful of the planet, Vonnegut also returns in *Slapstick* to the problem of the right use of technology. Thanks to the benign catastrophe of wildly fluctuating gravity, machinery rusts and human beings find themselves forced to decrease their needs solely to those required for survival. Within sight of the old New York Stock Exchange, now in ruins, a family of "food-gatherers . . . fish off docks . . . mine for canned goods[,] . . . pick fruits and berries[,] . . .grow . . . tomatoes[,] . . . potatoes and radishes" (82). War, although never eliminated, returns to a human footing. They key lay in the president's realization that "nations could never acknowledge their own wars as tragedies, but . . . families not only could but had to" (214). Those who volunteer for war, those who want to kill are rejected as unfit for combat. People are allowed to fight *only* if they recognize the terrible price in human life that wars exact (213–14). With extended families of thousands of relatives—identified as Daffodils, Chipmunks, or whatever—spread all across the country, each family will have relatives on every side in any war. As happened to many families during the American Civil War, individuals realize that if they go to fight they will injure and possibly kill people related to them, rather than the less-than-human enemy, say, created by the propaganda on both sides during World War II. It is, indeed, "a game our dreams remade" (230).

Slapstick actualizes Vonnegut's vision of a better world through fantasy yet that game or dream might become clearer for most readers if it were not blurred because of the ill-defined way it is told. Unlike in *Slaughterhouse-Five*, where Vonnegut puts himself clearly in the role of narrator with a minor part in the action, or in *Breakfast of Champions*, where his surrogate narrator plays a major role in the action, in *Slapstick* Vonnegut apparently drops out of sight as narrator after writing the prologue to reappear only in the epilogue. This absence represents a formal, conventional relation of author to narrator to story rather than one of Vonnegut's more innovative relations such as that of a prominent "character in [his] . . . works," that he talked about when he earlier announced his return to fiction writing (*Between Time and Timbuktu* xv).

At once fantastic and serious utopian fiction, *Slapstick* is also a book about waiting—Vonnegut waiting to ascertain the future direction of his life and fiction, waiting for inspiration and viable plots—as well as a book about loss. Gone is the exuberance of *Breakfast of Champions*—no one would ever describe either the author or the narrator of *Slapstick* as metaphorically "crossing the spine of a roof"—and missing is the frenzied activity of *The Sirens of Titan*. In their place is the daydream Vonnegut has as he flies to his uncle's funeral and meditates on the loss of his sister to cancer several years before. "It would have been catastrophic if I had forgotten my sister at once," he writes. Although he had never mentioned it, his sister Alice became the audience for whom he wrote. She thus became, as he says, for him the "secret of whatever artistic unity I had ever achieved . . . the secret of my technique" (*Slapstick* 15). The novel is thus framed by the anticipated funeral of his uncle and by the remembered one of his sister. It is a novel of a tired person, one worn down a bit by events, by the trials and tragedies of human life, and one who confesses to "experimenting with being old" (19). Even its moral tag sounds tired in context. It is the famous Hippocratic oath that all physicians must swear: "If you can do no good, at least do no harm" (Hippocrates).

Hippocrates's injunction, like the novel itself, is reminiscent of the Nixon years—that time when America itself appeared tired and unwilling to face squarely moral issues, whether in domestic politics or in foreign policy. Wilbur Daffodil-11 Swain, who in *Slapstick* is the current president of the United States, assesses his predecessor Richard Milhous Nixon, the only president of the United States ever forced to resign from office. "Mr. Nixon and his associates had been unbalanced by [extreme] loneliness. . . . [N]ot basically criminals . . . they yearned to partake of the brotherhood they saw in Organized Crime" (166).[18] Although somewhat tongue-in-cheek, Swain's comment points to the key issue of America's failure either to provide true extended families for its citizens or to deal with omnipresent American loneliness. "No matter how old we are, we are going to be bored and lonely during what remains of our lives," wisely observes Vonnegut in *Palm Sunday* (180). Americans, he believes, have a deep-seated need for a real human community that will genuinely care about individuals. Yet, with the demise of the folk family and peasant village and, almost at the same time, a huge increase in American personal mobility, how could such artificial extended families as pictured in *Slapstick* provide the comfort, aid, and meaning Vonnegut seeks? In novel after novel and story after story, Vonnegut's protagonists remain alone—"like a little bit of grit in the middle of the steppe," as Samuel Beckett puts it in *Endgame* (36). As if to emphasize this difficulty, in all Vonnegut's fiction it is hard, if not impossible, to find characters able and willing to bond with others. Rather than Emerson's self-reliant individual, readers encounter representatives of America's atomistic, lonely society in the nonbonding loner. Matthew Arnold admirably caught this high degree of personal isolation a century ago in his poem, "To Marguerite in Returning a Volume of the Letters of Ortis":

> Yes: in the sea of life enisl'd
> With echoing straits between us thrown,
> Dotting the shoreless watery wild,
> We mortal millions live *alone*.
>   The islands feel the enclasping flow,
> And then their endless bounds they know. (ll. 1–6)

Slapstick thus remains Vonnegut's very real cry against the loneliness Americans experience, and his assertion that there is little or no comfort to be found in traditional religion nor any consolation to be derived from traditional notions of an afterlife. Religion and a belief in an afterlife are satirically treated in *Slapstick* through another of Vonnegut's invented religions: The Church of Jesus Christ the Kidnapped that would in time take its place as the "most popular American religion of all time" (184). Believers behave ridiculously, exaggeratedly as they search with great optimism for their kidnapped savior. For example, one young man comically jerked his head this way and that, as if anticipating catching a person looking at him from in back of a potted palm or some piece of hotel lobby furnishings or perhaps looking down at him from the chandelier overhead. The satiric edge, so evident in The Church of God the Utterly Indifferent in *The Sirens of Titan* or in the religion of Bokonon in *Cat's Cradle*, appears somewhat dulled here. Mild amusement at the comic action of the devoted replaces the savage satire of *The Sirens of Titan* and the playful yet serious inventiveness of *Cat's Cradle*. All of which may help account for *Slapstick*'s slack quality. Yet the target of the satire remains clear. "America . . . is inevitably the most millenarian of all nations even though so far it has avoided the two extremes of modern millenarianism, fascism and Marxist-Leninism" (Bloom 155). But still the United States has experienced most of the millenarian spectrum between those two dictatorial extremes. Of the estimated 300-plus religions in the United States a majority are millennial in belief and outlook. Even mainstream Protestantism and Catholicism often dips into this turbulent water. "A nation whose quasi-official high priest is the reverend Billy Graham, author of *Approaching Hoofbeats: The Four Horsemen of the Apocalypse*, is rather clearly more likely than most other countries to have strong intimations of the Millennium," maintains Harold Bloom (3). And he is right. There are American television and radio stations and at least one television network whose total programming consists of discussions of and preaching on apocalypse.

Against this background, Vonnegut satirizes conventional notions of the afterlife. Rather than in the Golden City, the faithful find themselves stuck on a "badly run turkey farm" (231). A character in Beckett's radio play, *Embers*, might have been speaking of *Slapstick*'s picture of the Next World when he says: "[t]hat's what hell will be like, small chat to the babbling of the Lethe about the good old days when we wished we were dead" (96). Or as Wilbur's sister Eliza says "Whoever designed this place [the afterlife] knew nothing about human beings" (234). The novel's satire pokes fun at "the idea of a purposeful universe with a place established for humanity and in which a rational eschatology justifies and explains the seemingly unjust course of this life" (Blackford, "Definition" 194).

Rather than the spectacular consolations of eschatology, *Slapstick* offers more modest ones. "In *Slapstick* the absurdity of life fosters social neurosis, which one can at least begin to treat, rather than metaphysical alienation, which is beyond all cure" (Gill 78). According to the narrator of the novel, the great human inventions are those which help things to run more smoothly and/or make us feel more comfortable. We have and use *Robert's Rules of Order* (216), for example, to give everyone and no one an advantage in public meetings as demonstrated by the nine year old who runs a superbly ordered meeting in *Slapstick.*[19]

But disorder rather than order characterizes the novel's action itself as "civilization crumbles into absurdities that are bizarre even for a Vonnegut novel" (Gill 78). Some of those absurdities show the danger for Vonnegut in dismissing Kilgore Trout, as he did at the conclusion of *Breakfast of Champions*. *Slapstick* cries out for the failed hack science-fiction writer to wash out some of the unrealized parts of the plot, such as the shrinking microscopic Chinese and the Martian invasion in the form of flu germs. Such events might function far better in plots for failed Kilgore Trout novels than they do as part of a serious Vonnegut book. In several interviews Vonnegut noted that anything he wrote after *Slaughterhouse-Five* would be published without alterations since he had become a best-selling author. The downside of that arrangement becomes all too apparent with *Slapstick*. Vonnegut "felt rushed in getting the book into print. . . . [T]he completed manuscript was immediately computer-set and distributed for book club consideration," claims Loree Rackstraw ("Dancing" 129). "My publishers won't tell me honestly what they think of my work, since their opinion doesn't mean a damn thing commercially," Vonnegut complained. "Nobody's opinion matters commercially. We just publish, and off we go" (Rackstraw, "Dancing" 129). So apparently this is a Vonnegut novel somewhat "in the raw"—one that could have benefited from a last rewrite.[20]

Balanced against all of these negative considerations, however, lies *Slapstick's* pivotal place in understanding Vonnegut's work overall: first, it emphasizes ameliorating the loneliness of Americans that Vonnegut dealt with originally in several short stories and in *Player Piano* but did not return to in most of his later novels. Second, it points toward several new possible directions his fiction could take as he follows his dictum to write about what actually happens.[21] In *Breakfast of Champions* the narrator urges his fellow writers to do exactly that in order to help persuade fellow citizens who are not writers that, given the lack of order in the world, "we must adapt ourselves to the requirements of chaos instead" (210). Each of Vonnegut's novels beginning with *Breakfast of Champions* and including *Slapstick*, attempts in various ways to "adapt . . . to the requirements of chaos."

Slapstick will continue to be, like Vonnegut's play *Happy Birthday, Wanda June* (1970), more interesting as a transitional than as a wholly successful Vonnegut novel. Time has simply disproved his assertion that *Slapstick* will be the nearest thing he would write to an autobiography (1). *Palm Sunday,* published some years after *Slapstick*, proved a splendid, revealing autobiography in which Vonnegut talks about himself as writer, father, husband, citizen, and human being, while *Fates Worse Than Death: An Autobiographical Collage of the 1980s* is by turns insightful, argumentative, and revealing. In the late 1970s, Richard Giannone saw *Breakfast of Champions* and *Slapstick* as providing "a fictive guide to our lost culture" (*Vonnegut* 126)—a large claim that he attempted to substantiate through a close reading of these novels (98–126). "Without essentially altering his established material or practiced style," Giannone concludes, "Vonnegut advances his art in *Slapstick* through tone. Doom is handled quietly, philosophically, in the way that Laurel and Hardy throw pies with thoughtful poise" (*Vonnegut* 114). Hence the small sections of prose within abbreviated chapters that will become a hallmark of Vonnegut's later work—each section deliberately, carefully thrown. Yet the conclusion is foregone: dead Eliza summons Wilbur to join her quickly to alleviate the boredom of the Turkey Farm. Wilbur kept sane and functioning by drugs, has one final vision of himself as King of Candlesticks. But he has little else to show for a life that began disastrously, was maintained through pain and loss, evaded every promise it held, and brought considerable tragedy and suffering. Like Laurel and Hardy "bargaining in good faith with destiny" (2), Swain goes on to the end writing his necessarily incomplete autobiography—a work addressed, like the prayers of religious skeptics, "To Whom It May Concern" (19, 21).

The materials of *Slapstick*, like those of *Slaughterhouse-Five*, are about nothing less than the total inexplicability of life, death, and suffering. Giannone may believe that "*Slapstick* comes across as an abbreviated *Journey to the End of the Night*, during which Wilbur visualizes death on the American installment plan" (*Vonnegut* 115), but there remains a significant difference between Céline and Vonnegut in the intimacy achieved through the speaking voice in *Slapstick*'s prologue and epilogue that frame Wilbur's story. The novel's action is set against the background of Vonnegut's flight to his Uncle Alex's funeral. He and his widowed brother Bernard sit on either side of an empty seat reserved for their dead sister, Alice. Characteristically, there is a noticeable lack of whining, there is no special pleading, and there are no outbursts of righteous indignation over "man's rude slapstick, yes, and god's" (230). Things are the way they are. Humans simply must accept that this is so—as Laurel and Hardy accepted the pie in the face, the fender ripped from the car, or as Vonnegut's sister Alice accepted the train going over the open drawbridge and into the river, which killed her husband only hours before her own death (*Slapstick* 12). When talking about her own impending death, Alice would call the event "Slapstick" (11). Yet death is not the last word for "this game our dreams remade," as that is reserved for the story of Melody. "Vonnegut . . . has it both ways," claims R. B. Gill of the novel: "Bargaining in good faith, he realistically refuses a comic transformation of events, but he keeps alive that faint 'and yet' of idealism. . . . [He] creates the mature laughter that indicates a secure sense of superiority to the restrictions of life" (83). This laughter may be experienced through Melody, who appears as a "famished child, pregnant and clasping a Dresden candlestick."[22] Arriving on the Island of Death with the candlestick, she proves a love child in a fairy story that itself completes and counterpoints the fantastic tale of Eliza and Wilbur, the monstrous twins separated and thrown out of their Edenic paradise into a hostile lonely world. Together these tales join to create the "grotesque situational poetry" suggesting "what life *feels* like" to Vonnegut and to many of his readers, since "confident answers are more popular and easier to assert than bargaining in good faith" (Gill 90). Finally, *Slapstick* appears a gentle, quiet, but occasionally tired book. While Vonnegut does not again return to the furious activity of *Breakfast of Champions* or *The Sirens of Titan*, he will go on to write with far more authority in *Jailbird* and *Deadeye Dick*, with more consistency in the well-developed science-fiction novel, *Galápagos*, and with more unity and craft in *Bluebeard* and *Hocus Pocus*. Only *Timequake* will suffer from a similarly perceived lack of edge.

POOR SOULS

In imagining being an American, Vonnegut excoriates *both* American capitalism and American communism as lost opportunities because both failed to serve either the citizens or the economy very well. In *Jailbird*, for example, Mary Kathleen O'Looney illustrates both the out-of-control quality of the American corporate world and the ineffectiveness of the naïf communist revolutionary. While in earlier novels Vonnegut had satirized the inexplicable— because inhuman—world of high finance in the acquisitive Malachi Constant of *The Sirens of Titan* and the philanthropic Eliot Rosewater of *God Bless You, Mr. Rosewater*, in *Jailbird* he extends his satire to yet another stereotype: the richest person in the world. But Vonnegut makes this person female, rather than male and, ironically, a bag lady rather than an expensively dressed high-powered CEO. Mary Kathleen O'Looney may issue the expected order—"Acquire! Acquire! Acquire!"—but as a bag lady she will enjoy none of the trappings or appurtenances of the caricatured cigar-champing capitalist. At most, she may play the role of a fairy godmother that waves her magic wand creating instant vice presidents of RAMJAC, the world's largest corporation, which she owns.

But at the same time Vonnegut also presciently uses O'Looney to satirize those who believe the world's ills will be cured by a revolution of the proletariat. O'Looney's political effectiveness is a joke as she labors every day to bring about the communist revolution, calling those she meets on the street "capitalist fats" (*Jailbird* 184). But few, if any, of the targets of her vituperation even understand the words she is saying! When she attempts to bring about her own economic revolution through her will by leaving the world's largest corporation to all the citizens of the United States (218), her idealistic plans fail to take into account even the simplest economic reality. As the narrator of *Jailbird* observes: "Most of those businesses, rigged only to make profits, were as indifferent to the needs of people as, say, thunderstorms. Mary Kathleen might as well have left one-fifth of the weather to the people" (272).[23] So hers is a double defeat: first as a communist revolutionary and second as a capitalist radical. In *God Bless You, Mr. Rosewater*, Eliot Rosewater failed to change society in any meaningful way since money proves an impotent force for good.

Rather than helping the poor, O'Looney's unreflective gift of the RAMJAC Corporation to the American people, as if they were a first cousin or a daughter rather than a *granfalloon*, ironically benefits not ordinary citizens but 20,000 new bureaucrats, most of them already-rich lawyers.

Similarly unfounded optimism led young Walter Starbuck, in addition to joining the communist movement, to believe that the highest calling in a democratic society is to spend one's life in government service, a view that conspicuously fails to take into account any context, such as a Richard Nixon becoming president. Starbuck thus compounds his naïveté by ignoring the immediate political context of his acts. He accepts a position in the Nixon administration as a reward for helping to bring the obscure freshman congressman onto the front pages of the nation's newspapers, and from there ultimately to the presidency of the United States. But his help entailed considerable cost as one of the friends he exposed went to jail. Worse, Starbuck, like O'Looney and Bob Fender, learns the wrong lesson from his experience, since he later goes to jail rather than expose some of the Watergate conspirators, who are hardly worth sheltering from the law.

"The world of *Jailbird* is peopled with poor souls who do not have the ability to counteract their ill fate," concludes R. B. Gill (79). When they, and especially Starbuck, do act "in an inept attempt to be helpful" (Gill 79), the results are disastrous. Bob Fender, the veterinarian and science-fiction writer lands in jail for life for naïvely sheltering a North Korean spy, as if she were a wounded doe (102–04). Starbuck joins the Communist party in his youth, but instead of dramatically changing the way society operates economically or socially, he succeeds only in sending his best friend to jail when he guilelessly names him as a known communist before Nixon's Congressional Investigating Committee. None of these people—certainly not Walter Starbuck—is evil, and each acts out of the best of motives, but each fails in Vonnegut's view because youthful idealism becomes a poor guide for adult behavior.

Irving Howe, describing the conclusion of several twentieth-century American political novels by Dos Passos, Lionel Trilling, and Robert Penn Warren, might also have been speaking about *Jailbird* when he wrote: "The images raised by all these critical scenes [at the end of the novels] is one of isolation, an isolation that a wounded intelligence is trying desperately to transform into the composure of solitude" (*Politics* 200). But in *Jailbird*, only the minor character Bob Fender, alias the recidivist Kilgore Trout, achieves this "composure of solitude" as he serves out his life sentence in prison. By contrast, O'Looney lives out her whole life in ignorance, and Starbuck finds solitude only in his jail cell.

Nixon, an American isolato, as solitary as Melville's Bartleby, was, says Vonnegut, the "first President to hate the American people and all they stand for" (*Wampeters, Foma & Granfalloons* xxiii). Vonnegut satirizes this notoriously humorless man through his portrait of his nonrelation with his youth adviser and by having him tell "one good joke."[24] During the emergency meeting Nixon called to discuss how to handle the Ohio National Guard's killing of four Kent State University students during a student demonstration against the war in Vietnam, Starbuck, as the president's youth adviser, becomes excessively nervous. Lighting cigarette after cigarette until he has three lit at the same time, he then begins to light up another.

> The President himself at last noticed the column of smoke rising from my place, and he stopped all business to stare at me. . . .
> "We will pause in our business," he said, "while our special advisor on youth affairs gives us a demonstration of how to put out a campfire."
> There was laughter all around. (*Jailbird* 76)

Nixon fiddles, while Kent State burns. The model for the special adviser, whom Nixon never consults, may well have been his Secretary of the Interior Wally Hickel. After the Kent State debacle, Hickel sent Nixon some advice in "a well-publicized letter" (Leuchtenburg 246–47). "The President, his secretary of the interior recommended, ought to make himself more accessible to youth and to members of his Cabinet, while [Vice President] Agnew's abrasive alliteration should be heard less." Aside from the publicity, the letter produced no discernible results (summarized in Leuchtenburg 247)—exactly as Starbuck's many reports lie forever unread in the White House basement.

Vonnegut saves his sharpest satire in *Jailbird* for the corrosive effects of the Nixon presidency by placing them within a larger historical context—the McCarthy-Nixon witchhunts of the 1950s, the Sacco and Vanzetti executions of the 1920s, and the labor strikes in the early twentieth century.[25] The easy fantasy of Kilgore Trout's stories highlights by contrast the fantastic true story of the historical miscarriage of justice in the trial and deaths of Sacco and Vanzetti who, Vonnegut believes, were innocent of the charges of murder, yet sentenced to death. Their judge had already determined they were guilty before the trial began. After the trial was over and after he had sentenced them to death, the judge boasted: "Did you see what I did to those anarchist bastards the other day?" (*Jailbird* 222).

Typically, Vonnegut employs understatements when describing the effects of Sacco and Vanzetti's execution: it did not "cause an irresistible mania for justice to the common people" (*Jailbird* 51). Instead, it became lost in the dusty pages of history—much as the Dresden massacre was lost until Vonnegut published *Slaughterhouse-Five* thus helping bring it into the light of day. In similar fashion, the forced resignation of Nixon's vice president, Spiro Agnew, the various Watergate convictions, and even Nixon's own impending impeachment and subsequent resignation in disgrace, failed to usher in a new era of honesty or sensitivity to the public trust among political appointees, which is evident in the corruption, indictments, and resignations of the scandal-ridden Reagan administration and the various frontpage ignominies of the Clinton administration. "History. . . . Read it and weep!" laments Bokonon in *Cat's Cradle* (168), while Vonnegut—almost without emotion and certainly more in sorrow than in anger—calmly observes that "[v]anity rather than wisdom determines how the world is run" (*Palm Sunday* 299). This judgment proves especially true in *Jailbird* that itself "embraces almost a century of agonized national experience, including turn-of-the-century labor clashes, World War One beggar-veterans, Sacco and Vanzetti, Prohibition, the Crash and Depression, Nazi death-camps, the Korean War, Kent State, and then Watergate" (Vanderbilt 169).[26]

When "[t]he best lack all conviction," then, as Yeats memorably wrote, the worst may well prove "full of passionate intensity" ("The Second Coming"). If many writers dwell on the passionate intensity of the worst, such as Robert Coover who mercilessly rakes Nixon over the satiric coals in *The Public Burning* (1977), Vonnegut by contrast more quietly laments the loss of conviction among "the best." Starbuck's is a *reductio ad absurdum* portrait of the idealistic liberal who becomes a communist revolutionary in his youth, then a dedicated public servant in maturity. The loss, first, of the revolutionary spirit, such as it ever was, and, second, of the idealization of government service given Nixon's cynical manipulations is quietly mourned, rather than righteously denounced.[27]

All Vonnegut's novels, while permeated with an air of defeat, nevertheless underplay pain and suffering—something he may have learned from listening to the 1930s radio comedians who had to deal with the country's feelings of defeat caused by the Great Depression. This lack of any special pleading serves him well both in his fiction and autobiography. Describing his divorce, for example, he deadpanned "We have been through some terrible, unavoidable accident that we are ill-equipped to understand. . . . We only just arrived on this planet and we were doing the best we could. We never saw what hit us" (*Palm Sunday* 188). This description of the feelings such an event engenders juxtaposes the suffering occasioned by separation, divorce, and the end of a long-term marriage to three clichés usually reserved for other subjects. "We only just arrived" (travel story), "we were doing the best we could" (problem solving or excuse), and "We never saw what hit us" (disastrous accident). *Jailbird* is filled with such slightly comic, self-deprecating, and at the same time exact descriptions, which help account for its resigned tone, its minor key.

Throughout his career Vonnegut has never been given full—or, often, even partial—credit for his more radical experiments with form. He melded drawings with text in *Slaughterhouse-Five*, *Breakfast of Champions*, and *Hocus Pocus*, interleaved recipes in *Deadeye Dick*, and divided text up into radically smaller and smaller packages from *The Sirens of Titan* through *Slapstick* to *Hocus Pocus*. *Jailbird* is part of his ongoing experiment with the forms of fiction. The novel comes complete with a splendid index that gives equal time and value to both fiction and nonfiction, citing both simply by page number without labeling which is which. In *Cat's Cradle* the Mintons warn the journalist narrator against ever indexing his own book, because of what it could reveal about the character, personality, and experience of the indexer. In the way that life has of imitating art, after *Cat's Cradle* was published, Vonnegut found himself in correspondence with the Society of Indexers for having cited it in that novel. When he came to publish *Jailbird*, he "asked Dell [his publisher] if they would please hire an indexer. . . . So they did, and then the juxtapositions [between fictional and real persons] became quite marvelous," explained Vonnegut. "They are an easy way to make a comic work of art" ("A Conversation" 12).

Here are two such comic juxtapositions selected at random: First, the concluding "C" sequence.

> Cleveland, Grover
> Clewes, Leland
> Clewes, Sarah Wyatt
> Cohn, Roy M.
> Colson, Charles W.
> Custer, George. (286)

In this listing the factual (Cleveland) and fictional (Clewes) meet, and the nationally renowned liars and losers from McCarthy (Cohn) to Watergate (Colson) culminate in that name—most synonymous with defeat in American history—General Custer. The effect is both comic and sobering. Second, here is the F sequence in its entirety:

> *Failey, Bonnie* [hero in Vonnegut's fictional ballad about the tragic, but also fictional Cuyahoga Bridge and Iron strike]
> *Fender, Robert* [newest incarnation of Kilgore Trout]
> *Figler, John* [young man who wrote Vonnegut summarizing the "message" in his novels to date]
> *Fonda, Jane* [who in the novel is employed by RAMJAC and attends a Starbuck party in his New York duplex, while in her other life outside the novel she is, of course, Jane Fonda]

Beginning with a made-up victim memorialized in an equally fictional, if tragic ballad, the list proceeds through one of the best known—although also fictional—science-fiction authors, includes an attractive young person who corresponds with Vonnegut, and concludes with Ms. Fonda, who after a minor film career, achieved fame with her workout videos and makes a cameo appearance in *Jailbird*. As a result of this comic innovation, *Jailbird* looks and resembles other books, other *nonfiction* books, thereby illustrating Vonnegut's contention that "I tend to do things that look like books" ("A Conversation" 6) but which upon closer inspection turn out to be "wildly experimental" ("A Conversation" 5).

Finally, Vonnegut uses a deceptively simple, direct style to communicate his sense of loss in *Jailbird*. His voice echoes the United States not of either coast, but of the more conservative Middle-west. Vonnegut has never denied his Indianapolis origins and credits them, in part, for his distinctive voice: "I . . . sound like a person from Indianapolis" (*Palm Sunday* 79). "Vonnegut's values," Giannone adumbrates, "are those we associate with middle-class virtues. Decency, respect, neighborliness, success, and security are what his characters look for; and in the end, that commonplace search is rendered so tenderly that we can say that middle America also gave Vonnegut a moral scale" (*Preface* 5). To which Meyer strongly objects: "Giannone does much more than mislead the reader—he absolutely *obscures* [his emphasis] the enlightenment that is at the core of Vonnegut's fiction," which Meyer goes on to define as his being "passionately concerned about the aesthetic future of America" ("Kurt

Vonnegut" 104). But Vonnegut's concern, however small or great it may be, with "the aesthetic future of America" does not in any way preclude or negate the correctness of Giannone's observation that "middle America gave Vonnegut a moral scale." That scale undergirds all his satire and provides the measure by which his characters stand defeated. Howard Campbell, bereft of decency in*Mother Night*, Eliot Rosewater, losing all respect in *God Bless You, Mr. Rosewater*, Rudy Waltz, forfeiting any chance at friendship or intimate relationship in *Deadeye Dick*, Paul Proteus and Wilbur Swain, relinquishing any security they once had in *Player Piano* and *Slapstick*, and almost any character in any novel who remains lost, defeated, and unable to succeed. Kay Hoyle Nelson makes a good case for *Jailbird* with its emphsis on defeat as an "anti-fairy tale" or "farce fairy tale" as defined by Max Luthi in *The Fairytale as Art Form and Portrait of Man* (1985). According to Luthi, "the hero fails in the face of every difficulty, avoids everything requiring any effort, and always takes the easiest way out; he moves backward, not forward; he regresses." [This hero, totally dependent on helpers is] "the *receiver* (*der Begabte*) par excellence" (137–38 quoted in Nelson 112n3). "If you can do no good, at least do no evil," advised Hippocrates to the medical profession, and that appears the most to which Starbuck can aspire.

Ruth Starbuck, Walter's late and much-lamented wife, may be at least partially correct that human beings "could only create meaningless tragedies . . . since they weren't nearly intelligent enough to accomplish all the good they meant to do" (67).[28] Yet, *Jailbird* itself—as opposed to the ineffectual characters within it—offers a partial exception. As a writer, Vonnegut tells stories not simply to entertain, but also to educate—as a service to society. "The highest service," he claims, "is to the community" ("Serenity" 26, reprint 18). *Jailbird* performs this service first by calling attention to the Sermon on the Mount as a positive guide to ethical living, decision making, and even public policy—a standard now, unfortunately, largely abandoned (*Fates Worse Than Death* 163). Second, the novel calls attention forcibly to "a typical outrage in America, the sort of miscarriage of justice that's possible, because of ruling class conspiracy and xenophobia and so forth, let's keep the Sacco and Vanzetti thing alive" ("A Conversation" 10). Vonnegut says of that miscarriage: "I thought it was reason enough to write a book, political reason enough to write the book, just to talk about Sacco and Vanzetti again" (10). As with Dresden, Vonnegut's fiction functions once again to bring back into living memory a tragic event that many would like to forget or keep forgotten.

"ZANG REEPA DOP. FAAAAAAAAAAAAAAAAA!"

Although Vonnegut has said that he is "particularly fond of [*Deadeye Dick*] for personal reasons," this novel remains the least written about, least commented on, and least favored by critics. One reason is not hard to find. Leonard Mustazza astutely observes the striking similarity between Billy Pilgrim and Rudy: "both are tormented souls for whom one can feel pity but not much affinity" (*Genesis* 161). But unlike Billy, Rudy's escape from his terrible world lacks the pizzazz of coming unstuck in time or being kidnapped together with a beautiful woman and taken in a flying saucer to another galaxy, there to mate as an exhibit in a zoo. Instead, Rudy escapes into domesticity—especially cooking—composes little playlets about what should have happened, and scat sings the blues away.

The book itself is, as Vonnegut said, "a good book," "more literary and deeper" than many of his others, and includes innovations that other writers have picked up and turned into popular clichés. The inserted recipes, perhaps the best example of a Vonnegut original innovation is one he wisely limits to this one book. His imitators have, however, exploited it to the extent that there is now something of a fad of writers inserting recipes into their books. Tamar Myers, for example, has produced a series of "Pennsylvania Dutch Mysteries with Recipes," which now includes *Too Many Cooks Spoil the Broth* (1994), *Parsley, Sage, Rosemary and Crime* (1995), *No Use Crying Over Spilt Milk* (1996), and so forth. Diane Mott Davidson includes extensive recipes in *Catering to Nobody* (1990), *Dying for Chocolate* (1992), and *The Cereal Murders* (1993). Perhaps the most famous chef in mystery novels, an amateur like Rudy, remains Spenser of Robert B. Parker's numerous Spenser mysteries who often enthusiastically shares ingredients and cooking techniques—but no recipes—with readers.

Why then has *Deadeye Dick* been critically ignored, when so much of Vonnegut has been rediscovered and written about? Gary Giddens' review of the novel describes both its excellence and its difficulty, since they are one and the same: "Vonnegut is a masterly stylist, much in the way Count Basie is a masterly stylist—economic, droll, rhythmic. Consequently, many people think that they have no style; but try and imitate them—it can't be done" (253). Many a would-be Count Basie has sat down at the piano and with one finger of the right hand played a series of syncopated notes with disastrous results. Similarly, the grace with which Vonnegut uses his deceptively simple style here and, especially later in *Hocus Pocus*, helps to hide its artifice. Such a style is notoriously open to self-parody and there are places in *Deadeye Dick* where Vonnegut appears to have succumbed. "There must be two dozen sentences that position a climatic phrase after a colon (i.e., 'The words were these: Deadeye Dick') and in almost every instance the colon strains the humor," as Giddens maintians (253). Strains it because the colon throws the timing off—much like the Count Basie imitator who failing to stay on the leading edge of the beat reproduces nothing but clichés by playing directly on or after the beat.

Secondly, *Deadeye Dick* draws on many familiar Vonnegut assumptions about life that many critics reject outright. Benjamin DeMott in a favorable review describes the novel as "a riot of randomness" (245) where

the grand old Vonnegutian comedy of causelessness still holds center stage. . . . Why do human beings take satisfaction in creating a neutron bomb that destroys "only" human beings, not their accouterments? . . . Why should grief-struck Rudy Waltz, headed for a presumably moving moment at his parents' graveside, allow his train of thought to light on a certain cookie, whereupon . . . instead of grief we're provided with a recipe for almond macaroons?

Don't ask. . . . Sentence on sentence, paragraph on paragraph, chapter on chapter, so it goes: a tissue of unanswerables. . . . The good reader is aware that the allegedly solid, cause and effect, ask a good question get a good answer world is, in fact, pure scam.[29] (247)

All of this causelessness, however, relates back to and reflects off of the initial causeless, thoughtless act that destroyed Rudy's life: the double murder he committed without thinking when he fired a rifle in the air in the naïf belief that nothing bad would happen. Yet from just such a random incident all events and relationships in his life radiate including his received nickname, Deadeye Dick.

To imagine being an American in Vonnegut's America as pictured in *Deadeye Dick* involves participating in random events, causeless actions, negligible relationships, and, usually, almost inevitably the experience of defeat. If *Jailbird* focuses on Walter Starbuck's defeat in the political realm, *Deadeye Dick* shifts to Rudy Waltz's defeat in the personal realm. Like two other paradigms of defeat, Job and Melville's Bartleby, wherever Rudy turns he encounters a blank wall rather than life. "Within strict limits," and however faintly, his life echoes that of Job who complained,

> Why did I not die at birth,
> come forth from the womb and expire?
>
> For then I should have lain down and been quiet;
> I should have slept; then I should have been at rest,
> with kings and counselors of the earth
> who rebuilt ruins for themselves. (Job 3.11–14)

In "Bartleby, the Scrivener," Melville borrows Job's phrase, "with kings and councilors," to suggest the scrivener's equally desperate isolation (511). Bartleby may once have worked in the Dead Letter Office of the United States Post Office in Washington, DC. Can anything be more depressing, asks the narrator, than the "continual handling [of] these dead letters, and assorting them for the flames? . . . On errands of life, these letters speed to death," exactly as Bartleby himself speeds to death as more and more he "prefers not to" participate in work, leisure, or life itself.

Likewise, Rudy also "prefers not to" participate in life. Similarly to Billy Pilgrim, Rudy resists acting and instead "acquiesce[s] in the logic of things" (Mustazza, *Genesis* 164). For example, he reveals: "I have never made love to anyone. Nor have I tasted alcohol . . ." (99); and, later, "It seemed safest and wisest to be as cold as ice . . . to everyone" (110). Clearly, most contemporary psychologists, such as Abraham O. Maslow, would judge Rudy, "as far as motivational status is concerned," as unhealthy. "Healthy people," writes Maslow,

have sufficiently gratified their basic needs for safety, belongingness, love, respect and self-esteem so that they are motivated primarily by trends to self-actualization (defined as ongoing actualization of potentials, capacities and talents), as fulfillment of mission (or call, fate, destiny, or vocation), as a fuller knowledge of, and acceptance of, the person's own intrinsic nature, as an unceasing trend toward unity, integration or synergy within the person. (25)

But Rudy feels powerless to do any of this and so remains far, far from any self-actualization. Life appears to wall in and defeat him, as it walled in Bartleby until the latter died of physical, emotional, and spiritual starvation curled up in a fetal position facing the base of a brick wall "of amazing thickness . . . his head touching the cold stones" (510, 511). Like Bartleby and Job, Rudy believes that he does not "really belong on this particular planet" (176).

Earlier, in *God Bless You, Mr. Rosewater*, Diana Moon Glampers, like Rudy, also appears to have no focus and no center to her life. But she at least could telephone Eliot Rosewater late at night for the consolation of hearing another human being who will neither condemn nor ignore her. Rudy, not being as fortunate, has no one to call. This "neutered pharmacist" (xiii), who never knows love, never has any fun, never tastes any of the sins or delights of life, appears psychologically starving for love as he also appears in need of Thoreau's "morning work" or something real to do with his life. But, as life presents him with no one and nothing, instead of deepening relationships or meaningful work, he simply grows fat on his own cooking.

Rudy offers the reader almost a case study of what Maslow calls essential "deficits in the organism, empty holes, so to speak, which must be filled for health's sake, and furthermore must be filled from without by human beings *other* than the subject . . ." (22–23). But there are no significant others in Rudy's life. His growing bulk and his increasing isolation suggest the lack of any real emotional life. His life effectively ended at age twelve.[30] As the result of his double murder, "[h]e only spends one night in jail because of his age, but his mind is imprisoned forever in the tragic past" (Berryman, "After the Fall" 97). From then on he lives what Maslow would call a much-diminished life (Maslow 14).

Much of *Deadeye Dick* focuses on Rudy's attempts to overcome those "deficits in the organism," to fill those "empty holes" through his lavish care for his parents' every need. In doing so he follows the pattern of compensatory care giving described in several psychological studies, such as John Bowlby's *Attachment and Loss*, that examine in depth the importance of the parental relationship to mental health in children. Bowlby demonstrates that "some individuals respond to loss by concerning themselves intensely and to an excessive degree with the welfare of others" (206).[31] Rudy is (in Bowlby's use of the word) a psychopath—as are several other Vonnegut characters, including Dwayne Hoover (*Breakfast of Champions*) and Beatrice Rumfoord (*The Sirens of Titan*).[32]

One critic, however, believes to the contrary that Rudy does live a fulfilled life. Based upon very slim evidence, he contends that

The essential narrative principle of this novel . . . is the most important key to its meaning, which is that it is told in retrospect by a narrator who after great struggle with his own soul has learned to deal with his compulsions and to recreate himself through art. . . . Like Walter Starbuck, a scapegoat and Shaman [sic], Rudy possesses the awareness, imagination, and nerve to bear the sins and the shame of his family, his nation, and his world. (Broer, *Sanity Plea* 141, 142)

But this description conveniently ignores Vonnegut's repeated emphasis on Rudy's life being over when he shoots a pregnant housewife on Mother's Day. Like Chidiock Tichborne, who filled the time before his execution in the Tower of London by writing an elegy on his unlived life, Rudy, too, laments: "And now I live, and now my life is done":

> My prime of youth is but a frost of cares,
>   My feast of joy is but a dish of pain,
> My crop of corn is but a field of tares,
>   And all my good is but vain hope of gain;
>   The day is past, and yet I saw no sun,
>   And now I live, and now my life is done.
>
> My tale was heard and yet it was not told,
>   My fruit is fallen and yet my leaves are green,
> My youth is spent and yet I am not old,
>   I saw the world and yet I was not seen;
>   My thread is cut and yet it is not spun,
>   And now I live, and now my life is done.

Rudy's metaphoric leaves of life are indeed forever green for the fruit of his life does not ripen but only rots. He becomes an appropriately self-described neuter (compare Jake Barnes in *The Sun Also Rises* [1926]) and his life experience lies in striking opposition to any possible self-actualization. If his story as a neuter ends, as he decides, either at Celia Hoover's funeral when he experiences forgiveness, or with the death of his mother, then all the rest is epilogue (210). Like Bartleby in the Tombs, all Rudy has left is the wait before inevitable death.

Nor does the "essential narrative principle" of retrospection (Broer, *Sanity Plea* 141)—by itself—alter the empty nature of Rudy's character or condition. Here again, the parallel with Melville's short story is instructive: Melville also employed a narrator in "Bartleby" to tell his tale in retrospect, but that narrator gives little evidence he has fundamentally changed because of his encounter with the "incurably forlorn" scrivener. For a time, it is true, the lawyer narrator was inconvenienced. He did indeed entertain momentary glimpses of Bartleby's isolation, which he compares to "a bit of wreck in the mid-Atlantic" (493), and at the end he was actually moved enough by the waste of Bartleby's life to exclaim, "Ah, Bartleby, Ah, Humanity!" (512). But when his business calls him back to the world of Wall Street he returns to doing "a snug business among rich men's bonds." As he himself tells us in the story's opening sentences long after all the events have transpired and long after Bartleby has died, he still follows his "profound conviction that the easiest way is the best" (466). For a moment at most, he sees into the depths of human isolation and aloneness through the plight of the scrivener, but then he quickly withdraws to return to his comfortable life. The only time he betrays any emotion, as he tells his story, is not over Bartleby's starving to death but over the loss of his position as Master in Chancery, a position that brought him a good dependable income for very little work.

Rudy, like Bartleby, does not participate in life, although he tries to defend himself against it as best he can by making playlets out of the great crises in his life that usually turn out to be those painful moments of confrontation with others (83–84). Rather than positively recreating "himself through art" (Broer, *Sanity Plea* 141) or "creat[ing] honest myths to live by" (Broer 150) through Rudy's writing drama (Broer 146), Rudy's dramatic activity simply reinforces his defeat.[33] His full-length play fails to attract an audience and receives terrible reviews, because, in part, as Mustazza suggests, it is not a public, but a private, personal document. And he is of no help at all to the cast of the play, since he fails to answer "their questions, even obvious ones" (*Genesis* 162). But far more important are those small playlets Rudy devises to help him create some aesthetic distance between the painful-to-recall events and that person, himself, to whom they happened. Within the playlets, his person simply fades into the background, implying that whatever happened must have happened to someone else. Instead of becoming a creator or an artist, Rudy in this situation becomes merely an actor repeating lines, as if written and directed by someone else (see *Timequake* for an extensive exploration of this metaphor). The parts Rudy is given to play, rather than allowing him "to absorb and transform trauma into healing, personal truth" (Broer, *Sanity Plea* 146), simply drive him further into his neuter status as each involves his personal and, almost always, deep humiliation. Rather than increasing his autonomy as Maslow claims is necessary for growth (26), these playlets actually decrease it. As Bokonon remarked in *Cat's Cradle*: "God never wrote a good play in His Life" (161) and neither did Rudy Waltz. Moreover, in a detailed analysis of Rudy and his play acting in *Deadeye Dick*, Michelle Persell comments extensively on his handling of his role in the production of *Katmandu*. "[I]n essence," she concludes, "the formulaic writing takes on a life of its own." As evidence she quotes Rudy's excuse for wrecking his brother's marriage. "It was an accidentprone time in my life, just as it was an accident- prone time when I shot Mrs. Metzger. That's all I can say" (*Deadeye Dick* 147). She comments: "Claiming to be at a loss for words in an absurd yet deterministic universe, Rudy would absolve himself of self-authorship. In its stead, he would live out a pre-proscribed position in a plot that is 'prone' to occur. Of course, the very fact that he has just conveyed this scene of confrontation in the form of a play puts the lie to this approach" (46).

Rudy's uses other distancing techniques, such as the recipes and scat singing, to help keep the world and other people at bay. While the recipes may be Vonnegut's highly original fictional innovation, that originality remains his as novelist, rather than Rudy's as character. Vonnegut in the preface to the novel describes the several recipes in this book "as musical interludes for the salivary glands"—a culinary pause in the narrative (ix).[34] These interludes and pauses are designed to distract Rudy and the reader from the gaping hole at the center of his life where love, friendship, a sense of vocation could be, but are not. Similarly, Rudy's scat singing nonsense syllables to chase the blues helps fill his empty time the way that cooking helps fill in the gaps in his story where love or life should be. Neither leads to a "greater freshness of appreciation and richness of emotional reaction" that Maslow asserts characterize an authentic self (26) and both, by continually breaking the narrative, reinforce the lack of involvement of reader and character.

In imagining being an American, Vonnegut may also have a special obligation as an American writer to work with American materials and themes. Although often praising *Deadeye Dick*, one critic still faults Vonnegut in this and all his fiction for not solving the basic problem which that critic sees facing the American writer:

has Vonnegut really succeeded in *lasting* [his emphasis] fashion in coping with the special problem of the author or "word smith" . . . the inability of the writer to match saying with seeing . . . I hardly think that Vonnegut has . . . [s]ome lack of serious penetration into the evolution of American prose some failure to grasp the essence of Emerson's warning that "what a little of all we know is said" may keep Vonnegut out of the pantheon of our "clean well lighted place," may keep him in both his accomplishments and failures as the *doubly* [his emphasis] ironic "man with nothing to say." (Meyer, "Kurt Vonnegut" 107)[35]

The vague, if grandiose charge that Vonnegut somehow failed in a "serious penetration into the evolution of American prose," might be more appropriately directed at critics, rather than at a creative writer. Also, at the very least, when Vonnegut describes America in his novels, he does not regress to such abstractions as: "the 'essence' [his quotations] of the New World, the cold blooded murder of the social Word by the solitary Eye [his capitals]" (Meyer, "Kurt Vonnegut" 95). (Vonnegut years ago dismissed such formulas as irrelevant to his work ["Two Conversations" 215]). Also critical *aperçu*, such as "some lack of serious penetration [sic] into the evolution of American prose," might well prompt Tallulah Bankhead's famous remark, "There's less in this than meets the eye." Finally, any writer or artist deserves to be judged by accomplishments and not on what the critic thinks he has failed to do.

Vonnegut has indeed matched "saying with seeing." His novels focus on the great moral, social and political issues of our time, such as, genocide, racism, the destruction of nature, first amendment rights, and the need for human community. They do result in "the elevation of America," but, as is clear in most of them and especially in *Deadeye Dick*, Vonnegut's America reflects substantial, irreparable loss or defeat with no belief in gods, progress, revolution, political wisdom, or justice for all—an America much like the wandering ghost of Will Fairchild in *Deadeye Dick*, who is killed while doing an airplane stunt who now searches in vain and far too late for a parachute. Having lost something valuable, this America remains at the end of the twentieth century uncertain about exactly where to look for it. "Maybe my own country's life as a story ended after the Second World War, when it was the richest and most powerful nation on earth, when it was going to ensure peace and justice everywhere, since it alone had the atom bomb," speculates Rudy (206).

Furthermore, this critic's own comments on the end of *Deadeye Dick* illustrate how easy it is to misread this novel: "The book concludes, as do so many American works, with the continuing 'search' for Eldorado or Shangri la or the beckoning West 'Territories': 'Will Fairchild is *looking for* his parachute'" (Meyer, *Kurt Vonnegut* 104 his emphasis). But this formula conveniently ignores the considerable difference between the live Huck Finn lighting out for the territory at the end of Twain's novel and the long dead Will Fairchild at the end of this one. Huck having spent his life outside the hypocrisies of civilization tries, at the end of the novel, to continue doing what he has done throughout his voyage down the Mississippi "to light out for the Territory ahead of the rest" (226). In contrast, Will Fairchild's ghost tries to do in death what he *failed* to accomplish in life. The ghost is not trying to find Eldorado or Shangri La but simply, practically, to locate—too late—a life-saving parachute.

In *Deadeye Dick*'s larger context, Rudy's story of an individual suffering inevitable defeat parallels that of nations, leaders of nations, and planet Earth itself. Within such baleful circumstances, substituting wishful thinking for responsible action leads to disaster as witnessed most trenchantly in the belief in progress and the prospects for a better world after the war, such as Mrs. Eleanor Roosevelt declares in *Deadeye Dick* (59).[36] Subsequent events seriously undercut Mrs. Roosevelt's optimism. Immediately after her visit to the Waltz's home, Rudy goes upstairs to the gun room and fires the shot heard round Midland City, thus ending his prospects for a better world and forever arresting his social progress. In *Deadeye Dick*, Vonnegut rejects any belief in progress and all conventional images of progress. Instead, he offers the changing image of the John Fortune farm in Midland City as a symbol of the true "progress" enjoyed by large portions of the United States. In the 1930s the farm was self-sustaining and productive until the Great Depression wiped out its economic viability, whereupon the owner, Fortune, set off on his fruitless search for Shangri La. In the 1940s the farm symbolizes not productivity but destruction as the United States armed forces fighting in World War II use it for a tank proving ground. In the sixties the farm, transformed once more—this time into "Avondale," archetypal tract housing—the farm comes to symbolize suburban America. Abruptly, in the 1980s the farm disappears completely from the map when it becomes a test area for the neutron bomb probably dropped under orders of the United States government[37]—Midland City being the least objectionable place on which to test such a weapon (234). The farm and all of Midland City symbolize American indifference to the fate of its once self-sustaining small cities. "What I showed happening to Midland City," comments Vonnegut, is "the indifference of our government to the closing down of these towns." The example he gives of such a destroyed town or city is Terra Haute, Indiana:

The last business just closed down there—Columbia Records closed down its plant there permanently. . . . [T]his place has got twenty-seven churches, . . . a railroad yard, it's got all this, and it might as well have been neutron bombed, and so there was that analogy . . . if a neutron bomb did go off accidentally in Terra Haute, it would be on the news for about three days because the feeling is that these people weren't really of any importance. (Reed, "Interview" 9)

Unlike Vonnegut, who continually comments on serious public issues and is deeply engaged in life, writing, and public debate, Rudy Waltz lives up to his

name and waltzes through life skating on its surface as the stars of the Ice
Capades used to do. Never permitting anything to penetrate his shielded core, he
always kept covered those empty holes at his center. His character or, rather, his
lack of character helps account for much of the unique quality of *Deadeye
Dick*—a quality that has irritated when it has not baffled critics. In Maslow's
terms, Vonnegut tells the story of someone who is "deficiency need gratification
bent" rather than, as is more usual in American fiction, someone who is "growth
dominated . . . or growth motivated or self-actualizing" (27). Unlike those
rugged individuals found throughout American novels, Rudy essentially fails to
grow, fails to authenticate his existence, fails to recognize, deal with, or answer
his basic needs. Creating and sustaining such a unique protagonist is a difficult
task for any writer but one that Vonnegut accomplishes both with good grace
and considerable ingenuity—a story that raises important issues for public
policy as well as for private morality in imagining being an American.

NOTES

1. Psychologists believe that suicide often appears a positive choice for children of
suicides as Vonnegut, whose mother committed suicide in 1944, was and is aware. He
discusses the dreadful legacy of a parent's suicide in *God Bless You, Mr. Rosewater*
(103). For a lucid, extensive study of writers and artists who have suffered from
depression similar to Vonnegut's, consult Kay Redfield Jamison, *Touched with Fire:
Manic-Depressive Illness and the Artistic Temperament* (see especially 104–47).

2. Vonnegut credits writing with actually saving his life during this terribly painful
experience (*Palm Sunday* 322). He decides to continue writing, and to write about what
he knows well from his own experience: the distressing self-destructive bent of human
beings, the necessity for establishing some form of viable human community, and the
process of rebirth and rejoining humanity. As the reborn hero of *Slapstick* predicts, when
people "experience . . . companionship . . . [it] allow[s] them to climb the evolutionary
ladder [and] . . . become human beings, after having been for so many years . . .
centipedes[,] . . . slugs[,] . . . earwigs and worms" (177).

3. Unfortunately, most publishers would probably never consider publishing *Breakfast
of Champions* as a first novel by an unknown writer. Berryman claims that Vonnegut
withheld *Breakfast of Champions* from publication for several years fearing that his
audience would expect a sequel to *Slaughterhouse-Five* ("Comic Persona" 163–64). The
film version of the novel had many good moments and some truly excellent
characterizations by Bruce Willis as Dwayne Hoover, Nick Nolte as Harry LeSabre, and
Glenne Headly as Francine Pefko, plus a sharp satire on American advertising as a
substitute for culture. Yet because there was no narrator, much of Vonnegut's satiric
punch became lost. In its place there appeared first a portrait of a dysfunctional and
essentially crazy American family who came together at the end and second, a Kilgore
Trout who had extensive fantasies of a better world of eternal youth. Neither portrait
demonstrated much originality—unlike Vonnegut's book.

4. This "air of defeat" pervades all of Vonnegut's novels and governs his heroes from
Paul Proteus in *Player Piano*—used then abandoned by the corporation, his wife, and the
revolution—to Eugene Debs Hartke, the incarcerated hero of *Hocus Pocus*, who leaves
behind a horrendous trail of wounded, dead, and/or emotionally maimed. With the
possible exceptions of the "Vonnegut" who at fifty narrates *Breakfast of Champions*, the
"happy meat" of Rabo Karabekian at the conclusion of *Bluebeard*, the narrator of
Timequake at the great clambake, and—more ambiguously still—Eliot Rosewater in *God*

Bless You, Mr. Rosewater, all the rest of Vonnegut's heroes lie dead at their story's end (*The Sirens of Titan, Slaughterhouse-Five, Slapstick, Bluebeard*) or defeated (*Player Piano, Mother Night, Cat's Cradle, Jailbird, Deadeye Dick, Hocus Pocus*). Leon Trout in *Galápagos* does not fit easily within these categories. A relatively happy ghost in the rigging of a wonderfully inventive novel, he nevertheless died over a million years ago and continually refuses to go into the tunnel leading to the afterlife because his father waits to greet him there.

5. Perhaps such dead-end lives are linked imaginatively to Vonnegut's mother's suicide and his father's withdrawal from actively participating in life after the Great Depression wiped out his career as an architect. Small wonder that he concluded, "So an air of defeat has always been a companion of mine" (*Jailbird* 13).

6. Meyer's argument proves somewhat reductive when he insists on characterizing Vonnegut's experience as merely personal.

7. Vonnegut's mother killed herself the night before Vonnegut arrived home on a brief leave from the army during World War II to celebrate Mother's Day (Hume, "Myths and Symbols" 433).

8. Creed Greer maintains that "in a schizophrenic text . . . every time you try to settle the problem of who is real, the problem itself becomes unsettled because the terms that define the problem become indistinct. *Breakfast of Champions* argues the impossibility of the real/unreal dichotomy" (315). Fair enough, but Greer's essay proves impossibly ponderous often belaboring the obvious, such as the fact that Vonnegut did not write *Venus on the Half-Shell,* but Phillip José Farmer did as part of his *Fictional Authors Series.* (Surely it is time to lay to rest that controversy so well documented in interviews and writing by both authors.)

9. Berryman apparently had a change of mind some years after writing this essay, since his later essay, "Vonnegut's Comic Persona" (1990) lavishly praises *Breakfast of Champions.*

10 See *Timequake* for a serious reflection on events in Vonnegut's life and fiction writing as opposed to the parodies of his values and incidents in his life in *Breakfast of Champions.*

11. This unfinished novel takes place in heaven, where to the narrator's dismay, his "father . . . chose to be only nine years old." And from there on his father torments him extensively. "It insisted on being a very unfriendly story, so I quit writing it," Vonnegut confesses (*Jailbird* 13, 15).

12. There is an irony here at the expense of the narrator when he compares his action with that of Thomas Jefferson freeing his slaves under similar circumstances. When Jefferson went to free his slaves, found he could not because they were too heavily mortgaged. As for Vonnegut freeing Kilgore Trout, John Leonard accurately observes, "readers hate this, which is why Conan Doyle had to bring back Sherlock Holmes" (302) and Vonnegut had to bring back Trout albeit with an alias as early as *Jailbird.*

13. The sibyl of Cumae was much beloved of Apollo who offered to grant her anything she might wish for. She wished for life eternal and despite his entreaties refused to renounce or change her wish. Knowing the consequences but powerless to retract his word, Apollo granted her wish. Consequently, she could not die but equally she could age since she did not also wish for eternal youth. Eventually, she wizened up into a smaller and smaller crone until she could be kept in a cage. Her one wish then was to die. T. S. Eliot recounts her story in his notes to *The Wasteland.*

14. Tralfamadorians, on the other hand, could never understand or have fairytales as part of their literature, since for them there is no ending, happy or otherwise. Only humans, who experience mortality and therefore tragedy, can appreciate the intervention of the good fairy that makes everything all right again. Rosewater, for instance, acts as

the good fairy bringing about the magic ending to what might otherwise have been a sordid tale. (See Nelson for further comparisons.)

15. What Klinkowitz says about *Slapstick* applies to several Vonnegut novels, including *Galápagos*. Klinkowitz maintains that Vonnegut "uses the freedom of fiction to dream up a better reality, a set of new conventions more appropriate to present needs" ("Review" 188).

16. Nor is Vonnegut alone in his concern for the lack of community in America. Hume reports that in her *American Dream, American Nightmare: Fiction Since 1960* "forty or so of approximately one hundred books discussed are concerned with community in fairly central ways" ("Melancholy" 234).

17. In *The Eternal Footman* (1999), James Morrow elaborates a set of values with which Vonnegut would be in substantial agreement: "If the coming era must have a religion, then let it be a religion of everyday miracles and quotidian epiphanies, of short eternities and little myths. In the post-theistic-age, let Christianity become merely kindness, salvation transmute into art, truth defer to knowledge, and faith embrace a vibrant doubt" (34).

18. Vonnegut will deal more directly and more creatively with Watergate, its aftermath, and the issues it raises for Americans and America in *Jailbird*, which he judges a more successful novel than *Slapstick* (see *Palm Sunday* 311–12). In an interview published in 1973, Vonnegut talks about writing a Kilgore Trout novel with a plot similar to *Slapstick*'s (see *Wampeters, Foma & Granfalloons* 247–49).

19. Swain enumerates what he believes are the four finest American innovations, which include the principles of Alcoholics Anonymous, the Bill of Rights in the U. S. Constitution, *Robert's Rules of Order*, and, finally, Eliza and his artificial extended families (216).

20. Commendably, Vonnegut takes full responsibility for the quality or lack of it in *Slapstick*, giving the novel a D when grading his work from *Deadeye Dick* through *Jailbird* (*Palm Sunday* 311–12). He grades his play, *Happy Birthday, Wanda June* "D," *Breakfast of Champions* "C"—judgments that many readers would say are far too harsh. *Between Time and Timbuktu* goes entirely unmentioned because Vonnegut had no control over how his work was turned into the script (*Palm Sunday* 312)

21. Rackstraw says, for instance, "I believe this novel was an important aesthetic turning point, and that understanding his use of parody in *Slapstick* can be a key to the richness and intent of his more successful later works" (129). She then elaborates her thesis that *Slapstick* is "a parody of Friedrich Nietzche's classic study of the interplay of opposites in the origin of Greek drama, *The Birth of Tragedy*" (126). She also reads *Jailbird* as a parody of Dante's *Commedia* and *Bluebeard* as a parody of Joyce Cary's *The Horse's Mouth*. While such identifications may be too specific for Vonnegut's novels, these parallel parodied works provide Rackstraw with the occasion for insightful comments on Vonnegut's late novels.

22. Rackstraw reads the Dresden candlestick brought by Melody as "a brilliant *mise en abyme*, one of those internal reflecting mirrors that Vonnegut often uses to signal the dual nature of the text as both artifice and an aspect of the larger cultural context" (131). She then proceeds through each of the sketchy details given about the candlestick, including the figure of the flirtatious nobleman, the shepherdess, and the extensive vines and flowers (*Slapstick* 240), relating each of them to Vonnegut's life and work and *Slapstick*. But placing far too much weight on fragile details leads to their collapse, as in this example: "The nobleman's flirtation with the shepherdess surely [sic] suggests the interplay of Nietzche's Apollo and Dionysus, of *Slapstick*'s Wilbur and Eliza, of the 'real' Vonnegut and his sister, and of the archetypal Adam and Eve—about to 'put their

heads together' beneath the mythic Tree for the endless generation of creative imagination in the slapstick dance of life" (131).

But the figures on the candlestick are no more Adam and Eve than they are Wilbur and Eliza—and they definitely are not Vonnegut and his sister, Alice (compare *Slapstick* 240). Whatever else they may have been, all members of these three pairs were most definitely equals whereas the nobleman and shepherdess depicted on the candlestick are most definitely not. The nobleman obviously comes from a much higher economic and social class than the shepherdess, who is simply a commoner. In the language of such depictions, the flirtation is transparently between socially unequal people. Second, if the tree on the candlestick is indeed the Tree of the Knowledge of Good and Evil in the Garden of Eden, then somewhere there should also be depicted the fruit of that Tree, which in English-speaking countries since Milton's *Paradise Lost* has usually been symbolized as an apple. But no fruit is depicted anywhere on the candlestick, only "flowering vines" which, given the context, suggests entanglement—something the nobleman would wish to avoid. Rackstraw believes that: "The vines around the tree trunk are an artistic restatement of the [Dresden] firestorm, transformed into the Dionysian embrace that resolves paradox in Vonnegut's literary inventions" and so on (131). But a simpler, more appropriate, if less inventive, observation might focus on the fact that this is a *Dresden* candlestick and therefore symbolizes all that was beautiful and lost in that tragic firestorm, rather than the firestorm itself—and certainly not any "Dionysian embrace."

23. Klinkowitz reads this action in *Jailbird* far more optimistically than I do. He claims that "The bulk of *Jailbird*, then, is given over to the reinvention of America's dream. Property is ill distributed, *God Bless You, Mr. Rosewater* claimed; *Jailbird* redistributes it, as the massive holdings of the RAMJAC Corporation are broken up into a million parts and deeded back to the citizens of the USA" (*Kurt Vonnegut* 81–82). But surely Vonnegut's point is that this is a phony redistribution of wealth enriching, as it does, those already rich lawyers.

24. In *Palm Sunday: An Autobiographical Collage* Vonnegut reveals that he once applied for a job as a writer for the famous Bob and Ray comedy team, but does not say if he ever applied for a job as a writer for Nixon (141).

25. There is a strong obvious parallel between events and people in the invented labor strike replete with the Ohio National Guard with live ammunition in the prologue to *Jailbird* and the Kent State calamity.

26. The background for *Jailbird* includes Vonnegut's made-up chapter in labor history, the 1894 strike against Daniel McCone's Cuyahoga Bridge and Iron Company. While the strike and company are fictional, the details are familiar from American labor history. In *Timequake* Vonnegut also writes admiringly and at length about labor history, recalling the early strikes that proved highly effective in gaining decent wages and working conditions, much improved safety measures in the workplace, and even a measure of respect for working men and women. Targets of those strikes included railroads, coal mines, textile and steel factories, and several others. People were beaten and some died in these strikes that to a majority of Vonnegut's writer-peers appeared as worthwhile and justified as any armed conflict against a foreign power (151).

27. Of the many good portraits of Nixon's alleged crimes, one of the most succinct may be found in Hodgson, especially 40–44.

28. But as *Galápagos* shows, humans were intelligent enough to threaten all life on the planet, and, as *Jailbird* demonstrates, their partial intelligence could lead to some really bad snafus and misplaced philanthropy.

29. DeMott singles out two scenes for high praise: Midland City after being hit by the neutron bomb and Rudy's interrogation at the police headquarters.

30. Vonnegut describes how he dreamt that he had killed an old woman in the distant past (*Palm Sunday* 189–90) and proceeds to puzzle through what meaning the dream might hold for him. In an interview with Zoltán Abádi-Nagy, he reveals, however, that also when he was quite young "I did that. I didn't kill anybody. But I fired a rifle, out over Indianapolis. I didn't hit anybody as far as I know. . . . I never told anybody about it until I was an adult. I cleaned the gun and put it away." The interviewer asks: "What was it that frightened you in the experience?" To which Vonnegut replies: "That I was such a person. That I could be that silly" ("Serenity" 28, reprint 22).

31. Rudy's becoming overly concerned with his parents is characteristic of certain personalities prone to psychological disorder when faced with loss (see Bowlby 206–207). See Bowlby also for an accounting of the feeling of helplessness and hopelessness from which Rudy suffers (246.)

32. See Bowlby, Chapter 2, "The Place of Loss and Mourning in Psychopathology" (23–37).

33. Broer misreads Rudy's musings as strength rather than wistful thinking (compare *Deadeye Dick* 132). Clearly there is no sound basis for assuming that Rudy will actually act in the way Broer claims he will (147). The proof that he will not lies earlier in the paragraph from which Broer detaches his quotation. There, Rudy declares "I wasn't going home again, either. I would get a job as a pharmacist somewhere in New York" (132). That, too, never happens: "The morning after *Katmandu* opened and closed, Felix [his brother] and I were flying over a landscape as white and blank as our lives. . . . I was the laughingstock of New York" (*Deadeye Dick* 148). Rudy heads directly home to Midland City his tail between his legs with no thought of staying in New York much less establishing a home of his own or "pairing off with this kind of person or that one, to see how that went." Rudy is not a person who experiments with or in life.

34. In contrast to Rudy's using food to divorce himself from life, Vonnegut suggests that food and recipes are "a swell way to celebrate life . . . no matter how bad it gets" ("A Conversation" 7).

35. Meyer's opinion that Vonnegut has not succeeded in "matching saying with seeing" appears somewhat contradictory to the praise he lavishes upon *Deadeye Dick* for exactly this reason (compare, especially, 104–106). His hyperactive prose used throughout this essay on Vonnegut employs excessive italics, puns, and out-of-context quotations. It is, however, idiosyncratically his as he employs it in other published essays. See, for example, "The Unwelcomed Presupposition of *American* Philosophy—Eye Epistemology: An Essay Far Beyond the Bounds of Current Interdisciplinary Scholarship" where, some seven years later, he recycles his awful pun "O Say Can *YOU* See" (93).

36. Such substituting of wishful thinking for responsible action may also be seen in the omnipresent pollution in *Breakfast of Champions*, the brutal child-rearing in *Slapstick*, the naïve collaboration with evil in *Mother Night*, the multiple failures of Richard Nixon in *Jailbird*, the destruction of the earth in *Galápagos*, and so on and so forth.

37. Klinkowitz unaccountably describes this neutron bomb disaster as "a localized nuclear accident (or perhaps fiendishly amoral test)" ("Ultimate" 194).

6

Thinking Intelligently, Thinking Ethically about Science, Art, and War

"Science fiction presents a strangeness the reader did not imagine could exist in the world; fantasy tells the reader the world is strange beyond his belief," according to James Gunn ("The Horror" 137). Gunn draws a useful distinction between fantasy and science fiction in this memorable aphorism. After the fantasies of *Breakfast of Champions* and *Slapstick*, Vonnegut returns in *Galápagos* for the first time since the phenomenally successful *Slaughterhouse-Five* to fantasy's "non-identical twin, science fiction" (Kroeber 1).[1] There are, however, significant differences between *Galápagos*, this 1980s extrapolated comic look at the dubious future of humankind, and Vonnegut's earlier science-fiction novels. Gone is the freneticism of *The Sirens of Titan*, the cataclysmic destruction of *Cat's Cradle*, and the satiric extrapolation of *Player Piano*. Missing also is the Tralfamadorian or God's eye view of all time found in *Slaughterhouse-Five*, and in its place is a sweeping view back to the near future from one million years ahead. Vonnegut maintains that *Galápagos* as contemporary science fiction "had to be responsible in terms of the theory of evolution, the theory of natural selection . . . [since good science fiction will] make people think intelligently about science and what it can or cannot do. That's what we must *do* now" ("Serenity" 30–31, reprint 25). Some critics believe that such an endeavor is much too late. Veronica Hollinger, for instance, argues that "our love/hate relationship with our own technology and our very real and world-wide ecological crises have, as it were, caught up with SF [science fiction]. From the perspective of a postmodernism as ongoing crisis, it is indeed no longer necessary to write SF, since the future has already arrived" (30). But *Galápagos* leapfrogs over this contemporary problem of science fiction, by postulating a future beyond the vision of the present and most contemporary science fiction. Yet, what Hollinger goes on to say applies most aptly to *Galápagos*: "it is the imagery of the literature of the future that seems mostly appropriate to a description of the present" (Hollinger 33).

"All fiction is metaphor. Science fiction is a metaphor. . . . The future, in fiction, is a metaphor" as Ursula K. Le Guin contends ("Introduction"). Using science fiction to set the novel a million years in the future becomes for Vonnegut a way of communicating the ethical imperative that "God doesn't care what becomes of us, and neither does Nature, so we'd better care. We're all there is to care" ("Serenity" 31, reprint 25). In the metaphoric future of *Galápagos*, latter-day human beings evolve over eons away from destructive, grasping, and war-making to far more lovable, furry beings, thus ensuring their own survival along with that of other flora, fauna, and the very planet itself. The slow, steady, truly Darwinian evolution Vonnegut pictures in *Galápagos* takes place over one million years triggered by a change in the environment and the advent of a tiny virus that eats human eggs in utero. Not simply another apocalyptic, post-nuclear holocaust disaster novel of the kind so prevalent in the 1950s and 1960s,[2] *Galápagos* presents a far more sweeping indictment of human failure as this metaphor of the egg-eating-in-utero virus makes clear.[3] Where other apocalyptic novels provide for a human remnant surviving the post-nuclear holocaust environment by way of, say, a bomb shelter sentimentality or, perhaps, a superior survivalist strategy, no such big-brain scheme allows humankind to overcome or sidestep the virus present in *Galápagos*. "The worst is not so long as we can say this is the worst," said Tom in *King Lear*. Vonnegut echoes his words by suggesting that while being preoccupied with nuclear war—the worst we can imagine—humans may well be on the road to extinction by any number of other unforeseen causes, such as pollution or environmental degradation and destruction. Either end is, of course, not only final but also our own fault.

In *Galápagos*, humans return to a pre-Fall innocence: swimming in the sea, hunting fish, making love once or twice a year, but unable to read *King Lear* or any of Shakespeare's other plays—in fact, unable to read anything at all.[4] Humans evolve from the passengers aboard the cruise ship, *The Bahía de Darwin*, an improbable latter-day Noah's ark. After the elimination of the less fit, such as a successful businessman, inventive con man, and brilliant computer man, the ark carries one blatantly inept male plus nine females, eight of them fertile (and all of them uninfected by the virus because of having been totally isolated). This island of fertility in a sea of sterility might strike many readers as wildly implausible but it nevertheless has considerable scientific validity as attested to by Stephen Jay Gould. Upon reading *Galápagos* Gould "thought it was a wonderful *roman à clef* about evolutionary theory" (letter quoted by Vonnegut in "Skull Session" 252). Theory but not fact. For Vonnegut does not "present the evolution of the human race—as he imagines it will be," as at least one critic contends (Bianculli 276). Instead, he offers a clear, if metaphoric, warning about the dire straits humanity has entered upon and, therefore, the pressing need for humanity to change course to prevent the ecocide of planet Earth. This urgent need to take responsible action in the present leads Mustazza to argue persuasively that *Galápagos* "[u]ltimately, . . . is not concerned with either the past or the future but the present, is not predictive but cautionary, is not about science or religion but about the way we treat one another here and now" ("Darwinian Eden" 286).

Vonnegut starts from the now-almost-too-familiar premise that unless human beings stop destroying their environment by polluting it with their own garbage and increasing its temperature, then this beautiful, fragile planet will become uninhabitable—a theme first sounded in *Cat's Cradle* then revisited in *Breakfast of Champions, Slapstick, Jailbird*, and still later in *Hocus Pocus*. As a novelist and increasingly as a public speaker, Vonnegut has become progressively preoccupied with humans destroying their natural habitat and, even worse, with their widespread ignorance of nature that encourages such destruction. Moreover, he has become convinced, along with many other thoughtful people, that contemporary humans apparently lack the will to identify "The Problem" as themselves, and that in turn prevents them from doing anything effective about it. Writing in *The New York Times* in 1990, Vonnegut concluded that: "one-day . . . we would go belly-up like guppies in a neglected fishbowl" (*Fates Worse Than Death* 185).

Where *Galápagos* examines the misuse of human reason and invention as the principal danger to life on planet Earth, *Bluebeard* looks at both greed and the misuse of human creativity as endangering true art and imagination. The Rabo Karabekian who narrates this novel is a far more complex character than the Rabo Karabekian honored for artistic achievement in *Breakfast of Champions* by the Midland Arts Festival together with the writer manqué, Kilgore Trout. Now a reformed Abstract Expressionist painter with "what is the most important collection of Abstract Expressionist paintings still in private hands" (8), Karabekian wrestles at the end of his life with the nature and meaning of his life and his art. Clearly, Vonnegut rethought the Karabekian character in light of his desire to write a novel with a painter as hero. That idea for a novel came to him in turn because of an essay commissioned by *Esquire* on the Abstract Expressionist painter, Jackson Pollock (*Fates Worse Than Death* 41). Much of *Bluebeard* concerns the value or lack of it in Abstract Expressionist art—a subject on which Vonnegut has written extensively. In his essay on Jackson Pollock, for instance, Vonnegut argues that Abstract Expressionist painting with its marked absence of people, nature, and human artifacts, arose when it did because World War II was followed immediately by the revelations of the death camps, and then by the shock of the explosion of the first atomic bomb. Not even the old romantic moon or domesticated oranges could be used in painting if the artist recalled that a full moon was often given the title "bomber's moon." Oranges became suspect to those who recalled that the "Commandant of Auschwitz[,] . . . his wife and children, under the greasy smoke from the ovens" enjoyed good meals daily (*Fates Worse Than Death* 44). After World War II, Abstract Expressionism dominated American painting for several decades. Hilton Kramer, the distinguished art critic recalls that "[i]n the heady atmosphere of the 1960s, abstraction was not merely chic; for many its most ardent acolytes it represented the artistic equivalent of the promised land" (94).

In *Breakfast of Champions*, Karabekian's painting, *The Temptation of St. Anthony*, is part of the Promised Land of Abstract Expressionism—there are no persons, artifacts, or allusions to nature in it. Together with a Henry Moore sculpture, it becomes one of only two pieces in the collection of the Mildred Barry Memorial Arts Center. Before the Midland Arts Festival begins, however, a cocktail waitress confronts Karabekian directly and challenges him about the value of his painting. She directs her anger at the painting's cost, its subject, its technique, as well as at the painter himself. (Vonnegut elsewhere suggests that becoming angry over any work of art is about as sensible as "getting really mad at a banana split" [*Fates Worse Than Death* 48].) This painting cost the Arts Center $50,000 and, like all Abstract Expressionist art, it did not appear to refer very directly to its subject, if it referred to it at all. Utilizing a green wall paint called "Hawaiian Avocado," Karabekian's huge painting, measuring some twenty by sixteen feet, consisted entirely of a vertically running strip of Day-Glo orange reflecting tape against the green field (*Breakfast of Champions* 208).[5] Not much for $50,000. Still, Karabekian mounts a spirited defense of his work. First, he claims that his painting communicates what is really important in life. According to Karabekian, his work reveals "everything about life which truly matters. . . . [It shows] the awareness . . . the immaterial core . . . the 'I am' . . . all that is alive in . . . us." He concludes that this "unwavering and pure" awareness will remain "no matter what preposterous adventure may befall us" (221). Such speculations parody much of the criticism of Abstract Expressionism, which, in a more extreme form, appears in Tom Wolfe's spirited, if highly opinionated, book on the necessity of theory for modern art, *The Painted Word.*[6] Although *The Temptation of St. Anthony*—like all Karabekian's paintings—has no content and is about absolutely nothing except itself, Karabekian ascribes considerable significance to it, especially to that Day-Glo orange strip. If another creature or person were near St. Anthony, then he would have to add another strip of tape to indicate what is "alive and maybe sacred" in that second subject. Alternatively, anything other than awareness is simply "dead machinery" (221).

What is striking about Karabekian's defense—besides its articulate self-confidence that it shares with much of contemporary theorizing about modern art—is the slight, if any, relation these assertions bear to the painting itself. The painting is wholly free of content consisting as it does of a simple vertical band of Day-Glo orange dividing a green field. Vonnegut here satirically suggests that beauty no longer resides in the eye of the beholder, but artistic significance lies wholly within the head of the observer who looks at the painting and theorizes, whether that observer be an artist, critic, or gallery-viewer. If such a discussion of the nature and value of art is somewhat peripheral to *Breakfast of Champions*, it becomes central to *Bluebeard*. The latter novel raises the perennial issue of what art is and who the real artist is by contrasting Karabekian and his Abstract Expressionist painter friends with Dan Gregory, the illustrator who paints things more real than they appear to the eye.

In *Galápagos*, it was the great big human brains that were to blame for the pending destruction of the planet, but in *Hocus Pocus* Vonnegut identifies the enemy more narrowly as human indifference. He illustrates this indifference with a parable: Humanity's representative, six-year-old Bruce Bergeron, stands trapped in an elevator stuck between floors in a large department store. Mistakenly, "Little Bruce believed himself to be at the center of a major event in American history" (165)—as most six-year-olds will do. When at last the elevator becomes freed, it moves to the next floor where it deposits its passengers safely. Bruce, who "survived" the ordeal, discovers to his shock that no one else is remotely interested in his or his fellow passengers' predicament, as the rest of humanity either impatiently waits for the next elevator or madly participates in the department store's white sale. "There wasn't even somebody from the management of the store to offer an anxious apology, to make certain that everybody was all right" (166). Whether inside or outside the elevator, people are so completely immersed in their own activities and desires that they have no room left for anyone else's concerns—much less for any vision of society's needs as a whole. Discussing *Hocus Pocus*, Vonnegut once quipped that the majority of people were only interested in making things and no one appeared interested any longer in doing "maintenance . . . there goes the ball game. Meanwhile, truth, jokes, and music help at least a little bit" (*Fates Worse Than Death* 201; compare *Hocus Pocus* 240). But truth, jokes, and music, which may offer some solace, do not and cannot replace Eugene Debs's now-abandoned ideal of a United States free of poverty and injustice. In any event, America at the end of the twentieth century all too often appears content with ignorance, sentimentality, and noise.

Besides this story of trapped humanity faced with an indifferent universe, Vonnegut more specifically focuses on the state of the United States as an imperial power. The main character in *Hocus Pocus* for him becomes imperialism, which he defines as using an army and navy employing up-to-the-minute weapons to conquer people, steal their personal property, and seize their land (*Fates Worse Than Death* 130). But even imperial actions have consequences not just politically, but also socially, ethically, and economically for the state as well as for individuals. The United States at the end of the twentieth century appears in *Hocus Pocus* as a country with its aspirations frozen—a land that promised much but delivered little. John Leonard tells the story of a time when he and Vonnegut were walking in New Hampshire. "We happened, in an orchard, upon stricken boughs of black apples. Helicopters had sprayed Stop Drop on these apples during the October picking season, and then an early frost had killed them off, and so they hung there, very Japanese" (301). Yes, very Japanese in the sense of those aesthetically satisfying, brilliantly compact haiku, seventeen syllable Japanese poems so widely imitated at one time by American poets.[7] But *Hocus Pocus* focuses not on the aesthetic beauty but on the waste and inediblity of those black apples on those "stricken boughs."

At the center of *Hocus Pocus* lie the preserved black apples of several crucial, if disastrous, events of the twentieth century—each vividly illustrating humanity's inhumanity: The Bomb, which that came to symbolize the utter, sudden destruction of life; Auschwitz, which came to symbolize human ingenuity in the service of destruction; Vietnam, which came to symbolize the utter futility of war: Attica the maximum security prison, which came to symbolize the failure of American society to give meaningful work, life, or hope to all citizens. These late-twentieth-century symbols are joined by the first century binge of 6,000 crucifixions that resulted from putting down the slave revolt led by Spartacus and the Japanese Army's 1937 Rape of Nanking. Behind these appalling events that span the globe and 2,000 years of human history, lies "the complicated futility of ignorance" (14). Ignorance that may dream of impossible perpetual motion machines that look lovely and do nothing, but which in day-to-day life practices brutality, prefers ugliness, indulges in mind-numbing drugs, and willingly follows orders to perform the most inhuman and inhumane acts. Hartke discovers again and again first as a college teacher and then later as a prison teacher that for most people information is useless "except as entertainment" (67). A harsh if fair judgment on the United States in the fictional year 2001.

If there is nothing rational or sane to say after a massacre, as the narrator of *Slaughterhouse-Five* maintains, then what is there to say about deeds of brutality, ignorance, duplicity, and mayhem? What little there is to say, Vonnegut says: Such deeds were done in the past out of ignorance of the humanity of others who were once classified as the enemy. Thanks to modern communications and transportation, humans have explored all of the Earth's surface and discovered in the process that the only enemy left on planet Earth consists of fellow human beings no different from us. Because of this discovery, humans no longer can get such a kick out of killing their enemies. In fact, says Vonnegut, "Killing enemies has so lost its zing that no sane citizen of the United States would feel anything but horror if our country were to kill practically everybody in Moscow[,] . . . Leningrad and Kiev. Or in Nagasaki, Japan" (*Fates Worse Than Death* 147).[8]

And there is the point. During World War II Americans had the luxury of demonizing their enemies as those enemies in their turn demonized them, and there was little, if any, means of correcting the resulting caricatures (see almost any ad for U. S. World War II Savings Bonds).[9] Not so with Vietnam. Vietnam has long been on Vonnegut's mind and conscience. In *Slaughterhouse-Five*, Billy Pilgrim wakes to find his son standing by his bed wearing the green beret uniform made famous by the Vietnam War (189–90), while in *Jailbird* there is the infamous Nixon cabinet meeting called to discuss the Kent State disaster after raw untrained national guardsmen were issued live ammunition and used it to kill four students, some of whom were protesting the war. In his 1983 sermon preached at St. John the Divine Cathedral in New York City, Vonnegut speculated about why Vietnam veterans appear so distinctively, so unnervingly different. Why are they so "unwholesomely mature?" He concludes that they are different from older generations of veterans in that they have "*never* had illusions about war." For the first time, we encounter soldiers who from childhood on have seen and heard "so many pictures of actual and re-staged battles, [that they realized] . . . war is meaningless butchery of ordinary people like themselves" (*Fates Worse Than Death* 146). Hartke's experience during the Fall of Saigon replicates numerous Americans trapped in that debacle. On the twenty-fifth anniversary of the end of the Vietnam War, *Newsweek* published reflections by some of the key people involved. That of CIA analyst Frank

Snepp has much in common with Hartke's experience (see 32–51, especially 32–46). Snepp's book, *Decent Interval*, was the subject of a famous successful suit by the CIA in 1978. In addressing the 1973 international P.E.N. conference held in Stockholm, Vonnegut recalled the frustration of writers who vociferously opposed the Vietnam War.

We all raised hell about the war for years . . . with novels[,] . . . poems[,] . . . plays and short stories. We dropped on our complacent society the literary equivalent of a hydrogen bomb.
   I will now report [that] . . . such a bomb . . . has the explosive force of a very large banana-cream pie (*Wampeters, Foma & Granfalloons* 226)

When reread in the twenty-first century in light of President Clinton's end-of-the-century trip to Vietnam, perhaps *Hocus Pocus* may help Americans recall some of the lessons to be learned from that sad episode. How in arrogance the country neglected, or perhaps momentarily forgot, its own ideals that had led to imagining being an American—ideals that had also inspired other countries to fight for their freedom and may yet inspire Vietnam itself gradually to become democratic.

WINNERS AND LOSERS

"The two real political parties in America are the *Winners* and the *Losers*," wrote Vonnegut in *Harper's Magazine* (1972). The Winners' religion is "a harsh interpretation of *Darwinism*, which argues that it is the will of the universe that only the fittest should survive" (*Wampeters, Foma & Granfalloons* 185–86). To which he added, "every Winner knows: one must behave heartlessly toward Losers, if one hopes to survive" (187). What Vonnegut describes, of course, is not scientific but social Darwinism, which he long ago identified as brutally inhuman and an excuse for winner-take-all social and political practices.[10] Unfortunately, in imagining being an American quite often the survival of the fittest socially and economically becomes substituted for the ideal of freedom and equality for all. *Galápagos* plays with this substitution. The basic irony in the novel rests on the elimination of the fittest, as defined by social Darwinism, and the survival of the fittest, as defined by Darwinian evolution. Judged by the ability to adapt to changing conditions that Darwinian evolution emphasizes rather than the ability to "get ahead" that social Darwinism values, fur not brilliance contributes to survival in *Galápagos*. Aikio, the furry mutant therefore becomes the new Eve rather than her rich, successful father becoming the new Adam. Vonnegut thus

turns into its opposite the traditional science-fiction motif of man's evolution into an ever more perfect species: On the very islands on which Darwin once conceived of his theory, mankind's fate is decided through evolutionary regression, an obvious mistake in the development of the species is corrected, and man is relieved of his destructive brain. (Freese, "Religions" 160)

The result in *Galápagos* is not, however, a dark tale of doom and gloom but a sprightly story told with evident good humor and irony. Much of the wit of *Galápagos* lies in Vonnegut's reversing the usual picture of evolution as life evolving over eons from simple to more and more complex forms until voila! the ultimate, the pinnacle of evolution is at last achieved with the appearance of humanity.[11] Instead, a million years in the future, humans in *Galápagos* have moved from complex brain-ridden creatures to far more innocent, polymorphously perverse, aquatic creatures. Their lives become dedicated to hunting and eating, sex and procreating—a simpler and perhaps more reasonable agenda than the one currently followed by those big-brained creatures who often appear hell-bent on destroying themselves and their planet.

Galápagos itself cautions against this disastrous, low budget, fatal choice. Unlike many novels that contain a similar warning, including *Slapstick* (Vonnegut's weakest novel), *Galápagos* does not postulate an idealized picture of a reversion to some preindustrial state where society becomes once again feudal in outlook, organization, and technology,[12] but somehow most of the good things from the contemporary world remain. Instead, "the movement in the narrative [of *Galápagos*] is bidirectional [sic], progressive in that it applies a Darwinian solution to the problem of moral error, retrogressive insofar as the state of innocence that is ultimately achieved is allusively linked to primal mythic innocence," as Mustazza declares ("Eden" 279). "This was," as the narrator says, "a very innocent planet, except for the great big brains" (*Galápagos* 9).

Galápagos is, therefore, one of the very few science-fiction novels that questions the unchallenged assumption that a technologically advanced society is preferable to one less advanced.[13] Unlike the fatuous General Electric advertising slogan of the fifties and sixties, in this novel "Progress Is [not] Our Most Important Product" (compare *Breakfast of Champions* 290). Worse, so-called technological "progress" may well lead not to peace and plenty but to the destruction of humanity and its world (a thesis to be further elaborated on in the tale of the B-36 sisters in *Timequake*). In *Fates Worse Than Death*, Vonnegut suggests humans could hope to be saved from "our inventiveness, just as the dinosaurs may have prayed to be rescued from their massiveness" (145).

Popular views of progress often equate it with increasing complexity as well as with motion and speed. The widespread belief that life must always advance toward more and more complex forms comes about in part through misconstruing Darwin's observation that local adaptability to changed or changing conditions leads to the establishment of new species.

Everybody knows that organisms get better as they evolve. They get more advanced, more modern, and less primitive. And everybody knows . . . that organisms get more complex as they evolve. From the first cell that coalesced in the primordial soup to the magnificent intricacies of *Homo sapiens*, the evolution of life—as everybody knows— has been one long drive toward greater complexity. The only trouble with what everybody knows . . . is that there is no evidence it's true [ellipsis in original]. (Lori Oliwenstein quoted in Gould 212)

Reasoning from dead-end or unsuccessful experiments in evolving creatures, such as horses or humans, many place humanity at the pinnacle of evolution as they once placed humanity at the very pinnacle of creation. But substituting evolution for creation still leaves unresolved the problem of the absence of evidence for assuming that humans are the goal of evolution rather than simply another example of an adaptation to local conditions. Paleontologist Stephen Jay Gould contends, "We are glorious accidents of an unpredictable process with no drive to complexity, not the expected results of evolutionary principles that yearn to produce a creature capable of understanding the mode of its own necessary constructing" (Gould 216).

In *Galápagos*, Vonnegut reverses the evolutionary cliché of humanity marching ever-onward and upward. Adapting to local conditions and taking advantage of accidents and serendipity, *exactly as evolution has always done*, humans in this novel return to the sea. Darwin's best examples of evolution were found on the Galápagos Islands where he encountered isolated animals—like the humans in *Galápagos*—that had evolved into new species. Neither the strongest nor the most complex survived, but the fastest and best at adaptation. Rather than viewing species as superior or inferior, Darwin emphasized their differences, especially those differences that enabled certain species to survive changing conditions. The elephant that evolved into the wooly mammoth did so to survive in a new age of ice. To say that the wooly mammoth is somehow superior to his ancestor the elephant establishes an indefensible scale of value. Similarly, the animals of Australia evolved to live under incredibly difficult conditions of small erratic rainfalls, scarce food, and intense heat. The kangaroo, for instance, leaps rather than runs because leaping over long distances uses only a fraction of the energy that running does. The wombat and a sheep have about equal body mass, but one being perfectly adapted to scarcity requires only a small fraction of the other's daily intake of food to survive.

Initially, the conditions described in *Galápagos* appear more benign than, say, a world subjected to radioactive fallout but they prove equally as effective as the atomic bomb in eliminating humans. The vast majority of humanity mysteriously becomes sterile and, therefore, fails to reproduce. This scenario, derided as too improbable by some critics, appeared, at the end of the twentieth century as all too plausible. In a large area in Siberia, for example, the human and animal population lies under threat of extinction from the huge amount of leaking nuclear waste deposits. For decades, the atmosphere there has been polluted with radiation. Should that waste leach into the Arctic Sea, as appears now possible, then the poisoning of all northern latitudes of the globe will become a distinct possibility. The much-vaunted human technology could yet destroy all humanity. Gould warns that

accumulating technological "progress" need not lead to cultural improvement in a visceral or moral sense—and may just as well end in destruction, if not extinction, as various plausible scenarios, from nuclear holocaust to environmental poisoning, suggest. I have long been impressed by a potential solution . . . to the problem of why we haven't been contacted by the plethora of advanced civilizations that ought to inhabit other solar systems in our universe. Perhaps any society that could build a technology for such interplanetary, if not intergalactic, travel must first pass through a period of potential destruction where technological capacity outstrips social or moral restraint. And perhaps no, or very few, societies can ever emerge intact from such a crucial episode. (223)

Vonnegut's novels emphasize the huge discrepancy between our much-vaunted technological ingenuity and such social and moral restraint as Gould describes. When in *Deadeye Dick* a neutron bomb wipes out Midland City, it produces not so much as a murmur from an uncaring, callous, indifferent world. In *Cat's Cradle* Ice-9 precipitates the extinction of most life on the planet. Ants remain an exception. In *Slaughterhouse-Five* a careless Tralfamadorian test pilot accidentally terminates the whole universe. In *Galápagos*, when the human population on most of the planet fails to reproduce only a small saving remnant survives on the new ark of the Galápagos Islands. There, humanity evolves into the smaller brained, aquatic creatures minus either the hands or fingers that had caused so much damage to the environment.[14] Mustazza summarizes the action as "nature, with the help of an unwitting humanity, going about the business of correcting its errors, of gradually reforming people by re-forming them, bringing humankind's form and priorities into line with those of the rest of the animal kingdom" ("Darwinian Eden" 279). As fast swimmers, these future humans live in harmony with the natural world as they return to their first and most natural element, the Earth's seas. The fittest survive, as Darwin predicted they would, but rather than following human priorities, it is an ironic nature which determines who proves fittest.

Thomas Disch, in his perceptive review of *Galápagos*, correctly asserts:

In designing the tale that supports this thesis Vonnegut commands almost the full spectrum of comic possibility. He is a masterful debunker, a superb monologuist, an ingenious *farceur*, and has a quick and wicked tongue. Like Chaplin he can switch from farce to sentiment in the batting of an eyelash. All that he lacks to be an all-round champion of comedy is the mimetic genius of Dickens, but though Vonnegut is a shrewd observer of character, his dramatic strategy would militate against ventriloquism, even if he had the knack. (1267)

Part of this spectrum of comedy is Vonnegut's omniscient, invisible narrator, Leon Trout (son of the nefarious Kilgore Trout), who reads minds, discerns motivation, and predicts events accurately over the millennia of his tale. He sees his role as writer as "Nature's experiment with insatiable voyeurism, as my father was Nature's experiment with cynicism" (82). Moreover, Leon writes purely for art's sake, since there is not the remotest possibility of one of the latter-day sea-going humans reading anything at all (257).[15] As an ageless, headless ghost, Trout becomes symbolic of one solution to the great big brain problem—decapitation. Charles Berryman extends the metaphor to include Vonnegut himself: "When crossing the ocean in a terrible storm the narrator's ghost is seen at the mast of the ship holding gallantly to his severed head. What a perfect image for Vonnegut's place in contemporary literature!" ("Evolution" 198). [16]

The patently ephemeral nature of Trout's writing, along with his nonexistent medium and total lack of audience, raises issues central to many discussions of contemporary art that Vonnegut will explore more fully in *Bluebeard*. When as a ghost in the rigging of a ghost ship sailing the seas Leon Trout narrates *Galápagos* by writing on air he goes John Keats epitaph one better. [17] That epitaph famously proclaimed: "Here lies one who's life was writ in water."[18] Tom Wolfe tells a story similar to Trout's invisible novel about a masterpiece created by the greatest artist in the history of the world:

Suppose the greatest artist in the history of the world, impoverished and unknown at the time, had been sitting at a table in the old Automat at Union Square [in New York City], cadging some free water and hoping to cop a leftover crust of toasted corn muffin . . . and suddenly he got the inspiration for the greatest work of art in the history of the world. Possessing not even so much as a pencil or a burnt match, he dipped his forefinger into the glass of water and began recording this greatest of all inspirations . . . on a paper napkin, with New York tap water as his paint. In a matter of seconds . . . the water had diffused through the paper and the grand design vanished, whereupon the greatest artist in the history of the world slumped to the table and died of a broken heart, and the manager came over, and he thought that here was nothing more than a dead wino with a wet napkin. Now, the question is: Would that have been the greatest work of art in the history of the world?

Vonnegut improves on Wolfe's joke, while sharpening its point, by having his narrator die *before* he writes his masterpiece, and by having him write it in air and on air rather than in water on a paper napkin. The fantastic result is an invisible novel written by an author already dead for a million years.

This fiction of an omniscient narrator writing in the future for no discernible or possible audience, and of the surprising aquatic nature of future humans also provides Vonnegut with many opportunities to comment on the incredible penchant humans evince for self-destruction. Looked at objectively, the history of humanity appears dedicated to conceiving better and better ways to destroy itself, its artifacts, and the planet. In a memorable passage in *Galápagos*, the narrator recounts with an absolutely incredulous tone, from his perspective of a million years in the future, what humans appear to do best of all. What he sees are the large-brained, terribly mobile, inquisitive creatures, whose

big brains . . . would tell their owners, . . . "Here is a crazy thing we could actually do, probably, but we would never do it, of course. It's just fun to think about."
And then, as though in trances, the people would really do it—have slaves fight each other to the death in the Colosseum, or burn people alive in the public square for holding opinions which were locally unpopular, or build factories whose only purpose was to kill people in industrial quantities, or to blow up whole cities, and on and on. (*Galápagos* 266)

Such events and acts are so unbelievable, are such violations of good sense, as well as of human self-interest, that they do require a radical explanation. Leon Trout, like a doctor diagnosing the illness of a patient, supplies one: "the only real villain in my story: the oversize human brain" (270).

This most objective-of-all-narrators thus becomes the perfect vehicle for satirizing the mind that delights in devising engines of destruction. In describing an exploding rocket, for instance, his open-mouthed wonder emphasizes not human ingenuity, but human lack of foresight in applying thinking to the problem of how to better and more efficiently destroy things rather than applying thinking to the problem of survival. Rather than moral outrage, he adopts the stance of neutral amazement as he ironically discusses "the collective achievement" represented by this device: "No single human being could claim credit for that rocket, which was going to work so perfectly. It was the collective achievement of all who had ever put their big brains to work on the problem of how to capture and compress the diffuse violence of which nature was capable, and drop it in relatively small packages on their enemies" (189–90). The delight in watching a rocket explode as if it were part of a Fourth of July fireworks display and the horror at the resulting brutal damage and death creates a contrast between fabulous human creativity and equally fabulous human destructiveness. Comparing the meeting of the rocket and its target—the moment of mating—with human sexual consummation all in a deadpan delivery followed by a famous Shakespearean quotation reinforces this discontinuity (190). Trout begins the sequence by recalling the exploding rockets he saw while fighting in Vietnam, yet even those pale beside what happens "when that Peruvian rocket put the tip of its nose, that part of its body most richly supplied with exposed nerve endings, into that Ecuadorian radar dish" (190). Instead of completing this overtly sexual image, Trout breaks the narration to insert an apparently irrelevant comment about art in the far future: "No one is interested in sculpture. . . . Who could handle a chisel or a welding torch with their flippers or their mouths?" (190).[19] This violent wrenching away from the sexual imagery used to describe the rocket about to hit its target to an objective statement of the lack of sculpture in the far future not only breaks the narrative flow while pointing to the loss of creativity through violence, but also sets up the next comic effect by suspending, but not abandoning, the imagery of sexual consummation. Trout pictures a sculpture that would juxtapose humanity's creativity, art, and sexual drive with the human ingenuity embodied in the rocket's overt destructive power.

Into the lava plinth beneath it these words might be incised, expressing the sentiments of all who had had a hand in the design and manufacture and sale and purchase and launch of the rocket, and of all to whom high explosives were a branch of the entertainment industry:

> . . . 'Tis a consummation
> Devoutly to be wish'd.
> William Shakespeare (1564–1616). (190)

But destruction not reproduction—war not love—prove to be the consummation humanity devoutly wish'd for.

Throughout *Galápagos*, similar quotations from poets, dramatists, novelists, statesmen, and philosophers appear juxtaposed to the picture of the downward slide of humanity into the sea—a slide caused, at least in part, by the human failure to listen to the wisdom contained in such quotations. Moreover, by failing to protect those who love from the effects of war, and by insisting on following the fascinating path of destruction as exemplified in the rocket's explosive power, humans neglect the very survival of the species itself. Vonnegut's comedy, therefore, reflects human shortcomings and failures and warns against approaching disaster, yet does so without lapsing into moralizing, preaching, or declaiming.

"Maturity . . . is a bitter disappointment for which no remedy exists, unless laughter can be said to remedy anything," wrote Bokonon, the spurious holy man in *Cat's Cradle* (134). As an antithesis, *Galápagos* suggests that laughter and good humor may yet enable humanity to survive the bitter disappointment of the inevitable discovery that the world, humanity, and, yes, human beings themselves are not only an imperfect, but also an endangered species. It is not "finally just another bitter and pessimistic comment on man's tendency toward self-annihilation," nor does it "prescribe a remedy against mankind's impending self-annihilation" (Freese, "Surviving" 170)—that would be to take its central metaphor too seriously and literally. Nor is *Galápagos* simply "an extended joke" (Freese 171)—that would be to take its central metaphor not seriously enough. When filling out a police identification form, Bokonon was asked what his avocation might be. He wrote, "Being alive." When asked his occupation, he dutifully filled in the blank with "Being dead" (*Cat's Cradle* 95). Where *Cat's Cradle* concentrates on human myopia that willfully chooses the human vocation of death with the result that just about all life—not only human life— perishes, *Galápagos* emphasizes the human avocation of being alive as all life survives even at the cost of the human species mutating. Rather than the dark apocalyptic humor of *Cat's Cradle*, *Galápagos's* comedy proves lighter and more positive. Brian Aldiss sums up the novel's strengths as "Sprightly, funny, suspenseful, *Candide*-like, and endearingly ingenious in its telling" (*Spree* 329). "The book's a joy," he exclaims (letter to author). Other readers agree: "it is a triumph of style, originality and warped yet consistent logic," declares David Bianculli (275), while Vonnegut himself was pleased. "I think technically what I undertook was impossible. I think I solved the technical problems, and it was miraculous to me that I was able to do that," he said in an interview ("Skull Session" 259). [20] Only *Timequake* a decade later would present Vonnegut with a set of still more difficult technical problems to be solved.

Despite its disaster scenario, *Galápagos* retains an air of optimism and joy, rather than defeat and sorrow. Only *Galápagos*, *Bluebeard*, and *Timequake* among Vonnegut's novels may be said to celebrate life and to escape the air of defeat that pervades all the others. Observing widely what humans do, reflecting long on what consolation might exist for their shortsightedness and stupidity, Vonnegut opts for the tragic joy of life that leads not to the laughter from the grin on the face of the death's head skull, but to the laughter of self-recognition and wonder as he imagines being an American—well, being human—a million years in the future.

THE "MORNING WORK" OF THE ARTIST

Life is painting a picture not doing a sum.
                                    —Justice Oliver Wendell Holmes

Numbered among the world's oppressed and outcast, Rabo Karabekian's
Armenian parents imagined becoming Americans, and so immigrated to the
United States, the land of promise. Along with so many other immigrants, they
believed that they were about to become rich, but they discovered instead that
hard work and relative poverty were to be their lot. Both of them had already
survived the great Turkish massacre of the Armenians that added the word
genocide to the languages of the world (*Bluebeard* 3). Their son lived to witness
the end of the most cataclysmic war yet fought on European soil, where a
megalomaniac again practiced genocide in his attempt to exterminate
systematically a portion of the human race. Against this background,
Vonnegut's hoax autobiography, *Bluebeard*, demonstrates that through self-
acceptance and the serious, if playful, use of human imagination and creativity,
human beings can become reconciled to their weakness and fragility, while
remaining outraged at human stupidity, greed, and the many disastrous self-
defeating schemes such big brained rational creatures concoct, let alone attempt
to implement.

Much of *Bluebeard* is preoccupied with the question of the nature and value
of art and the right use of the imagination—topics to which Vonnegut will return
in *Timequake*. In *Bluebeard* Dan Gregory functions as a negative example of the
wrong use of talent. While society, or the art market, makes him fabulously
wealthy by purchasing everything he paints, his work fails as art because it has
no emotional or spiritual content. Its purpose is simply to illustrate someone
else's ideas or someone else's feelings: it is "good painting about nothing,"[21] or
what Holger Cahill contemptuously dismisses as the "merely decorative."

Art is not merely decorative, a sort of unrelated accompaniment to life. In a genuine
sense it should have use; it should be interwoven with the very stuff and texture of human
experience, intensifying that experience, making it more profound, rich, clear, and
coherent. This can be accomplished only if the artist is functioning freely in relation to
society, and if society wants what he is able to offer. (473)

Gregory's illustrations, although painted in minute and exact detail, are
completely removed from "the very stuff and texture of human experience";
they prove, upon close examination, to be as void of content as Rabo
Karabekian's extremely well executed huge abstract canvasses. *Bluebeard* asks
repeatedly which works are art and, therefore, essential to life and which ones
are merely decoration and, therefore, nonessential. Are Dan Gregory's exact
illustrations, Karabekian's wall-sized paintings, or Terry Kitchen's spray gun
paintings? Are any of these valuable as art, or does each have value only as one
person's attempt to play with paint? How does each of the three measure up
against the great artists of other ages? Can a line be drawn from Rembrandt to
Pollock?[22] Or from Gregory to Karabekian?

Vonnegut places these questions within the context of the art world replete with its marketing and investment ploys. After examining the Abstract Expressionists, as represented by Karabekian's and others' exuberant splashing of paint on canvas, and after looking at the astronomical prices people willingly paid for such splashing, he comments wryly: "Tastes change."[23] "[M]uch of what I put in this book [*Bluebeard*] was inspired by the grotesque prices paid for works of art during the past century" ("Author's Note" n.p.). Vonnegut asks what is the role of those who collect, curate, write about, or deal in art? Clearly, they may "ridicule or reward grotesquely" (*Fates Worse Than Death* 46). Vonnegut's satire on the world of art, artists, connoisseurs, and critics provides a few provisional answers. "Artistic justice," for example, occurs in *Bluebeard* when Karabekian's paintings return, "thanks to unforeseen chemical reactions," after a few years to their pristine state as sized canvas: "people who had paid fifteen- or twenty- or even thirty thousand dollars for a picture . . . found themselves gazing at a blank canvas, all ready for a new picture, and ringlets of colored tapes and what looked like moldy Rice Krispies on the floor" (*Bluebeard* 18–19).[24] Perhaps Karabekian here unwittingly became a Conceptualist painter, one whose work exists only as a concept (compare "The Greatest Artist in the History of the World" and Leon Trout's invisible novel, *Galápagos*). Or perhaps he is only the latest example of "Now you see it, now you don't"—as stage magicians used to say during the Great Depression when the rabbit disappeared into the tall silk hat. Or, more likely, his success illustrates once again the truth articulated in the story of "the Emperor's New Clothes." Whatever the choice, Vonnegut's satire on the art world succeeds so well in *Bluebeard* because, in addition to its implied and stated criticism, he offers a positive alternative in Karabekian's final canvas, *Now It's the Women's Turn*. This monumental painting records in exact minute detail the moment Karabekian observed "when the sun came up the day the Second World War ended in Europe" (268) as Vonnegut himself had done (compare *Fates Worse Than Death* 216–20). But the meaning, the significance of that event, would reveal itself to him only over time, as the meaning or nonmeaning of Dresden also unfolded itself only over time.

Now It's the Women's Turn occupies a place in the sub-genre of painting known as the panoramic canvas. The nineteenth century offers numerous examples of such crowded canvases in the various panoramas that were, and are still, hugely popular as entertainment in Europe. Typical of such painters was W. P. Firth (1819–1909) who "became famous as a panoramic painter of Victorian actuality, with canvases crowded with the minutiae of everyday life, 'Derby Day,' 'Wymouth Sands,' 'The Railway Station' " (Carter 16). Looking at Karabekian's enormous eight-foot-by-sixty-four-foot canvas, an observer feels, correctly, that each of the hundreds, the thousands of miniscule characters in this huge painting has a story. Ironically, the 5,219 figures appear so convincingly real not because the artist saw or knew them but because, before creating their image on canvas, he invented a detailed war story for each, and only after doing that did he paint "the person it had happened to" (*Bluebeard* 270). His painting is at once as precise as Gregory's illustrations and, in some important ways, as imaginatively playful as an Abstract Expressionist canvas. Karabekian's work as serious, creative play, memorializing and giving life to these thousands of representative humans, contrasts vividly with Felix Hoenikker's frivolous, destructive play that ends the world in *Cat's Cradle*. Rather than become an artist by loving those who have no use, as Eliot Rosewater attempts unsuccessfully to do (*God Bless You, Mr. Rosewater* 36), Karabekian gives each person dignity and life through his great painting.

"In the land of the blind, the one-eyed man is king," runs the ancient proverb, and Karabekian, the one-eyed painter, becomes king in the blind land of art. With this last painting, this "last thing I have to give to the world," he discovers and fulfills his vocation as an artist, something he had been unable to do either as an Abstract Expressionist or as an illustrator. Karabekian thus finds his own answer to Thoreau's question of vocation and meaningful work. "Morning work! . . . what should be man's *morning work* in the world?" asked Thoreau in *Walden* (24). In painting *Now It Is the Women's Turn*, Karabekian finds his morning work to do. Confronting the murderous destructiveness of modern war, he compassionately transforms that blasted battlescape into an image of human hope. Now fully the painter, he grows satisfied in the sense that, ignoring the world, he becomes "intoxicated for hours[,] . . . days[,] . . . weeks[,] . . . years with what his . . . hands and eyes can do" (*Fates Worse Than Death* 47). Unlike his earlier work that allowed him "to ignore life utterly" (*Fates Worse Than Death* 44), his last monumental painting reflects his life-experience and feelings. It gives him peace, while eliciting positive responses from the common people who come to view it (*Bluebeard* 283). He thereby becomes an example of "the artist . . . functioning freely in relation to society, . . . society wants what he is able to offer" (Cahill 473). No longer does Karabekian have to browbeat his audience—whether a cocktail waitress in Midland City or one of his neighbors on Fire Island—into accepting what he has done as art.

Vonnegut advocates in *Bluebeard* that the true artist employ technique to serve human beings and their human feelings—whether it be putting paint on canvas or putting words on paper. He thereby aligns himself with painters, such as Adolph Gottlieb and Mark Rothko who challenged the "widely accepted notion among painters that it does not matter what one paints as long as it is well-painted. This is the essence of academism" (545). In an important statement printed in the column of the art critic, Edward Alden Jewell in *The New York Times* for 13 June 1943, they maintained as a positive alternative to "good painting about nothing" the proposition that "the subject is crucial and only subject-matter is valid which is tragic and timeless. . . . Consequently, if our work embodies these beliefs it must insult any one who is spiritually attuned to interior decoration; pictures for the home" (545).

In the end, Karabekian serves humanity not by providing it with more interior or exterior decoration but by depicting a "crucial [subject] . . . which is tragic and timeless." In so doing, he stands out in bold relief against the pale shadow of Dan Gregory who, during his whole professional life, remained merely a "decorator" despite his talent and enormous popular success. Like the notorious Andy Warhol, who "put an ad in *The Village Voice* saying he would endorse anything, anything at all, for money . . . and listing his telephone number" (Tom Wolfe 86), Gregory wields a brush available for hire; he is ready and able to illustrate or reproduce anything at all for anyone at all for money. In contrast, Karabekian, rather than merely illustrating someone else's idea or feeling, creates something genuine based on his own feeling and experience that reveals what James Joyce termed "the simple intuitions which are the tests of reality" (81). His last painting includes all life after the war: the lunatics, war prisoners, concentration camp victims, ragged remnants of an exhausted army, and civilians—the dead, dying, and living. "In Bluebeard's secret chamber is death; in Rabo's, a painting that depicts life and death, the survivors of a six-year nightmare of bloodletting caused by people who make Bluebeard look like Mr. Rogers," comments David Rampton (22). The emphasis in Karabekian's huge painting falls on all humanity gathered together as the sun comes up after the disaster—"a fair field full of folk," as Piers the Plowman said—rather than on the world worn out by war. Rampton points to the parallels between Karabekian's work and that of the fifteenth-century Florentine painter, Paolo Uccello:

Rabo Karabekian, Uccello's modern counterpart, does not paint a Flood or a Resurrection; he paints the survivors of a human disaster, a group representing all humanity, menaced by the cataclysmic events of World War II. His work, like Uccello's, is made up of an extraordinary number of scrupulously observed figures: old men and young, women and children, some clothed, some naked, most living, some dead, portrayed against a natural background. The self-destructive properties of Uccello's materials have left "The Flood" in a very poor state of repair. The decay of Rabo's materials leaves him with what is quite literally a *tabula rasa*, a canvas on which he can achieve in mimetic art what he could not as an abstract expressionist. (20)

Ohio painter and retired professor of art, Cliff McCarthy—who also crops up as a minor character in *Deadeye Dick* providing the means by which the Waltzes discover their house is radioactive (xi, 221–22)—went in search of what he calls Vonnegut's "real world" models among the paintings of New York Abstract Expressionists.

Rabo Karabekian's *Temptation of St. Anthony* . . . resembles a painting by a real world abstract expressionist, Barnett Newman. *Midnight Blue*, which Newman painted in 1970, the last year of his life, is an overall dark, royal blue. It contrasts sharply in color with *St. Anthony*, which is *Hawaiian Avocado*, a warm green, but compositionally, they are remarkably similar. Rabo has placed his vertical strip of orange tape on the left of his canvas while Newman's single stripe of light cerulean blue is located on the right; merely a detail of preference, I presume. (167)

But while Newman and Karabekian's paintings do bear a compositional resemblance, their elements vary in crucial ways. The similarities between the two canvases include their being painted in only one color with one vertical strip of a second color imposed over the field. Yet, the two contrast both in their choice of colors and in the placement and nature of their respective strips. The only detail in each canvas interrupting the solid color is that strip—one painted and the other made of tape. Given the limited elements involved in each painting's composition and the location of each strip on its respective canvas, some importance may attach to their being not on the same but on opposite sides of the painting. The two strips would, of course, appear on exactly the same side of each painting if one the paintings were to be hung upside down, but would that reversal also be "merely a detail of preference?" Apparently Vonnegut does not think so: "This Side Up" he suggests is a good motto for humans and for paintings (*Fates Worse Than Death* 45).[25]

Nor is Karabekian modeled on Dan Flavin for whom both McCarthy and Edward A. Kopper, Jr. attempt to make a case.[26] Surely it is no mere "detail of preference" that the Flavin composition, *the nominal three* that Kopper prefers as Vonnegut's model, consists not of one vertical neon tube but of six. Moreover, Flavin uses no "canvas or a panel of any kind to mount his neon tubes" (Auping 149–50 cited in McCarthy 171), whereas Karabekian employs one and one only vertical strip of Day-Glo orange reflecting tape rather than a neon tube (*Breakfast of Champions* 208). Plus the size and proportion of the two compositions vary greatly: Karabekian's *Temptation of St. Anthony* is a rectangle sixteen feet high and twenty feet wide (208), whereas Flavin's composition is a square with eight feet on each side. Flavin's work may well be, as McCarthy claims, "a twentieth-century art and technological miracle," but Karabekian's *Windsor Blue Number Seventeen* is not. Rather than a miracle of art or technology, the latter remains synonymous with "fiasco"—the kind of fiasco "in which a person causes total destruction of his own work and reputation through stupidity, carelessness or both" (*Bluebeard* 258). Part of the joy of *Now It's the Women's Turn* derives from Karabekian turning this stunning defeat into victory, this debacle into creativity, by using exactly the same canvas, that earlier was the occasion of his famous fiasco.[27]

In his vast painting, the sun shines on the first day without war in Europe, the first day of what could possibly be a new era "with hopeful people 'standing on the rim of a beautiful green valley in the springtime' " (Mustazza, *Genesis* 192). Historically, Vonnegut's own experience in the "Happy Valley" was not the one imagined and pictured in Karabekian's painting. While Karabekian made up all of the stories for the 5,219 figures on the canvas including the improbable Japanese soldier with his sword, Vonnegut being actually there, along with his buddy O'Hare confined himself to what he observed (*Fates Worse Than Death* 171). He writes in the appendix to *Fates Worse Than Death*, how in *Bluebeard* he pictured that valley "being stripped of everything edible . . . by liberated prisoners of war[,] . . . convicts, lunatics, concentration camp victims, . . . slave laborers, and . . . armed German soldiers" (217). But this locust plague suggests a continuation of the way things were and are, whereas the "Happy Valley" in Karabekian's painting suggests the way they should be—as does the title, *Now It's the Women's Turn*. For among other things, this title intimates that perhaps women will manage the affairs of the world better than men have thus far. Moreover, the painting is not just Vonnegut's rethinking, reorienting the scene in the Happy Valley; it is Karabekian's. When in Italy, Karabekian tells Marilee, "the coal miner's daughter" what that day was like when the war ended.[28] It is a full description of events and people brought back from the past at the end of World War II into the present by way of memory as he talks with Marilee, Countess Portomaggiore (226–28). But this conversation by itself does not lead to his beginning to paint this subject. The actual painting lay some years in the future, after Karabekian reclaimed his *Windsor Blue Number Seventeen*—"the largest painting in New York City" and perhaps the largest painting in the world (262)—after the disaster of the disappearing paint. He then had the blank canvas restretched and resized leaving it a dazzling white (263). Only after his second wife, Edith, dies does he create his last and greatest painting, which takes him six months working nonstop (265–66). Thus a seemingly unrelated event in the present, the death of his much-loved wife, triggers both the memory of the day the war ended in Europe and the desire once again to paint—a desire strong enough to overcome the inertia caused by the Sateen Dura Luxe fiasco. Psychologists studying the brain agree that part of what creates memory is an emotional stimulus. Complex recreations of past events in the present through memory, in fact, require some sort of emotional trigger. The more powerful the memory, the more potent must be the trigger.[29] Hence it took the death of Karabekian's wife to trigger the most powerful of all his memories—that of the day the war ended.

In Greek mythology, memory is the mother of the nine muses; that is, memory is the essential activity necessary for all the arts from theology to dance to history to painting to epic poetry. Without memory, no art can exist or be practiced. With memory all arts, including painting, become possible. (It could be said of Dan Gregory, the taxidermist, that remembering nothing, he must paint illustrations of other people's memories.) Karabekian's memory of the day World War II ended in the Happy Valley thus becomes the basis *but only the basis* for his great panoramic painting, the rest, equally essential for the creation of his art, comes from imagination and talent. "Art does not reproduce the visible. Rather, it makes visible," declared Paul Klee (5). Karabekian's night of loss and death thus turns into his day of creation and life. But the realization of that vision, the working out of all the myriad of details necessary for this huge panoramic painting with its cast of thousands requires hard and difficult work continuously for six months. Once finished, Karabekian can lock the barn and walk away knowing the secret that is inside, not Bluebeard's night of death— that great *No* of corpses, but his own great *Yes*. From that moment on his identity becomes synonymous with the barn and—like Bluebeard—with whatever secret it holds. No wonder he refuses to open the door—not even for colossal sums of money.

Like *Slaughterhouse-Five*, *Bluebeard* concludes with a vision of accepting life as it is after having "come face to face with the most horrific truths about humanity's potential for cruelty" (Rampton 23). But such accepting of life as it is must include accepting "that you have looked into the heart of something that is quintessentially meaningless" (Rampton 23). As David Rampton cogently argues: "The impact of such a vision will be profound, but to attempt to build a series of conceptual arguments on it or to countenance explanations of it would be like trying to get light from a black hole" (23). Neither *Slaughterhouse-Five* nor *Bluebeard* constructs a logical argument or even attempts to convince the reader that the protagonist's final vision is correct or good: it simply is what it is. In Wallace Stevens's words it becomes "a speech of the self" ("The Well Dressed Man with a Beard"). There is, however, a profound, significant distinction to be drawn between the visions embodied in these two very different novels. If *Slaughterhouse-Five* left the reader with Billy Pilgrim's vision of Tralfamadorian serenity—which, by definition, must remain extra-terrestrial and therefore unattainable by human beings—*Bluebeard* ends with a picture of the acceptance of human limits, whether of artists, oneself, friends, or parents. Nor is Karabekian a ghost in the rigging, like Leon Trout in *Galápagos*, condemned to spend a million years in the Sisyphusean task of recording on air his observations of human beings evolving back to the sea. Instead, Karabekian achieves his vocation as an artist, as one who creates a rich portrait of human hope to which others respond enthusiastically.[30]

Through Rabo Karabekian's triumph, Vonnegut celebrates human creatively, friendship, and community without which, as shown in *Galápagos*, these great big brains would be left on their own to become the ultimate threat to the survival of humanity, of all life, and of the very planet itself. "There may be nothing to say about things as monstrous as wars and massacres, but if the creative artist is to say anything, he must adapt whatever rules are available and use what talent he has to make something happen on canvas" (Rampton 21). And that is exactly what Karabekian has done to his great joy. At the end of *Bluebeard*, as at the end of so many other Vonnegut novels where the protagonist dies or is about to die, Karabekian dies but unlike other Vonnegut heroes, he ends life happily and at peace with himself as he celebrates his life and genuine accomplishments. He says of himself with all his heart: "Oh, happy Meat. Oh, happy Soul. Oh, happy Rabo Karabekian" (287). In so doing he becomes the fully imagined American as artist.

THE PARABLE OF THE STALLED ELEVATOR

> How embarrassing to be human.
> —Eugene Debs Hartke

The process of imagining being an American, a citizen of the most powerful and one of the largest and richest nations on Earth, rarely, if ever, includes the prospect of defeat, especially at the hands of one of the world's smallest, poorest, and weakest nations. Similarly, the process of imagining being an American usually includes all that America has promised in democracy, equality, and freedom. Only rarely does it include the often-rampant racism, the selling of the country's resources, or the incarcerating of more citizens per capita than any other country in the world, except Haiti and South Africa.[31] What are the implications for being an American in the conduct and subsequent loss of the Vietnam War? What happened to the promise that was America? And, asks Vonnegut, what happened to the country's social conscience embodied in, among others, Eugene Victor Debs (1855–1926) and his justly famous epitaph: "While there is a lower class I am in it. While there is a criminal element I am of it. While there is a soul in prison I am not free." Debs ran for president four times and in 1912 received close to a million votes.[32] Debs advocated and worked for a society composed of poverty-free, politically free and equal individuals, with well-maintained institutions that would, for instance, prevent youngsters from becoming criminals by giving them hope through the prospect of genuine economic and social equality. Looking back from the end of the twentieth century, Debs's dream of such a just society appears to have died with him in 1922.

Hocus Pocus records a similar death of a dream in the generous legacy establishing what will become Tarkington College. That legacy stipulated the creation of a free institution of higher education for all the children of that Finger Lake Valley—one to rival Harvard. Yet within a few short years the terms of the legacy would be first violated then ignored. This briefly free institution for local students quickly became a fee-paying college for the learning-disabled children of the rich from across the country.[33] So much for Debs's ideals of addressing the needs of "the lower class" or the goal of the legacy establishing Tarkington College to provide free education for the needy. The needs of the rich come first, since they are the ones with the power not only over educational institutions, such as Tarkington College, but also over social and political ones as well. "I think any form of government, not just Capitalism, is whatever the people who have all our money, drunk or sober, sane or insane, decide to do today," concludes Eugene Debs Hartke, the narrator of *Hocus Pocus* (242–43).

Named ironically for the great social reformer, Eugene Debs and for Indiana Senator, Vance Hartke,[34] "Hartke is a graduate of West Point and a veteran of the Vietnam War, a thoughtful but not tormented man who killed many human beings on the orders of the Government and dispensed many official lies as an information officer" (McInerney 309). He also learned first hand that war is meaningless butchery of ordinary people like himself. Like Howard Campbell and Walter Starbuck, Hartke writes his book in prison.[35] Another of Vonnegut's single-book authors, he questions the sanity of his time. Were not those in charge of Vietnam, for instance, a little like the governor and his wife in the second part of *Don Quixote*, that is, people so caught up in their illusions derived from fiction that they produced fake events for real people to participate in, rather than for actors on stage or television to act out?[36] Hartke, like the Knight of the Woeful Countenance, became the victim of someone else's script, spoke someone else's lines, while encouraging himself in a futile enterprise. "I was a genius of lethal hocus pocus!" he exclaims (154). Like Eliot Rosewater, Walter Starbuck, and Dr. Wilbur Swain, Hartke wanted to help his fellow humans through a life of service. His first choice of a career was journalism, but he ended up at West Point training to be a professional soldier. During that career, he kills dozens and dozens of his fellow humans—all quite legally, as he repeatedly points out. Some of those killings were regrettable, others shameful. Regrettable was the incident where Hartke tossed a hand grenade down a tunnel killing "a woman, her mother, and her baby hiding from helicopter gunships which had strafed her village. . . . Unforgettable" (252). (The incident is similar to Eliot Rosewater's killing of the unarmed firemen in World War II.) His action is, of course, unintentional, if unforgettable.[37]

Hartke's most shameful act committed while in uniform may also be unforgettable but it is clearly dishonorable because it is intentional. The last American in the last helicopter to leave the roof of the United States embassy in Saigon, Hartke makes it clear that all the Vietnamese on or near that roof were friends, not enemies.[38] His job, as he describes it, was "to keep Vietnamese *who had been on our side* from getting into helicopters that were [for] . . . Americans only" (52 emphasis added). And therein lies the double disgrace: not only were the Americans—of which he is the most prominent—leaving having been beaten, but they were abandoning their allies to imprisonment and possible death. "His final soldierly act" cannot, therefore, be described, as one critic does, as "not militant but merciful—the rescue of American personnel from the rooftop of the United States Embassy in Saigon" (Broer, "Heroes" 189). No American personnel, including Hartke, were in any danger and none needed rescuing. "The enemy could have shot down the helicopters and come up and captured or killed us, if they had wanted. But all they had ever wanted from us was that we go home," he reports (*Hocus Pocus* 52). The Vietnamese, on the other hand, those that Hartke prevented from getting on a helicopter met certain imprisonment and/or death. This last unenviable, but highly symbolic act, performed under orders, cost him his self-respect, he confesses, and led to his loss of faith in his country's leadership.

In his second career as a teacher at Tarkington College, a student informer betrays him, castigating him as an unfeeling cynic. A self-serving, ignorant, and arrogant board of trustees then fires him for having an affair with the wife of the college president. Crossing the Finger Lake Valley where the school is situated, he becomes a teacher of prisoners in the maximum-security prison, Athena.[39] When a massive prison break occurs, Hartke stands accused by racist authorities of masterminding the escape since, they reason fallaciously, in an all-black prison no inmate could possibly engineer, much less carry out, such a complicated break.[40] In Vietnam as an officer, Hartke dealt with a preponderance of black soldiers, so it may be ironically appropriate that he be accused of leading a black prison break. "Vonnegut's criminal narrators may be guilty of much, but they are typically innocent of the crime for which they are charged" maintains John Irving ("Vonnegut in Prison" 10): And Hartke is no exception to this rule.

From his earliest childhood, Hartke has had no illusions about anything from his parents and his relationship to them, his abilities and talents, to his freedom to choose or not to choose. It becomes, therefore, most appropriate that, almost as a pawn of fate, he should go to West Point and conclude his military career in Vietnam. If Eugene Debs identified with the outcast, the down and out, the lower classes, the jailed, Hartke does not. "I have no reforms to propose," he reiterates (242). Furthermore, he goes to jail, not because of sympathy toward those already incarcerated, but because of the white racism of those in authority. If Eugene Debs at the beginning of the twentieth century was an exponent of the Sermon on the Mount, Eugene Debs Hartke at the end of that century becomes an exponent of getting along by going along. He is not a man tormented by his conscience, though he has killed close to a hundred people. One of his defenses becomes listing both those he killed and those to whom he made love. "Quantification becomes the latest escape valve discovered by a Vonnegut narrator from a condition too troublesome for him to confront," claims Bill Mistichelli (322). "I could not love thee half so much loved I not honor more," intoned the Cavalier poet, but for Hartke life offers neither love nor honor but, instead, adulterous affairs and sanctioned killings.

Hartke proves a prime example of Kathryn Hume's teflon coated character whose emotions, if any lie buried beneath an impervious surface. Neither in adultery nor in killing does he evince any feeling or involvement. No conviction ever guides Hartke in any choice he makes for rarely, if ever, does he actually make choices himself, but rather follows those detours that present themselves. For example, he establishes and maintains a home for not one but two insane women, his wife and his mother-in-law—a difficult, compassionate act involving a considerable commitment of time, money, and energy. One day when he is not home, the authorities forcibly remove both women and incarcerate them in a public asylum without consulting him. His technique for surviving this and numerous other emotionally wrenching experiences is to appear laconically indifferent—in this instance, indifferent to the violence done to his wife and mother-in-law as well as to the sanctity of his home. Thus we have a compassionate act—providing a safe, congenial environment for two insane people—done without complaint or whining followed by almost brutal indifference to their sudden disappearance from his life. Like Walter Starbuck in *Jailbird*, whose prose style resembles his, Hartke appears capable of singing but only in a minor key and then only within a most limited range. Typically, readers appear to be left without authorial guidance here and elsewhere in *Hocus Pocus*—left to evaluate ethical issues of character, action, and value within an unresolved, opaque moral situation. The same cannot be said for social issues, however.

Vonnegut satirizes the extensive and increasing foreign ownership of American enterprise—a subject of considerable concern to many contemporary social critics of American values and economics. For instance, Robert Kuttner, economics correspondent for the *New Republic*, praises Martin and Susan Tolchin for providing "a comprehensive guide to . . . foreign penetration in their well documented and deftly written *Buying into America: How Foreign Money Is Changing the Face of Our Nation*" (9). What alarms the Tolchins, Kuttner, and Vonnegut in *Hocus Pocus* is that in less than fifteen years foreign investment in the United States increased over six times, soaring from $200 billion in 1974 to $1.3 trillion in 1987. Foreign purchases included banks, real estate, and failing American corporations. The Tolchins contend that this increase results in a disproportionately large foreign investment, one that threatens both the national interest and the national identity.[41] Kuttner agrees: "These [the facts] the authors have provided in abundance, precisely and persuasively" (9). As so often in his works, Vonnegut takes an economic or social analysis, such as this one, and satirically extrapolates the data into the new millennium.

In addition to economics, Vonnegut focuses on two related social issues: the neglect of society's real needs and the privatization of social services. The example of the Athena prison in *Hocus Pocus* contracted to a private Japanese firm to manage proved all too prophetic. The results, as played out in the novel, are as disastrous as they were predictable. Vonnegut's criticism of such and similar schemes to privatize public institutions and services, especially prisons, is particularly pertinent as several states' legislatures and/or governors advocate contracting out their prison service, school systems, hospitals, and welfare services, as if society had no responsibility for these institutions other than their financing. In *Hocus Pocus*, Japanese businesspeople run prisons and hospitals, although "they were smart enough to pass on our inner city schools" (Leonard 305).[42] The breakdown of social organizations and values, increases in personal danger, and the reversal of social achievements are also targeted for Vonnegut's criticism, besides excessive foreign ownership and society's neglect of its responsibilities and institutions, and the reintroduction of vicious racism.

"Ultimately," contends Mistichelli, "the success of *Hocus Pocus* is that it fails to resolve the questions and issues it poses" (322). But such irresolution appears to other, more hostile readers as Vonnegut's failure of nerve as author or, worse, his indifference to moral values or, still worse, his inattention to important fictional techniques. One prominent reviewer announced at the beginning of his omnibus review of recent fiction in a prestigious journal that "with one exception, unless a book took seed and flourished in the imagination, I have chosen not to review it. . . . The exception has been made because it is a work by a greatly admired American writer, even a cult figure, whose garden . . . has become an overworked and arid little patch" (Philips 133). Seeing himself as an agent of the public good, the white knight of book reviewers, he proceeds to dismiss *Hocus Pocus* as "almost totally devoid of some standard ingredients of fiction" (135), rather than see Vonnegut's not relying on "dialogue, form, confrontation, coherent plot" as innovative and, perhaps, even daring. Similarly, he refuses to see irony, even where it is obvious, as in Hartke's declaring "There is still so much we have to learn about TV!" (*Hocus Pocus* 57).[43] And he simply misreads the novel when he claims that Hartke and through him Vonnegut "disparages rich kids, Japanese entrepreneurs and all prosperous foreigners, optimists, and people who are mentally ill" (135).

Finally, in his haste to criticize, this reviewer neglects completely Hartke's service as a professional soldier in Vietnam, which becomes the vehicle for so much of Vonnegut's criticism of that misguided adventure. He also declines to allow Hartke his role as an idiosyncratic, first time book writer who, like so many writers in prison, must use whatever odds and ends of paper may come to hand but ridicules Vonnegut for dividing pages into sections to represent these often small bits: "The narrator did not have access to uniform writing paper, see? The writer, locked up in a library and facing trial, was desperate [sic] to express himself. . . . The snippet technique soon begins to wear" (Phillips 135). Perhaps it does—clearly it did within a few pages for the reviewer and yet those dividing lines do serve to remind readers that this book is being written in jail. It was on just such snippets of paper in 1963—actually on the edges of pages of *The New York Times*—that Martin Luther King, Jr. wrote his *Letter from Birmingham Jail*, his prophetic call to resist and end racism in America. *Hocus Pocus*, read in its entirety, also proves a ringing denunciation of both the Vietnam debacle and American racism. Hartke's story also typifies many prison narratives in its tentative nature. He probably started writing "impulsively, having no idea it would become a book, scribbling words on a scrap which happened to be right at hand," says the unnamed editor of *Hocus Pocus* (vii). If Rabelais built his language cairns by piling one extravagant instance on top of another until the whole work tumbled over under its own weight, Vonnegut in *Hocus Pocus* prefers to build his one small stone or piece of paper at a time over several hundred pages until there is a sizable pile whose stability the novel tests. Rather than analyze the effect of this technique, some reviewers too simply and too derisively dismissed it (see, for example, Phillips 135).

Hostility and an ill-concealed posture of superiority typify the negative half-digested reactions masquerading as serious book reviews that Vonnegut has had to endure throughout his career. This is particularly true when a reviewer admits in the course of a review that he had already determined not to like or approve of *any* new novel from "a cult figure['s] . . . overworked and arid little patch" even *before he read it* (Phillips 133). Although this specific reviewer expects a reader to empathize with his own plight as an overworked reviewer who must read "through the cartons of fiction submitted for this chronicle" (133), few will sympathize with his deliberately choosing to review a book that he knows he will not like by an author with whom he is out of sympathy. C. S. Lewis years ago warned against choosing to review books with which a person had no empathy since the task must, of necessity, be odious, the results a foregone conclusion, and the review inevitably dishonest. In contrast, Vonnegut's fellow novelists, Jay McInerney and John Irving, who do empathize with his work, conclude in their reviews that *Hocus Pocus* may be "the most richly detailed and textured of Mr. Vonnegut's renderings of this particular planet" (McInerney 311) and "as good as the best of his novels" (Irving, "Vonnegut in Prison" 10).

"American fiction since the sixties has been . . . particularly obsessed with its own past—literary, social, and historical. Perhaps this occupation is (or was) tied in part to a need to find a particularly American voice within a culturally dominant Eurocentric tradition" Linda Hutcheon contends (12). True, but this search for a unique American voice is as old as American literature. Even before Emerson proclaimed the coming of the American Scholar who would create a literature using American materials, subjects, and language, literature in the New World records its attempt to break free of European literary roots—exactly as the newly formed United States' in its politics and history attempted also to break free from European dominance. American Romanticism made this project an imperative. Looking back, we recognize the success of Emerson, Thoreau, Hawthorne, Melville, and Twain, as well as Dickinson and Whitman, both individually and collectively, in creating a distinctively American voice in literature. Vonnegut's fictional voice, clearly and distinctively American in cadence, vocabulary, subject, attitude, and focus, calls attention once again in *Hocus Pocus* to the American emphasis on the issue of means and ends so familiar from these classic nineteenth-century American writers. At the beginning of his career as a novelist (1952–1969), Vonnegut concentrated on the firebombing of Dresden, a horrendous act as means, but done for the purpose of "shortening the war" surely an exemplary end. Toward the last phase of his career (1973–1990), he focuses on Vietnam as means, a series of horrendous acts done also for an exemplary end—to save "democracy and freedom" in Southeast Asia and to prevent other countries from succumbing to communism like so many dominoes toppling down.[44] As Billy Pilgrim symbolizes the innocent child playing at war, which Vonnegut submits characterizes World War II soldiers, so Eugene Debs Hartke symbolizes the disgraced adolescent playing at saving nations from themselves, which Vonnegut suggests characterized American policymakers in Vietnam.[45] Morally and politically bankrupt, the Vietnam War "was about nothing but the ammunition business" (*Hocus Pocus* 2).

Stories of defeat, such as the United States in Vietnam, may not be good for morale, as Jason Wilder the hypocritical talk show host and Tarkington trustee in *Hocus Pocus* observes (126–27). But they do serve the far more important function of roughing up human pride, chastening mindless patriotism, and giving poor mortals a realistic perspective on themselves as individuals, on the human race in general, and on the planet they inhabit. Further, such stories form an integral part of American history and as such become crucial in imagining what it means to be an American. Washington Irving in "Rip Van Winkle" provided one of the clearest examples in American fiction of the negative effects of ignoring history. Through the character of Rip, Irving's story "explores what it means for a society to close its eyes to history, to sleep through the historical moments that transform reality, and to live as if history were only a fiction narrated from afar" (Budick 302). The Tarkington trustees are themselves people who choose to sleep through the historical moments that transform reality. Rather than acknowledge either their own unimportance or their country's defeat, they, like Rip, close their eyes to history in favor of punishing the messenger who brings the news, thus sending Hartke off on a new tangent as prison teacher.[46]

Hartke's life itself may be viewed as a series of detours caused by others, as in this last phase of teaching in Athena Prison. As an adolescent, for instance, he wanted to go to the University of Michigan and become a journalist. Instead, he went to West Point and became a soldier. As an adult, he wanted to teach the young for which he had some real talent. Instead, he was fired from Tarkington for cynicism and began teaching adults in prison. As someone once said, "Life is what happens while you're making other plans." Hartke's marriage also develops a huge detour since he, in effect, married a time bomb, a woman who carries within her the destructive genes of insanity, as did her mother before her. (In order to marry at all, his future wife had to leave her hometown and move to a place where no one knew either herself or her family with its reputation for inherited insanity.) Their two children, once they learn of their terrible legacy, escape from home leaving behind no forwarding address. "What a metaphor," exclaims John Irving ("Vonnegut in Prison" 10). With this one metaphor, Vonnegut captures the plight of person, country, and planet in the late twentieth century. What could be more demented than to transmit congenital insanity to innocent children, or to subvert American values in the name of education, or to destroy the Earth because we would not spend the money to clean up pollution, or make the sacrifices necessary to save the planet from devastation (*Hocus Pocus* 143). What the Hartke family, the United States, and Earth itself have in common is precisely that time bomb buried deep within, ticking away. It is only a matter of time before insanity catches up with the United States and the Earth—*if* it has not already done so—exactly as it caught up with the Hartkes.

As the end of the twentieth century approached and the United States awaited the new millennium, it became clear in Vonnegut's fiction, especially in *Hocus Pocus*, that Mars was in the ascendant—Mars, the God of War not Venus, the Goddess of Love, ruled human affairs. After he dies, Hartke wishes to have engraved on his tombstone "a number that represents both my 100 percent-legal military kills and my adulteries" (322) and not, as one critic contends, "the names of the women he has loved" (Broer, "Heroes" 191).[47] Only the number. Nothing else. The number dedicated to Venus and the number dedicated to Mars since the number of his adulteries coincidentally matches exactly the number of people he killed legally in war. In both instances—making love or killing—Hartke evinces no feeling, no emotion, no involvement. His epitaph neglects completely to mention the poor, the criminals, or those imprisoned—all prominently mentioned in his namesake Eugene Debs's epitaph. But Eugene Debs had convictions by which he lived his life. No conviction ever guides Eugene Debs Hartke in any choice he makes for he rarely, if ever, actually makes choices himself, but rather follows detours. Events in *Hocus Pocus* appear to be controlled by "the worst [who] are full of passionate intensity." That "rough beast," once envisioned by W. B. Yeats, that famously "slouches toward Bethlehem to be born" in "The Second Coming" has already arrived in Vonnegut's world, as in Hartke's, and been all but ignored by a humankind preoccupied with its own petty problems.

At the beginning of the twentieth-first century, life on Earth resembles far more a Vonnegut novel than Stanley Kubrick's famous film of Arthur C. Clarke's novel *2001: A Space Odyssey*. In *2001*, despite HAL, the rogue computer, humans do arrive on Jupiter's moons where a warm welcome awaits them prepared by cosmic beings who have solved not only most of the problems preoccupying humans but also many of the problems that humans have not yet even begun to identify. On Earth the great achievement of putting a man on the moon came too close to mid-century to reignite the popular imagination at century's end. All the promise of space flight of going from the moon to Mars to the planets to the galaxy and beyond has withered under the loss of imagination, the loss of will, the loss of investment. (And the investment in manned flight would have had to be huge, as Vonnegut pointed out several times.) In much science fiction, the universe appears but a playground for humans beings as they carry their wars, phobias, and diseases out beyond the solar system, but in

Vonnegut's fiction humans are redirected to look again at themselves and their planet. What they will see, as succinctly described by Don Gifford, should give them pause:

Apart from the possibility of nuclear immolation of the Earth and human time, there are the extraordinary ways in which industrialized-consumerized humanity has, in its preoccupation with immediate gratification and immediate profit, hastened the processes of evolution: expending in days the solar energy that took millennia to store in the Earth's horde, destroying ecosystems in weeks that took an ice age to evolve, accelerating the processes of extinction with use-it-up technology and pollution, speeding the processes of mutation (and speciation) through radioactive contamination. (95)

Set in the millennial year 2001, *Hocus Pocus* presents Vonnegut's view of that new millennium's possibilities. If the novel predicts anything, it predicts that if people continue following that "complicated futility of ignorance" (14), then events, and humans in the new century, in the new millennium, will continue much as they did in the old. The result will not be progress toward enlightenment or toward the new heavenly city or toward a better life, but toward apocalypse. Unlike in either Arthur C. Clarke's or Stanley Kubrick's *2001*, humans will not travel to other parts of the universe nor will they receive help from some mysterious source outside themselves. In Vonnegut's universe, help is not on the way to Earth and, therefore, humans have to realize they are alone and must of necessity become their own best resource.

Eugene Debs died early in the twentieth century—a century that would become tyrannized by Hitler, Stalin, and a host of all-too-successful dictators. In the closing years of that century, approaching the year 2001, tired, worn out by wars, racism, and the breakdown of social services, and living on an endangered planet, Americans could yet reverse each of these disasters, if they had the will. Yet many Americans take a kind of perverse pride in being or remaining ignorant. "They act as though their ignorance somehow made them charming," remarks a character in *Hocus Pocus* (288). She echoed Emerson who, in the last century, described "the mind of this country, taught to aim at low objects" (70). This novel, like Emerson's oration, "The American Scholar," is Vonnegut's attempt to awaken his fellow countrymen to action and to possibilities that are fast disappearing. Although the national or even planetary elevator in the parable of Bruce Bergeron may stall, effective action could still be taken to get it going again and to take it down to reality away from the fantasy and distraction of a never-ending department store white sale. Progress, Vonnegut maintains, is but an illusion of motion going somewhere (*The Sirens of Titan*), a delusion of society advancing (*Deadeye Dick*), or a series of chimerical detours through life (*Hocus Pocus*). Therefore, if action is to be taken, it must be taken by ordinary, responsible people who, overcoming indifference and inertia leave the department store sale of irrelevancies to work together and help save the child and those stranded on that stalled elevator. No one from management will arrive to apologize for the inconvenience.

NOTES

1. Kroeber writes: "this inwardness distinguishes fantasy from its non-identical twin, science fiction. Science fiction also appears when the supernatural has been driven out of enlightened society" (1).

2. For a review of the more lasting apocalyptic, postnuclear holocaust disaster novels, see Dorris and Erdich.

3. Perhaps one of the strangest interpretations of this in utero virus belongs to Loree Rackstraw who construes "this modern plague" as "suggest[ing] that world literature, which unknowingly debilitates the feminine, may eventually be the death of us all" ("Dancing" 135).

4. A second powerful metaphor of that super brain, computer Mandarax with its storehouse of quotations perishes in the sea swallowed by a shark like so many of the human characters in *Galápagos*. The blind-feeding shark who eats both Mary "Mother Nature" Hepburn and Mandarax the computer—one nourishing and the other indigestible—creates a complex metaphor of nature's success in creating the shark who cleans the ocean environment of debris and of nature's blindness to the danger of humans and their machinery. Vonnegut in *Gálapagos* eliminated the indigestible machinery, but retained the nourishing humans in the far future creating a far better natural balance in the overall scheme of things.

5. Loree Rackshaw sees "the image of the Dresden column of flame . . . central to *Slaughterhouse-Five* and pivotal in *God Bless You, Mr. Rosewater* . . . transformed into the abstract painting by Rabo Karabekian as an image of 'awareness,' that which is sacred to all life" ("Dancing" 123).

6. Unlike Wolfe, Vonnegut provides an example of a positive, genuinely artistic achievement in Karabekian's last painting.

7. Probably the most famous of these imitation haiku is Ezra Pound's "In a Station of the Metro."

8. Vonnegut's timing, as always, is impeccable and worthy of, say, Jack Benny, the master of the deadpan double-take. Here, the sting in the tail of the trail-away remark lies in that seemingly offhand, almost forgotten addendum, "Or in Nagasaki, Japan." Gottcha! Kilgore Trout commenting on the bombing of Nagasaki put it somewhat more crudely but very effectively when he suggested that obliterating Nagasaki could no longer be termed war but was strictly "*show biz* " (*Timequake* 9). For an alternative view of the necessity of using the atomic bomb on Nagasaki in order to save lives, see Fussell "Thank God for the Atom Bomb."

9. In *Timequake*, Vonnegut retells a Kilgore Trout short story, "No Laughing Matter," in which the Japanese are referred to by a racial epithet. The ever-helpful narrator of the novel comments that in those bygone days: "The little yellow bastards were called 'little yellow bastards'" (8). The repeated appellation implies that successful attempts to dehumanize people necessarily precede massacres.

10. Mustazza astutely notes that "in *Galápagos* . . . Charles Darwin, whose work— both directly applied (evolution) and as it has been spuriously interpreted (Social Darwinism)—informs Vonnegut's imaginative vision of the novel" ("Darwinian Eden" 279). See Mustazza's essay for an extensive discussion of Darwin's work and *Galápagos*.

11. Contrast Peter Høeg's fantasy, *The Woman and the Ape* (1996), which cleverly reverses current evolutionary assumptions that humans evolved from apes. In that novel a doctor says to a newly discovered specie of ape, "your ancestors, your race, after breaking away from us a million years ago on the shores of Lake Turkana, traveled northwards. And after that you outstripped us. We had it all wrong. . . We thought we

would learn something about one of those hominids which came before man. But you are not what went before. You are, rather what comes afterwards" (209).

12. For a negative view of such values, see Jackson (especially 141–56); and Hume, *Fantasy* (especially 28–38 and 127–29).

13. Kathryn Hume notes that "rarely do you see questioned within science fiction the assumption that a higher-tech society is better than a lower one" ("Postmodernism" 182).

14. Vonnegut has said that the model for his evolutionary changes are the tortoises who have survived on the Galápagos Islands and in Sumatra because the rodents that ate their eggs did not exist in either place. He concludes: "so these great big impractical animals still exist there and nowhere else" ("Skull Session" 251).

15. One critic unaccountably claims that Trout must narrate the story because "only . . . as a ghost who is arrested in the developmental stage of 1986, . . . [and] does not join in the mutation he is so pleased about, can he tell us about it" (Freese, "Surviving" 169). But this comment misses the point that in trying to write this novel Trout, the disembodied ghost, faces a far worse problem than even those seal-like creatures of a million years in the future would, should they attempt to write a novel. He must write as a ghost without even flippers to write with and with nothing to write on and with no one to write for. The moving nonexistent index finger writes and moves on.

16. In commenting on the narrator, Freese makes the point that *Galápagos* is "an intricate epistemological joke . . . a verbal game built on the premise of its very impossibility" ("Surviving" 170). But his assessment ignores the fact that many, if not most, science-fiction works are similarly built on the premise of their own impossibility. Yet such works are viewed neither as intricate epistemological jokes nor as verbal games. For instance, an alternative history, such as Philip K. Dick, *The Man in the High Castle* (1962) or a time travel tale into the past, such as George Gaylord Simpson, *The Dechronization of Sam Magrauder* (1996), are on the face of it impossible. "Built on the premise of [their] very impossibility," the history which they rewrite or which their characters become part of has by definition already happened and, therefore, cannot possibly be rewritten or, in these instances, even written.

17. Perhaps the most famous posthumous narrator is Brás Cubas who tells his story from beyond the grave in *The Posthumous Memoirs of Brás Cubas* by the Brazilian nineteenth-century author Machado de Assis. But Machado's author confines his narrative to his own personal biography rather than tell a story such as Trout's of a million-year history of all humankind.

18. Compare with Rabo Karabekian's disappearing paintings that might as well have been painted with tap water (*Bluebeard*) or Kilgore Trout's inability to find any writing implement in *Breakfast of Champions* (67).

19 Vonnegut toys with his reader here in much the same way that Laurence Sterne did in his novels by first raising the reader's expectations and then deliberately thwarting them.

20. For a slightly more pessimistic reading of the novel, see Berryman, "Vonnegut and Evolution" (especially 188 and 198).

21. Adolph Gottlieb and Mark Rothko, responding to Edward Alden Jewell, *The New York Times* art critic's criticism of their paintings, forcefully maintained that "There is no such thing as good painting about nothing" (545).

22. Although grouping some of the moderns with the Great Masters may appear either strained or pure errant nonsense, depending upon one's view of the moderns, at least one serious art critic lumped them all together—or, rather, in his inelegant prose, he "tossed [them] into one pot." "The pictures of de Kooning and Kline, it seemed to me, were suddenly tossed into one pot with Rembrandt and Giotto. All alike became painters of illusion" (Leo Steinburg quoted in Tom Wolfe 79).

23. Jacket blurb written and signed by Vonnegut, April 1, 1987, for the hardcover edition of *Bluebeard* and reproduced as an "Author's Note" in the paperback edition (n.p.).

24. The trade name of the disappearing paint changes from *Breakfast of Champions* to *Bluebeard* as casually as the names of characters shift between and among Vonnegut's stories and novels. Vonnegut says several times that such changes have no significance. See, for example: "Two Conversations" (203–204); but for a contrasting view see Hume, "Heraclitean Cosmos."

25. McCarthy's description of both Karabekian (1916–1988) and Newman (1905–1970), while meant to identify them, actually serves to illustrate how different they remain. "If Karabekian had been a successful husband, if he had been Jewish rather than of that tragic clan from Armenia, and if he had never drawn a recognizable image in his born days, his status as a Barnett Newman clone would have been established. But that was not to be" (168). There simply are too many conditional clauses in McCarthy's description to make it convincing. (Also, as McCarthy himself points out, Karabekian is not modeled on the Armenian Abstract Expressionist, Vosdanik Adoian who took the name, Arshile Gorky [168–69].) Rather than Newman's life, Newman's paintings may well have been Vonnegut's model for Karabekian's, especially those painted after January 29, 1948 when Newman invented his famous zip using masking tape. For example, according a descriptive note for *Adam* 1951–1952 purchased by the Tate Museum in London in 1968: "From the mid-1940s Newman had been preoccupied with the Jewish myth of Creation. The vertical strips in his paintings may relate to certain traditions that present God and man as a single beam of light" That "single beam" becomes an "unwavering band of light" in *Breakfast of Champions*—"the immaterial core of every animal," according to Karabekian (221). Yet there does appear an important difference between Newman's paintings and Karabekian's: *Adam*, for instance, utilizes a dark ochre background with two *painted* strips of vertical red (paint over masking tape) as is true of all Newman's paintings whereas Karabekian's *The Temptation of St. Anthony* is mixed media—paint and perishable *colored* tape.

26. Kopper confesses that "Vonnegut does not mention him [Flavin] among the fourteen actual artists who appear in the novel" (583), but silence appears to grant a license to hunt in this instance. (Vonnegut does, of course, mention Jackson Pollock, his avowed model for Karabekian, several times in *Bluebeard*.) Basing his discussion on a critical work that appeared in 1987—the same year as *Bluebeard* and some fourteen years after the publication of *Breakfast of Champions* thus virtually eliminating any possibility of Vonnegut's seeing or reading it before or while writing either novel—Kopper educes significant parallels between Karabekian's *Temptation of St. Anthony* and Flavin's *Diagonal of May 25, 1963* where "we find ourselves staring at a large expanse of wall which supports a single glowing fluorescent tube" (Michael Auping, ed. *Abstract Expressionism: The Critical Development* [1987], 149 quoted in Kopper 584). So far there is a parallel, but Kopper ventures on thin critical ice when he shifts his discussion to *Now It's the Women's Turn*: "The length of the neon tubes in *the nominal three* [a second Flavin composition] is also eight feet, the same length (or height) as the panels in *Now It's the Women's Turn*" (584). But the proportions are quite different since Flavin's composition is a symmetrical rectangle eight by about 10.3 whereas Karabekian's eight panels of 8-x-8-foot squares form a symmetrical rectangle 16 x 32 feet rather than 16 x 20.6—or is this another "detail of preference?" The proportions of Flavin's "*the nominal three (to William of Ockham)*" (8 x 10.3) and Karabekian's *The Temptation of St. Anthony* (16 x 20) are, however, very close. Kopper gives an incorrect size for Karabekian's huge painting, reducing it to a mere "512-square inch [sic] painting" (583).

But *Now It's the Women's Turn* measures 512 square *feet* (*Bluebeard* 259)—a significant difference surely.

27. McCarthy appears to forget that Karabekian is not a New York Abstract Expressionist painter, but a fictional character the details of whose life may well have been suggested to Vonnegut by one or several of the New York Abstract Expressionists (see *Fates Worse Than Death* 41–48). Karabekian does, however, share at least one important characteristic with Jackson Pollock. According to Vonnegut, Pollock was the presiding genius over making the United States and "especially New York City, the unchallenged center of innovative painting in . . . [the] world" (*Fates Worse Than Death* 41). Although he spent much of his life dripping paint onto canvas, Vonnegut emphasizes that, like Karabekian, Pollock could portray "in photographic detail" any scene desired. Pollock's teacher had been Thomas Hart Benton (42). (See also Cotter, especially B7.) If it is absolutely necessary to conjure up an actual model for Karabekian's painting then a likely candidate could be Newman's *Adam* 1951–1952 (see n28; Tate Museum 1968 purchase.)

28. The phrase, "a coal miner's daughter" was made popular by Loretta Lynn from Butcher Hollow, Kentucky, especially through her country and western recording and by the film of her life, *Coal Miner's Daughter*. Vonnegut has on occasion confessed to a partiality for Country and Western music (*Palm Sunday* 151–55).

29. See, for example, the extensive discussion of emotion and memory in Rosenfield who claims on the basis of recent research that "[e]motions are essential for creating and categorizing memories" (169).

30. Rampton notes that "Vonnegut's artist implicitly turns his back on the entire movement in modernist art criticism, from Clive Bell to Herbert Read to Mark Rothko, which systematically and inexorably rejected both the narrative and representational dimensions of visual art as irrelevant" (21).

31. *Hocus Pocus* focuses on a continuing and unacknowledged problem in American society that results from a rising rate of increasing incarceration without a comparable increase in crime. Rodger Doyle begins his essay in the *Scientific American* on "Why Do Prisons Grow?" with two conflicting statistics: "The U.S. has gone through a historically unparalleled expansion in its prison population—from fewer than 400,000 in 1970 to almost 2.1 million in 2000. The expansion continued vigorously even as crime rates fell sharply in recent years" (18). This results in, what Doyle terms, "profoundly disrupted minority communities" since "the Bureau of Justice Statistics estimates that 28 percent of black and 16 percent of Hispanic men will enter a state or federal prison during their lifetime" as opposed to only 4 percent of white men (18).

32. Debs's votes were, according to Daniel Bell, cast by "as unstable a compound as was ever mixed in modern history of political chemistry." This compound mingled rage at low wages and miserable working conditions with, as Bell says, "the puritan conscience of millionaire socialists, the boyish romanticism of a Jack London, the pale Christian piety of a George Herron, . . . the reckless braggadocio of a 'Wild Bill' Haywood, . . . the tepid social-work impulse of do-gooders, . . . the flaming discontent of the dispossessed farmers, the inarticulate and amorphous desire to 'belong' of the immigrant workers, the iconoclastic idol-breaking of the literary radicals, . . . and more" (*Marxist Socialism in the United States* [1996] 45 [quoted in Rorty 52 ellipsis in the original]).

33. Some of Hartke's experiences at Tarkington may reflect those of Vonnegut when he taught at a high school for the mentally disturbed children of the rich.

34. Vance Hartke narrowly won reelection in 1968 having bravely campaigned against the Vietnam War—one of the very few congressmen courageous enough to do so.

35. Jail, of course, is the very place where Miguel Cervantes invented or reinvented the modern prose novel.

36. Or, perhaps more obviously, for characters in a novel to follow—an issue Vonnegut explored at length in *Breakfast of Champions*.

37. Bob Kerrey, former United States Senator and now president of the New School of Social Research tells a similar story of civilian deaths in Vietnam. " 'The thing I remember, and will remember until the day I die, he said, "is walking into a village and finding, I don't know, 14 or so . . . women and children who were dead. [I was] expecting to find V.C. soldiers with weapons. That memory has blocked out almost everything else'"(Thomas 57 ellipsis in original).

38. According to Broer, Hartke is then involved in "throwing a suspected enemy agent out of a helicopter (203)" ("Heroes" 186), but there is no mention of this event on the page he cites nor any evidence in the novel as a whole to support such an assertion.

39. Vonnegut modeled Athena on Attica, the upper New York State maximum-security prison, and scene of one of the most famous prison uprisings in twentieth-century penal history.

40. Vonnegut also bitterly satirizes American racism in the resegregation of the prison system and though his invention of GRIOT, a computer program that foretells a person's future occupation, financial and social status, and so forth. The crucial information GRIOT needs and without which it will not function is the subject's "ethnic background" which is jargon for race. GRIOT's very name is satiric and quite possibly borrowed from Alex Haley's popular novel, *Roots* (1977), where the crucial role of the griot in black African society is clearly described: A griot spent years in studying the records of the ancestors until he knew "of the great deeds of the ancient kings, holy men, hunters, and warriors who came hundreds of rains before us" (Haley 116–17).

41. The Tolchins in their next book would discuss the national security implications of buying foreign microchips, for instance, rather than producing them at home.

42. The Japanese delay the collapse of the United States and planet Earth, but it is only a short delay and at the end of *Hocus Pocus* they too are desisting. "Their Army of Occupation in Business Suits" calls it quits and leaves (286).

43. Compare Phillips (135–36) where he omits the crucial qualifying word "still" (135).

44. The Domino Theory has since been relegated to the ash bin of history along with other slogans, such as "Making the World Safe for Democracy" of World War I.

45. "[Hartke] is fond of punching holes in complacent American pieties and conventional flag-waving beliefs. Included are data from his own experiences, like his frequent references to the brutalities he performed and witnessed in Vietnam" (Mistichelli 316).

46. Another Tarkington trustee berates Hartke because he informed his physics class truthfully that the Russians beat the Americans in producing a weapon-sized hydrogen bomb, that is, one that can be easily transported. Of course, some might argue that neither national nor human pride accrues to the winner of that lethal race to make such a weapon of oblivion.

47. Broer writes: "Just as the words on his namesake's tombstone reflect decency and caring, Eugene projects as his own epitaph the names of the women he has loved" (191). But nowhere in *Hocus Pocus* does Hartke say or do this. In Vonnegut's novel only a number will appear on Hartke's tombstone. That number will be the sum total of those women with whom he has had sex but excluding prostitutes and his wife (30) with whom he was indeed in love, at least for the first four years of their marriage. That number—to be carved enigmatically on his tombstone—will be over eighty. How that number "reflects decency and caring" in the way that Eugene Debs' epitaph does, "While there is

a lower class I am in it," Broer neglects to say. Later, Hartke makes up another brief list of women he has loved that has three or, at most, four names on it (101). This misreading of an important datum in the novel followed by unsubstantiated speculation is unfortunately typical of Broer's error-ridden essay.

7

Drowning the Book, Breaking the Staff

> The cords of all link back.
> —James Joyce, *Ulysses*

With the publication of *Timequake* in 1997, Kurt Vonnegut declared his novel-writing career at an end. Like Prospero in Shakespeare's *The Tempest*, he swore to break his magic staff and to "drown his book."

> But this rough magic
> I here abjure; . . . I'll break my staff,
> Bury it certain fathoms in the earth,
> And deeper than did ever plummet sound
> I'll drown my book.
> (*The Tempest* 5.1: 50–51, 54–57)

The Tempest, possibly Shakespeare's final play, became his fitting farewell to the stage and his career; so, too, *Timequake*—Vonnegut's self-proclaimed last novel—also forms an appropriate last chapter to his imagining being an American. Neither exclusively fiction nor exclusively autobiography, but a distinctive mixture of both, *Timequake* proves a fitting valedictory for a writer whose fiction and public utterances have long complemented one another. The result, as one reviewer observed, is "a highly entertaining consideration of the relationship between the writer's life and the writer's imagination. Some of its juxtapositions are unsettling, especially the fictional-nonfiction scenes of marriage. Some are hilarious" (Sayers 14). This relationship exists in the very description of *Timequake* itself: a novel in the form of a memoir or a memoir in the form of a novel or "the neatest trick yet played on a publishing world consumed with the furor over novel versus memoir" (Sayers 14).[1] As Ariel Swartley wrote in her review for *The Boston Globe*:

with his tat-a-tat delivery and keen ear for bathos, Vonnegut performs a kind of literary vaudeville where the plots trip over their shoelaces, rhetoric lands with a bump, and subversive humor becomes a moral farce. As on the stage, Vonnegut's vengeance melts imperceptibly into community, for even his villains—bomb-droppers, bureaucrats, bullies—are revealed as local boys who got drastically too big for their britches but may still, just possibly, be redeemed. (C2)

Four times so far in his writing career Vonnegut has announced that he was through either with novel writing or with writing entirely. The first time was just after completing *Slaughterhouse-Five* when he experienced a feeling of arriving at "the end of some sort of career" (*Wampeters, Foma & Granfalloons* 280). But "the end of some sort of career" did not mean the end of his writing novels, since after *Slaughterhouse-Five* came the transitional *Breakfast of Champions* and *Slapstick*, then a series of individually distinct but clearly recognizably Vonnegut novels from *Deadeye Dick* through *Hocus Pocus*. A second less serious farewell occurred in *Breakfast of Champions*, when he freed his characters in preparation for the new distinct years ahead. But as before, this renunciation proved either premature or simply part of the fiction as Kilgore Trout, his most famous character reappeared in the very next novel, *Jailbird*. A third and more serious renunciation of writing came about when Vonnegut published *Bluebeard* and exclaimed after listing all his other books, "Enough! Enough!" and "Most people my age are retired." Yet a short while later *Fates Worse Than Death*, his memoir of the 1990s, and *Hocus Pocus*, his Vietnam novel, appeared—both superior Vonnegut books. The "Kurt Vonnegut" who narrates *Timequake* and announces the end of his novel-writing career most closely resembles in attitude and tone the Vonnegut who looked back at *Slaughterhouse-Five* as a genuine accomplishment, seeing it a career end point, and the Vonnegut who thought seriously of retiring with the publication of *Bluebeard*.[2] He least resembles *Breakfast of Champions'* narrator who grandiosely bids good-bye to his characters, boasting that his act of freeing them emulates that of Leo Tolstoy when he freed his serfs or Thomas Jefferson's when he freed his slaves.

As if to underscore his emphatic retirement announcement in *Timequake*, Vonnegut repeated it incessantly in almost every interview he gave following the book's publication. Again and again he insisted that "this is my last book. I've put myself out of business 'cause I'm completely in print" ("Interviewing Kurt Vonnegut"). Having nothing more to say, realizing everything has been said, and everything that has been said is there still in print for anyone to read, he declared he would quit writing novels rather than become repetitious.[3] "Let somebody else write the books. . . . Human beings didn't use to live as long as I have. I'm old," he complained to one interviewer (Stone 78). Yet the Irish novelist, Francis Stuart, published a new novel late in the twentieth century, when he was almost ninety! Many other artists almost contemporary with Vonnegut, such as Pablo Picasso, Pablo Cassals, Vladimir Horowitz, and Samuel Beckett continued to create, perform, and/or write well into old age. *Timequake* may therefore mark the end of a subject and a theme in Vonnegut's work, but whether this is *the last Vonnegut novel* or only the end of a phase in his fiction with more novels to follow, time will tell. Probably readers should receive his pronouncements about retiring with some skepticism, *cum grano salis*.

Good-byes and farewells dominate *Timequake* as it alternates between the comic and the sad, the outrageous and the poignant. The book's epilogue focuses on the seriousness of having to leave life and the terrible reality of losing loved ones. All of this runs parallel to the reader's awakened knowledge that soon this author, too, will depart. Kilgore Trout returns to lead the chorus of good-byes and Vonnegut himself appears to thank his family, readers, and friends for their roles in his life and work. *Timequake* gathers together the strands of Vonnegut's life and fiction personified in the dedicatees of his novels, critics of his fiction, even characters drawn from his novels, people he has known, family members, the unknown and famous in Indianapolis and New York. They appear at the cast party of a 2001 amateur play production, a clambake on the beach at the writers' retreat, Xanadu in Rhode Island where the living, the fictional, and the dead receive equal attention. As the novel progresses, however, the numbers and importance of the dead increase—so much so that they begin to crowd out the living—Vonnegut's powerful metaphor for the experience of growing old while family members, friends, and acquaintances die. Those we love leave this life, while we, the living, must continue on without them. Vonnegut's sister, Alice, who died almost forty years before *Timequake*, has an important role in the book. His older brother, Barnard, also palpably present throughout the novel, was diagnosed with cancer as Vonnegut writes the last chapters, and dies a few days before he writes the epilogue. "Beyond the poignancy of the farewells in *Timequake*, nuggets endure, not least the generosity with which Vonnegut memorializes his late ex-wife, or recalls his tight-lipped sister's passion for that unfashionable form of humor, the pratfall: the body's most theatrical revenge on pretension" (Swartley C1). He also recalls his first agent, who advised him how to break into print and who later committed suicide. Remembered also is the late Seymour Lawrence, to whom *Timequake* is dedicated, who gave Vonnegut his famous three-book contract for *Slaughterhouse-Five*, *Breakfast of Champions*, and *Slapstick*. Dead also is friend after friend, acquaintance after acquaintance.

In the late twentieth century one physical place that most epitomizes loss for millions of Americans is the Vietnam Memorial in Washington, DC. Maya Lin, the young designer of the monument, says she conceived of it as a means of experiencing grief. "In the design of the memorial, a fundamental goal was to be honest about death, since we must accept that loss in order to begin to overcome it" (33). Similarly, Vonnegut in *Timequake* shares his grief by being honest about death. In memorializing his dead fellow writers along with his dead brother, sister, and ex-wife, he accepts the pain of loss—living with it in order to overcome it.

In a way that is at once personal and detached *Timequake* thus directly confronts death and loss—topics that often appear forbidden in American society and culture. During Vonnegut's career as a professional writer, American culture—its values and sense of worth—has been dominated by the values, taste, and buying power of the young rather than by the wisdom and discrimination of the old.[4] Because American youth behave, like all youth, as if immortal, rarely do the issues of death, mortality, and the end of life arise in late-twentieth-century American culture or society except under terrible circumstances, such as car accidents, plane crashes, or serial suicides. When such issues have forced their way into public consciousness, they quickly recede after a splash of television reporting and interviews. Alternately, those other events telling of "plain old death" (*Slaughterhouse-Five* 4), have usually been kept at a discreet distance. "Happy days! We thought we'd live forever," ironically summarizes the narrator of *Timequake* (148).

The death of any individual means the death of the universe that exists because that person observes it. Other universes remain in existence as other people observe them, but that particular universe vanishes with that individual. "Now I will destroy the whole world," rightly says the Bokononist when committing suicide (*Cat's Cradle* 160). Vonnegut's world, like the world of each one of his readers, will end with him. *Timequake* memorializes that world: his fiction, his public life, his family, and his readers. Toward the end of the book, the mostly comic and upbeat tone becomes elegiac as the accumulation of deaths and losses, especially of members of his family whom he loves deeply, takes its toll. Readers, too, become aware of that figure that waits for each person hovering near, but just out of sight in the shadows. "Death come creeping in the room," sang the bluesman, and death does come creeping into *Timequake*. Vonnegut's attitude of bemused acceptance toward the loss of loved ones, fellow writers, colleagues, valued friends, as well as his attitude toward the end of his own career as a full-time professional writer unsurprisingly proves identical with his attitude toward life throughout his long and fruitful career. If a touch of suffering makes the whole Earth kin, so the acceptance of mortality admits a person into the company of all fragile living creatures.

When we try to picture the future after we are dead, we almost never see ourselves as truly absent but somehow, somewhere we remain observing future events and people as if still present.[5] Hence in *Timequake* Vonnegut projects himself into a time when he is almost impossibly old. Of course, he may well make it to age eighty-eight or ninety-eight and beyond, but the actuarial odds grow ever more slim. Others, with the odds overwhelmingly in their favor, such as his daughter, Lily, who at the time of writing *Timequake* is thirteen years old, will in all likelihood still be alive. Such speculations about the future, couched as bittersweet, yet often-comic reflections, acknowledge continuity and change as the two coordinates of human life, much as space and time are the two coordinates of our physical universe. Our bodies move through space as our minds move through time, and, thanks to our minds and the use of our imaginations, we are able to travel in time backward by way of memory and forward by way of anticipation, yet remain always in the present. So *Timequake*, Janus-faced, looks backward at what has happened in Vonnegut's fiction and in his life and forward to what will happen "if the accident will" (*Slaughterhouse-Five* 2). Vonnegut thus stands on Thoreau's "meeting of two eternities, the past and the future, which is precisely the present moment" (10). Perhaps this double

vision helps account for the resigned acceptance that characterizes the novel—
an acceptance familiar from other valedictories including, what may be the most
famous one in English, "Valediction Forbidding Mourning" by the seventeenth
century poet John Donne:

> As virtuous men pass mildly away
> And whisper to their souls, to go,
> Whilst some of their sad friends do say,
> The breath goes now, and some say no. . . . (spelling modernized)

Allied to this valedictory attitude is *Timequake's* powerful lament for the loss
of imagination in contemporary society—something that Vonnegut had earlier
and more obliquely warned against in his famous *Playboy* interview. There, he
rightly pointed out that "we've changed from a society to an audience"
(*Wampeters, Foma & Granfalloons* 273). In *Timequake* Vonnegut recalls being
a part of theater audiences watching plays that then made a difference in his life,
thinking, and values in large measure because of his active involvement. "They
would have made no more impression on me than *Monday Night Football*, had I
been alone eating nachos and gazing into the face of a cathode-ray tube" (21–
22), he speculates.

Rather than isolated individuals staring at images, the theater is a social
occasion with live actors interacting with those in the audience. In abandoning
theater for television, Americans went from being active agents to becoming
passive spectators. Exactly as they also did when they stopped participating in
games and turned to watching them, from playing a musical instrument to
programming CDs, from arguing about political and social issues to checking
the latest polls, from finding drama in their own lives to observing it unfold on
the small or large screen. "Increasingly . . . we're spending the hours of our days
Elsewhere—inhabiting an abstract space, a simulacrum, which mimics the forms
of social life even as it confirms us in our isolation," rightly laments social critic
Mark Slouka (149) echoing Vonnegut in *Timequake*. A clear example of this
shift may be observed on school playgrounds. One experienced teacher "over
the course of a quarter-century . . . watched on the playground the mutation in
children's imaginations from exterior elaboration of internal fantasy to repetitive
imitation of televisual constructs" (Frick 204). Rather than spectator-centered
television, shopping, or advertising, individual-centered reading could help
create rich, meaningful, fulfilled lives for most Americans. Danger lies in
replacing the book in the hand with images on a screen. Whether the screen in
question be the ubiquitous television, the ever-encroaching computer, the old-
fashioned movie screen, or the more recent VCR or DVD, each decreases the
power of an individual's imagination by presenting an already fully formed
image to whomever is watching. Radio to some extent, but books preeminently,
nurture that autonomous imagination in contrast to these other electronic pre-
formed images that help kill it. "TV is an *eraser*," laments Vonnegut
(*Timequake* 193).[6] Television's ephemeral, constant stream of images along with
its instant events or instant replays replace and erase history, art, and literature,
damaging both individual and collective memory.[7] A medium almost devoid of

reflection, television exists exclusively in what William James calls, the "*specious* present" (1.609). Or, as Thomas Frick memorably phrases it, given

the insane and dangerous deviance of TV's seamlessly constructed counterworld, its darkly hermetic consistency, its manic paucity of human feeling and response. . . . [I]t appeared truly remarkable that we willingly installed such agents of insidious madness in our living rooms and bedrooms. We might as well be agreeing to neural implants by aliens. . . . We've allowed it to destroy our politics, our neighborhoods, and our common sense by sucking our attention up into its ubiquitous reification of the world *as view*, not of any particular thing but *as such*. (210–11)

Similarly, xerography by fully and accurately reproducing images, words, numbers, or whatever thereby lessens the need for memory and may actually contribute to its weakening. Without memory no art is possible; without imagination no art can be created. Vonnegut, richly blessed with both memory and imagination, offers readers of *Timequake* a melding of both in the very form of the work itself.

Some of *Timequake's* remembered events will occur paradoxically only in the future; that is, well after the book was published in 1997 since the novel is narrated variously in 1996, 2001, 1997, and 2010. Thanks to a timequake, a kind of cosmic hiccup caused by the universe ceasing to expand for almost a decade, time repeats itself. Living once again in 2001–2010 through events that have already taken place in 1991–2001 becomes for the characters a kind of living instant-cosmic-replay caused by the timequake. During this repeated decade, *déja vu* rules, as people become actors repeating lines in a play where all events are fully and completely determined. Obviously, an actor memorizing her lines, cues, entrances, and exits, rehearsing with the full company, and above all studying the script will know how, when, and where everything happens during the play. Yet night after night, actors appear continually surprised by events they witness or, even more remarkable, by events in which they participate. In other words, they "behave as though the future were a mystery" (*Timequake* 20). Exactly the same or a process similar to acting in a play occurred to everyone on Earth when the 2001 timequake "zapped us back to 1991" (20). In that instant, everyone began performing in a ten-year-long play where they "could remember everything . . . [they] had to say and do again when the time came" (20).

Obviously, free will cannot exist during such a replay. When the timequake finally does come to an end after almost ten years, disastrous consequences result from people continuing to behave not as free autonomous beings but as if they were still fully determined. It is as if they were—in Kilgore Trout's felicitous phrase—"on automatic pilot," rather than in charge of their lives and actions. The result leads to uncounted accidents big and small as riders fall from bicycles and planes plummet from the air, fire engines career out of control, cars pile up at intersections, pedestrians walk into walls, food burns on stoves. The timequake and the resulting cosmic-replay of events become metaphors for any occasion where people believe or accept that they must operate within the straightjacket of a system of rules and regulations. Common examples might include enlisting in the armed services, spending time in jail, playing games according to preset rules, accepting employment. More general instances might include writing fiction where committing words to paper limits alternative expression or, more perniciously, allowing others to take charge of one's life. (Of course, the most general example of all remains being mortal where the end is known in the beginning.) No wonder Thoreau, the guiding spirit behind *Timequake* said: "The mass of men lead lives of quiet desperation" (*Walden* 4), for at their peril they neglect to exercise whatever freedom they may have in a largely determined world. (Vonnegut echoes Thoreau's sentiments and repeats his very words [*Timequake* 2] as he expands on his own metaphor of the timequake.)

In the nineteenth century, Thoreau went to Walden Pond because, he said

I wished to live deliberately, to front only the essential facts of life, and see if I could not learn what it had to teach, and not, when I came to die, discover that I had not lived. . . . I wanted to live deep . . . to drive life into a corner, and reduce it to its lowest terms, and, if it proved to be mean, why then to get the whole and genuine meanness of it, and publish its meanness to the world; or if it were sublime, to know it by experience. (62–63)

Vonnegut's fiction has been his attempt a century after Thoreau also to drive life into a corner and also to publish what he found there. Each of Vonnegut's narrators, but especially the narrator of *Timequake*, appears—like Thoreau in *Walden*—as a "sojourner" (*Walden* 1); that is, someone who is only passing through, trying to make what sense she or he can out of life. Kilgore Trout's mantra, which he uses so effectively to wake people out of PTS or Post Timequake Syndrome, summarizes much of the imperative embodied in Thoreau's writing: "You were sick, but now you're well again, and there's work to do" (*Timequake* 169). Thoreau—above almost all other American thinkers—insisted on the importance of work for each individual. Not fake make-work but real work. Work that adds to rather than detracts or distracts from, life. Vonnegut, acting in the spirit of Thoreau, proposes in *Timequake* adding two amendments to the United States Constitution. Clearly, these amendments embody principles underlying all his novels and public addresses:

Article XXVIII: Every newborn shall be sincerely welcomed and cared for until maturity.
Article XXIX: Every adult who needs it shall be given meaningful work to do, at a living wage. (152)

The Kurt Vonnegut in *Timequake*, like Prospero in *The Tempest*, bids a sorrowful, stoical good-bye not only to his world of fiction, but also to his engaged readers represented at the gathering at Xanadu by Peter Reed, the first scholar to write a book-length study of Vonnegut's fiction; Marc Leeds, the editor of *The Vonnegut Encyclopedia*, that amazing compendium of all the characters in every book of Vonnegut's through *Hocus Pocus* and *Fates Worse Than Death*; John Leonard, the judicious book reviewer who has gone more than once to Vonnegut's defense in print; Loree Rackstraw, writer of numerous essays and reviews and editor of a book on Vonnegut's work; Robert Weide, who directed the film, *Mother Night*; Joe Pietrott, who taught Vonnegut how to silkscreen;[8] and Asa B. Pieratt, Jr. and Jerome Klinkowitz, the assiduous bibliographers of Vonnegut's works early and late (*Timequake* 206). All are included in—what the jazz standard calls—this "true live clam bake." They all come, however, not to see Vonnegut himself, but to meet and greet his most famous character, Kilgore Trout, since their interest lies in the author's work and not in the author's person. This may well be the highest compliment they could pay to a writer as opposed to a celebrity. Echoing Yeats's oft-quoted line, "My glory was I had such friends" ("The Municipal Gallery Revisited"), the novelist enumerates and celebrates his friends both living and dead. And painfully present are a myriad of now-dead writers, his first wife Jane, his sister Alice, his first agent, his most significant editor, and most painful of all, his older brother Bernard who dies as Vonnegut finishes the novel and readies it for publication.

If *Breakfast of Champions* entailed the metafictional act of Vonnegut freeing his characters through the "Vonnegut" stand-in narrator, and *Bluebeard*, published in his sixty-fifth year, turned out to be the appropriate novel for Vonnegut to announce his retirement, then *Timequake* in itself should prove a witty farewell to writing whatever the course of his subsequent life and career. Vonnegut might now decide to devote himself full-time to his painting as he has more than once suggested he might do, or he could elect to cultivate his garden as his famous predecessor and fellow satirist Voltaire, "the Humanists' Abraham" (*Timequake* 74), advised people to do in *Candide*. Whether he continues to write either fiction or prose, whether he continues his profession of public gadfly on the body politic, or does none or all of these—*Timequake* will remain a model valedictory fiction. For Vonnegut here says farewell to writing fiction within what itself is, arguably, a highly innovative work of fiction—"a political novel that's not a novel, a memoir that is not inclined to reveal the private details of the writer's life," as one reviewer described its peculiar form (Sayers 14).

Timequake is also quite clearly the work of an older writer thinking about aging and old age, death and loss. As such it belongs with a body of literature by writers who have attempted to present and interpret old age. W. B. Yeats, for example, wrote excellent poetry throughout his productive life, but he also had a magnificent late burst of creativity that engendered some of the finest poetry in English about the concerns, reflections, and values of old age. Similarly, *Galápagos*, *Bluebeard*, *Hocus Pocus*, and *Timequake* when taken together form a substantial body of work that reflects the cares and concerns of people in the last phase of their lives. These four novels are very different from earlier novels such as *Slapstick*, which, at the time of writing Vonnegut declared was his experiment with old age. Certainly *Slapstick* was such an experiment. But so much of that earlier book now appears the work of someone tired of life, deep in mourning, yet very much still in mid-career. In contrast, *Galápagos*, like Yeats's late, great "Crazy Jane" poems, employs an improbable persona using an inventive comic style to discuss the future, if any, of the human race. *Bluebeard*, on the other hand, focuses on the last weeks in the life of a person confronting his past and present until finally able to affirm all of life including mistakes and errors—much like any number of late Yeats poems. Both *Bluebeard* and *Galápagos* are joy-filled books as readers celebrate with Rabo Karabekian his accomplishment and marvel with Leon Trout at humanity's survival. Like Thoreau, who declared, "I regret nothing," Rabo Karabekian in his last days joyfully trumpets his acceptance of body, soul, and self: "Oh, happy Meat. Oh, happy Soul. Oh, happy Rabo Karabekian" (287). *Bluebeard* also reflects a late-life acceptance of what cannot be changed—part of the inevitable process of preparing to leave this life. The horror, waste, omnipresent suffering and death, so palpable in Vonnegut's earlier novels, recede into the background of *Bluebeard*, leaving life and the living in the foreground—exactly as pictured in Karabekian's great painting, *Now It's the Women's Turn*. This acceptance of life in all its fragility and mutability permeates *Timequake* as well, but the distinction between *Timequake* and *Bluebeard* inheres in *Bluebeard's* remaining clearly fiction, a novel, while *Timequake* mixes fiction mostly by and about Kilgore Trout with Vonnegut's autobiography thus bringing art and life together.

Bluebeard's affirmation becomes, in turn, balanced by Vonnegut's indignation over human short-sightedness, veniality, and pride—an emotion he also shares with Yeats—evident in his next and perhaps penultimate novel, *Hocus Pocus*, whose narrator is as morally complicit in causing suffering and death as was Howard W. Campbell, Jr. in *Mother Night*. Campbell had deluded himself by excusing all his acts that supported the Nazis as done to further his work as a double agent for the United States. Eugene Debs Hartke in *Hocus Pocus* does much the same thing not as a double agent but as a military publicist in Vietnam serving evil too openly and good too secretly, thus also committing the crime of his times. While Hartke does much that is good with his life, especially within his small family circle, he nevertheless leaves a huge trail of dead and emotionally maimed victims in his wake. On the positive side lies his caring for his insane mother and mother-in-law, the warm welcome he gives his unknown son, his dedicated teaching both at the private school and in prison. On the negative side, however, stand the over eighty people he killed legally and the over eighty love affairs he consummated. The scales hardly balance but dip precipitously down on the negative side. In *Hocus Pocus* the air of defeat that prevails in so much of Vonnegut's work dominates not only Hartke's life, but also that of his country, as the novel recalls in excruciating detail the United States leaving behind its Vietnamese allies when Saigon fell.

While *Hocus Pocus* and *Timequake* as late-life novels both focus on loss, there is a crucial difference between them. In *Hocus Pocus* there is a loss of self-respect occasioned by life's detours, other people's actions, as well as derived from following orders. These kinds of losses become hard to bear because they appear to be caused by the actions or inaction of others or inappropriate action by the protagonist. Each might have been preventable. But the losses that occur in *Timequake*, although equally difficult to bear, are in no sense preventable—they happen simply from time taking its toll.[9] Life becomes for most people a process of letting go not only of that which is no longer needed or required, but also of that which is still loved and desired.

Further, loss in *Timequake* becomes far more personal because more deeply rooted in Vonnegut's vocation. "I don't have survivor's syndrome from the second world war, but I sure do from the writing profession," he quipped in an interview after publishing *Timequake* (Stone 80). As evidence, the names of recently dead writers, such as Jerzy Kosinski, Nelson Algren, Isaac Asimov, Borden Deal, Tennessee Williams, and so forth, all appear in *Timequake* with considerable regularity. Vonnegut then couples this sense of loss to a sense of his own writing career coming to an end. This creates, in turn, what developmental psychologist, Erik H. Erikson calls a "meaningful interplay between beginning and end as well as some finite sense of summary and, possibly, a more active anticipation of dying" (63). Erikson also described what he called "the dominant antithesis in old age . . . *integrity* vs. *despair*" (61). Despair, of course, lies in regret, while integrity lies in acceptance of both life and death. For Erickson, integrity consists of a kind of "informed and detached concern with life itself in the face of death itself" (61) and that exactly describes *Timequake's* angle of vision. Although good-byes and farewells of all kinds dominate Vonnegut's last novel, still it never loses its "informed and detached concern with life itself in the face of death itself."

The many farewells and remembrances of now dead family members, friends, and colleagues also add to the evidence for identifying *Timequake* as a book of memory. They become what Jorge Luis Borges calls "Those odds and ends of memory [that] are the only wealth the rush of time leaves to us." As previously mentioned, the Greeks wisely acknowledged memory as the mother of the muses, for without memory there can be no art. But one could also argue equally forcefully, as clinical neurologist Oliver Sachs does, that memory is the very basis of our humanity for it provides us with "the capacity (and necessity) . . . to create our own histories, our lives" (xviii). In his significant study, *The Importance of Memory: A New View of the Brain*, Isaac Rosenfield argues that: "Each person . . . is unique: his or her perceptions are to some degree creations, and his or her memories are part of an ongoing process of imagination" (197). This power and significance of memory in relation to imagination—especially as encountered in *Timequake*—has been eloquently described by Borges in his poem "Cambridge."

> We are our memory
> we are that chimerical museum of shifting shapes,
> that pile of broken mirrors
>   (ll. 45–47)

The importance of this "chimerical museum" becomes hard to overemphasize, for *Timequake* makes explicit what all of Vonnegut's novels from *Player Piano* to *Hocus Pocus* imply and often state. That is, to imagine being an American in the latter half of the twentieth century involves creating an identity through memory—memory that should be as full and as complete as possible. Willfully selective memories inevitably lead to false imagining and equally false identity. For instance, erasing terrible memories, such as the 200-plus years of slavery in the United States, helps create contemporary racism. Omitting appalling memories, such as the massacre of 135,000 civilians in Dresden, the crucifixion of 6,000 slaves in Rome, or the defeat of the United States in Vietnam promotes false myths of national invincibility and righteousness. Ignoring the instant devastation of Hiroshima or, worse, ignoring the needless destruction of Nagasaki leads to a false notion of scientific progress, and so on. This function of memory differentiates Vonnegut's work at the end of the twentieth century from that of his predecessors in the nineteenth. Emerson, Whitman, and Thoreau had not so much to preserve and acknowledge memory, as they had to work to create the stuff of memory for future generations out of what they saw as unique in American history and experience. The process of imagination rooted in memory creates individuals, societies, and nations.

Kevin Alexander Boon points to Vonnegut's role as "a story teller in a scientific age . . . writing in a time of long-dead Gods and inhumane science." He concludes that Vonnegut "is a twentieth-century thinker struggling for humanity in a universe that neither the Gods nor the scientists have managed to improve" (*Chaos Theory* 168). Perhaps nothing can radically improve that universe, yet Vonnegut's writing does point the way toward a modest improvement that he believes might be possible based upon the one great gift that humanity brings to the universe—human awareness. First discussed at self-serving length by Rabo Karabekian in *Breakfast of Champions* when he defended his abstract painting *St. Anthony*, the concept of awareness returns at the end of *Timequake* when Kilgore Trout at Xanadu demonstrates rather than argues its importance. Unlike Karabekian, Trout does so not for any self-aggrandizing purpose but simply to reveal the truth behind life and, fortuitously, the truth behind *Timequake* itself. "Your awareness . . . is a new quality in the Universe, which exists only because there are human beings. Physicists must from now on, when pondering the secrets of the Cosmos, factor in not only energy and matter and time, but something very new and beautiful, which is *human awareness*" (213–14). To which Trout adds: "I have thought of a better word than *awareness*," he said. "Let us call it *soul*" (214). In the epilogue to *Timequake*, Vonnegut extends Trout's observation by citing his late-brother, Bernard's favorite quotation from Albert Einstein: "The most beautiful thing we can experience is the mysterious. It is the source of all true art and science" (215).

Rooted in this sense of wonder, Vonnegut's art confronts the mysterious. "Vonnegut's fiction points to the confluent boundary between the morbid and the sublime where humor and grief are inevitably conflated" (Boon, *Chaos Theory* 111n86). If there are no answers to the questions he asks in his fiction, that does not mean it is futile or foolish to pose them. Human beings are questioning creatures who never grow tired of asking: "Why, why, why?" (*Cat's Cradle* 124). "Why do I write?" asks Vonnegut at the end of *Timequake*—an almost inevitable question for a full time, professional writer whose career then spanned more than five decades. His reply is part of his career-long rebuttal of Senator Rosewater's notorious "The Golden Age of Rome" speech from *God Bless You, Mr. Rosewater* (26–27). In that early novel, the senator advocated forcing "Americans to be as good as they should be"—the opposite of what

Vonnegut has advocated over the years in each of his novels, but especially in *Timequake*, as well as in many of his public addresses and various essays. While Senator Rosewater promoted "a true Free Enterprise System, which has the sink-or-swim justice of Caesar Augustus built into it" (27), Vonnegut defends the principles of Eugene Debs. Where the senator envisions "a nation of swimmers, with the sinkers quietly disposing of themselves" (27), Vonnegut wants to improve the United States by having it provide meaningful work and caring for its young through his proposed constitutional amendments, articles twenty-eight and twenty-nine. Like all of Vonnegut's fiction, *Timequake* "bear[s] witness to a forgotten past" while revealing an "*empathic* capacity to identify with those different from us" (Kearney 255). Finally, unlike the senator who, from his superior moral position, lectures his fellow citizens in order to improve them, Vonnegut writes to fellow humans in order to confirm their common condition. "Many people need desperately to receive this message: 'I feel and think much as you do, care about many of the things you care about, although most people don't care about them. You are not alone' " (*Timequake* 193). His response echoes and even paraphrases Emerson's idea of the poet as representative of all humanity with which this study began. Emerson wrote

[The poet is] isolated among his contemporaries, by truth and by his art, but with this consolation in his pursuits, that they will draw all men sooner or later. For all men live by truth, and stand in need of expression. In love, in art, in avarice, in politics, in labor, in games, we study to utter our painful secret. (448)

Although help is not on the way to rescue humanity either collectively or individually, in fifteen novels, numerous short stories, essays, and public appearances, Vonnegut by "utter[ing] our painful secret" assures his readers that they are not alone in feeling and thinking as they do "about many of the things [they] . . . care about." This shared concern forms, in turn, the foundation for the genuinely human and humane community that lies at the core of this representative writer's imagining being an American.

NOTES

1. Klinkowitz agrees but suggests a slightly different formula: "In *Timequake*, novel and essay are united in a new form by which the author presents neither fiction nor nonfiction, but rather the autobiography of a novel" ("Essayist" 14).

2. He least resembles the bumbling, fumbling "Vonnegut" who narrates *Breakfast of Champions*, who often finds himself at the mercy of his fictional creations and whose hubris knows no bounds. That "Vonnegut" does not shrink from claiming to be "on a par with the Creator of the Universe" in his little fictional world (200).

3. To his credit, none of his novels so far repeat themselves. While they may employ a similar style making each recognizably his own, each distinctively creates and sustains its characters within its own fictional world. No one would, for instance, mistake a chapter in *Deadeye Dick* for one in *The Sirens of Titan*, or a chapter in *Hocus Pocus* for one in *God Bless You, Mr. Rosewater*. Nor would a reader confuse Rudy Waltz with Billy Pilgrim or Paul Proteus with Walter Starbuck, despite some similarities.

4. The potency and pervasive appeal of youth in America may be experienced through a thought experiment devised by gerontologist Tom Kirkwood. In this experiment, a person becomes forced to make life and death choices that clearly will be tipped toward either youth or age. Although too complicated to be recounted in full here, the essence of the experiment is that six people need to be rescued from a life-threatening storm. Only one can be rescued at a time and most likely only some of them can be rescued at all before the storm will capsize their boat leading to certain death for whoever remains in it (see Kirkwood 17–21). The group ranges from young to old, from single to married to widow, from productive to nonproductive, from involved in life to uninvolved, from contributors to noncontributors to the community. Obviously there is neither a right nor a wrong answer to the order in which they could be rescued. While the result of this experiment—the order in which a person chooses to rescue those in the boat—may depend on an individual's life experiences and values, the society and culture in which a person lives heavily condition both. In the United States in the second half of the twentieth century, most people's first choice would be the young since "they have all their lives ahead of them," while the old have had their chance. In contrast, other societies and cultures might well choose the most productive, involved members of society or still others might rescue the oldest people first because they will have the accumulated wisdom their society needs.

5. Tom Stoppard captures this paradox in *Rosencrantz & Guildenstern Are Dead*. Rosencrantz attempts to think about being dead "lying in a box with a lid on it," but concludes that "one thinks of it like being *alive* in a box, one keeps forgetting to take into account the fact that one is *dead*" (70).

6. The vacuity of television becomes the basis for Trout's short story "The B-36 Sisters" (17–18).

7. Nor will television aid in changing radically American society. As Mary O'Looney lamented in *Jailbird* " 'How can you base a revolution on *Lawrence Welk* and *Sesame Street* and *All in the Family*?' " (198–99). Such programs are so ephemeral that two or three decades later they may or may not be even recognized by most Americans.

8. For a discussion of Vonnegut's graphics, see Reed, "Appendix: The Graphics of Kurt Vonnegut" (206–22) and "Kurt Vonnegut's Fantastic Faces" (77–87).

9. Unlike earlier parodies in *Breakfast of Champions*, *Timequake* seriously reflects upon events in Vonnegut's life and fiction writing.

Works Cited and Consulted

WORKS CITED

Works by Kurt Vonnegut

Bagombo Snuff Box: Uncollected Short Fiction. New York: Putnam, 1999.
Bluebeard. New York: Dell, 1987.
Breakfast of Champions. 1973. New York: Dell, 1991.
Cat's Cradle. 1963. New York: Dell, 1970.
Deadeye Dick. 1982. New York: Dell, 1985.
Fates Worse Than Death: An Autobiographical Collage of the 1980s. 1991. New York: Vintage, 1992.
Galápagos. New York: Dell, 1985.
God Bless You, Mr. Rosewater, or Pearls Before Swine. 1965. New York: Dell, 1970.
Happy Birthday, Wanda June. New York: Dell, 1971.
Hocus Pocus. 1990. New York: Berkley, 1991.
Jailbird. 1979. New York: Dell, 1980.
Mother Night. 1961. New York: Dell, 1966.
Palm Sunday: An Autobiographical Collage. 1981. New York: Dell, 1984.
Player Piano. 1952. New York: Dell, 1980.
The Sirens of Titan. New York: Dell, 1959.
Slapstick or Lonesome No More. 1976. New York: Dell, 1989.
Slaughterhouse-Five. 1969. New York: Dell, 1991.
Timequake. New York: Putnam, 1997.
Wampeters, Foma & Granfalloons: Opinions. 1974. New York: Delacorte, 1976.
Welcome to the Monkey House. 1968. New York: Dell, 1970.
With Ivan Chermayeff. *Sun, Moon, Star*. New York: Harper & Row, 1980.
Letter to the author. 15 June 1992.
"Dear Friend." ACLU (American Civil Liberties Union) solicitation letter. N.d.
"50 Years Later: Hoosiers Remember WWII: Kurt Vonnegut, Frank Kibbe, Madge Minton, Alex Vraciu." *Traces of Indiana and Midwestern History* 3 (1991): 43–45.
"Foreword." Leeds and Reed, *Images*. ix.

"The Hocus Pocus Laundromat." Trans. (into Church Latin) John F. Collins. *The North American Review* 271 (December 1986): 29–35.

And David O'Dell. *Between Time and Timbuktu or Prometheus 5.* 1972. New York: Dell, 1973.

Interviews with Kurt Vonnegut

"The Art of Fiction." With David Hayman, David Michaelis, George Plimpton, and Richard Rhodes. *Paris Review* 69 (1977): 55–103. Reprinted in Allen, *Conversations.* 168–95.

"A Conversation with Kurt Vonnegut, 1982." With Peter J. Reed. Reed and Leeds, *Chronicles.* 3–14.

"A Talk with America's Greatest Living Saab Dealer." With Tom Carson. *Village Voice* 7 October 1997. 28–30, 35.

"Interviewing Kurt Vonnegut." Interview with Robert Siegel. *All Things Considered* National Public Radio. 22 September 1997.

"Interview with Kurt Vonnegut." Interview with William Rodney Allen and Paul Smith. Allen, *Conversations.* 265–301.

"Interview with Kurt Vonnegut." Writer's Workshop. SCTV, Public Broadcast Service, 1980.

"Kurt Vonnegut, Jr." Interview with John Casey and Joe David Bellamy. *The New Fiction: Interviews with Innovative American Writers.* Ed. Joe David Bellamy. Urbana: University of Illinois Press, 1974. 194–207. Reprinted in Allen, *Conversations.* 156–67.

"Kurt Vonnegut, Jr.: The Novelist Talks about His Life and Work." Interview with John Disney. Audio-Text Cassette. North Hollywood, CA: The Center for Cassette Studies, Inc., n.d. CBC758, 1970.

"On Art, Writing, Fellini, and *Time Quake* [sic], 1993." Interview with Peter J. Reed and Marc Leeds. Reed and Leeds, *Chronicles.* 35–44.

Playboy Interview. Interview with David Standish. *Playboy* 20 (July 1973): 57–60, 62, 66, 68, 70, 72, 74, 214, 216. Reprinted in Allen, *Conversations.* 76–110.

" 'Serenity,' 'Courage,' 'Wisdom': A Talk with Kurt Vonnegut." Interview with Zoltán Abádi-Nagy. *Hungarian Studies in English* 22 (1991): 23–37. Reprinted as "Serenity, Courage, Wisdom: A Talk with Kurt Vonnegut, 1989" in Reed and Leeds, *Chronicles.* 15–34.

"A Skull Session with Kurt Vonnegut." Interview with Hank Nuwer. *South Carolina Review* 19 (1987): 2–23. Reprinted in Allen, *Conversations.* 240–64.

"A Talk with Kurt Vonnegut, Jr." with Robert Scholes. *The Vonnegut Statement,* ed. Jerome Klinkowitz and John Somer. New York: Dell, 1973. 90–118. Reprinted in Allen, *Conversations.* 111–32.

"Two Conversations with Kurt Vonnegut" with Charlie Reilly, *College Literature.* 7 (1980): 1–29. Reprinted in Allen, *Conversations,* as "Two Conversations with Kurt Vonnegut" Charles [sic] Reilly." 196–229.

"Vonnegut Is Having Fun Doing a Play" with Mel Gussow, *The New York Times* 6 October 1970: 56. Reprinted in Allen, *Conversations.* 23–25.

Other Sources

Abádi-Nagy, Zoltán. "An Original Look at 'Original': Bokononism." *The Origins and Originality of American Culture.* Ed. Tibor Frank. Budapest: Akademiai Kiado, 1984.

601–08. Reprinted in Reed and Leeds, *Chronicles*, as "Bokononism as a Structure of Ironies." 85–90.

—. "Ironic Historicism in the American Novel of the Sixties." *John O'Hara Journal* 5.1&2: 83–89.

—. " 'The Skillful Seducer': Of Vonnegut's Brand of Comedy." *Hungarian Studies in English* 8 (1974): 45–56.

Aldiss, Brian. Letter to the author. 14 November 1988.

—. "Was Zilla Right?: Fantasy and Truth." *Journal of the Fantastic in the Arts* 1.1 (1988): 7–23.

Aldiss, Brian with David Wingrove. *The Trillion Year Spree*. New York: Atheneum, 1986.

Allen, William Rodney. *Conversations with Kurt Vonnegut*. Jackson: University Press of Mississippi, 1988.

—. *Understanding Kurt Vonnegut*. Columbia: University of South Carolina Press, 1991.

Amis, Martin. "Kurt Vonnegut: After the Slaughterhouse." *The Moronic Inferno and Other Visits to America*. 1986. Harmondsworth: Penguin, 1987. 132–37.

Andrews, David. "Vonnegut and Aesthetic Humanism." Boon, *Millennium*. 17–47.

Attebery, Brian. "Fantasy as an Anti-Utopian Mode." *Reflections on the Fantastic*. Ed. Michael R. Collings. Westport, CT: Greenwood Press, 1986. 3–8.

—. *The Fantasy Tradition in American Literature from Irving to Le Guin*. Bloomington: Indiana University Press, 1980.

Barthel, John. Letter to the author. 13 January 1999.

Beckett, Samuel. "Embers." *Collected Shorter Plays*. New York: Grove Press, 1984. 91–104.

—. *Endgame*. New York: Grove Press, 1958.

Bellah, Robert N., Richard Madsen, William M. Sullivan, Ann Swidler, and Steven M. Tipton. *Habits of the Heart: Individualism and Commitment in American Life*. Berkeley: University of California Press, 1985.

Berkove, Lawrence I. "The 'Poor Players' of *Huckleberry Finn*." *Papers of the Michigan Academy of Science, Arts, and Letters* 53 (1968): 291–310.

Berryman, Charles. "After the Fall: Kurt Vonnegut." *Critique* 26 (1985): 96–102.

—. "Vonnegut and Evolution: *Galápagos*." Merrill, *Critical Essays*. 188–99.

—. "Vonnegut's Comic Persona in *Breakfast of Champions*." Merrill, *Critical Essays*. 162–70.

Bianculli, David. "The Theory of Evolution, According to Vonnegut." *The Philadelphia Inquirer* 10 November 1985: S-6. Reprinted in Mustazza, *Response*. 275–77.

Birkerts, Sven. "The Fate of the Book." *Antioch Review* (1996). Reprinted in Birkerts, *Tolstoy's Dictaphone*. 189–99.

—, ed. *Tolstoy's Dictaphone: Technology and the Muse*. Saint Paul, MN: Graywolf Press, 1996.

Blackford, Russell. "The Definition of Love: Kurt Vonnegut's *Slapstick*." *Science Fiction* 2 (1980): 208–28. Reprinted in Mustazza, *Response*. 193–207.

—. "Physics and Fantasy: Scientific Mysticism, Kurt Vonnegut, and *Gravity's Rainbow*." *Journal of Popular Culture* 19:3 (1985): 35–44.

Blake, William. *The Complete Poems*. Ed. Alicia Ostriker. London: Penguin, 1977.

Boon, Kevin A[lexander]. *Chaos Theory and the Interpretation of Literary Texts: The Case of Kurt Vonnegut*. Lewiston, NY: Mellen Press, 1997.

—. "What to Do When a Pool-Pah Is Your Zah-Mah-Ki-Bo." Boon, *Millennium*. ix–xii.

—, ed. *At Millennium's End: New Essays on the Work of Kurt Vonnegut*. Albany: State University of New York Press: 2001.

Boon, Kevin Alexander, and David Pringle. "Vonnegut Films." Boon, *Millennium*. 167–96.

Borges, Jorge Luis. "Cambridge." *Selected Poems*. Trans. Hoyt Rogers. London: Penguin, 1999.

Bowlby, John. *Attachment and Loss*. Vol. 3. *Loss, Sadness and Depression*. 3 vols. London: Harmondsworth, 1980.

Boyer, Paul. *By the Bomb's Early Light: American Thought and Culture at the Dawn of the Atomic Age*. New York: Pantheon, 1985.

Brien, Alan. "Afterthought." Review of *Cat's Cradle*. *The Spectator* 2 August 1963: 158–59. Reprinted in Mustazza, *Response*. 63–65.

Broer, Lawrence R. "Hartke's Hearing: Vonnegut's Heroes on Trial." Reed and Leeds, *Chronicles*. 179–203.

—. *Sanity Plea: Schizophrenia in the Novels of Kurt Vonnegut*. 1989. Tuscaloosa: University of Alabama Press, 1994.

Brooke-Rose, Christine. *A Rhetoric of the Unreal: Studies in Narrative and Structure, Especially of the Fantastic*. Cambridge: Cambridge University Press, 1981.

Brooks, Van Wyck. *The Writer in America*. 1953. New York: Avon, 1964.

Budick, E. Miller. "The Origins of American Historical Romance." *The Early Republic: The Making of a Nation—The Making of a Culture*. Ed. Steve Ickringill, Zoltán Abádi-Nagy, and Aladár Sarbu. Amsterdam: Free University Press, 1988. 299–305.

Bunyan, John. *The Pilgrim's Progress*. Ed. James Blanton Wharey. Oxford: Clarendon Press, 1928.

Burhans, Clinton S., Jr. "Hemingway and Vonnegut: Diminishing Vision in a Dying Age." *Modern Fiction Studies* 21 (1975): 173–91.

Cahill, Holger. "The Federal Art Project." From *New Horizons in American Art*. New York: The Museum of Modern Art, 1936. Reprinted in Chipp, *Theories of Modern Art*. 471–73.

Carter, Angela. "Come unto These Yellow Sands." *Come unto These Yellow Sands: Four Radio Plays*. Newcastle upon Tyne: Bloodaxe Books, 1985.

Céline, Louis-Ferdinand. *Journey to the End of the Night*. Trans. John H. P. Marks. 1932. New York: New Directions, 1960.

Chabot, Barry. "*Slaughterhouse-Five* and the Comforts of Indifference." *Essays in Literature* 8 (1981): 45–51.

Chipp, Herschel B., ed. *Theories of Modern Art: A Source Book by Artists and Critics*. Berkeley: University of California Press, 1968.

Chrichton, J. Michael. "Sci-Fi and Vonnegut. Review of *Slaughterhouse-Five*." *The New Republic* 26 April 1969: 33–35. Reprinted in Mustazza, *Response*. 107–11.

Coates, Joseph. "Truly Subversive Vonnegut." Review of *Fates Worse Than Death* by Kurt Vonnegut. *Chicago Tribune* 1 September 1991: 4, 6.

Coleridge, Samuel Taylor. "Kubla Khan." *The Oxford Book of English Verse, 1250–1900*. Ed. Arthur Quiller-Couch. Oxford: Oxford University Press, 1926. 650–51.

Cook, Kenneth. "What's So Damn Funny?: Grim Humor in *The Mysterious Stranger* and *Cat's Cradle*." *Publications of the Missouri Philological Association* 7 (1982): 48–55.

Cooley, John R. "Kurt Vonnegut, Jr." *Savages and Naturals: Black Portraits by White Writers in Modern American Literature*. Newark: University of Delaware Press, 1982. 161–77.

Coover, Robert. *The Public Burning*. New York: Viking Press, 1977.

Cotter, Holland. "In the Jumble of Pollock's Earliest Work." *The New York Times* 21 October 1997: B1, B7.

Cowan, S. A. "Track of the Hound: Ancestors of Kazak in *The Sirens of Titan*." *Extrapolation* 24 (1983): 280–87.

Cowart, David. "Culture and Anarchy: Vonnegut's Later Career." Merrill, *Critical Essays*. 170–88.

Crane, Stephen. *The Red Badge of Courage*. 1895. Ed. Donald Pizer. 3rd ed. New York: Norton, 1994.

Davies, Paul. *About Time: Einstein's Unfinished Revolution*. New York: Penguin, 1995.

—. *The Last Three Minutes: Conjectures about the Ultimate Fate of the Universe*. New York: Basic Books, 1994.

DeMott, Benjamin. "A Riot of Randomness." *The New York Times Book Review* 17 October 1982: 1, 32–34. Reprinted in Mustazza, *Response*. 245–49.

Dewey, Joseph. *In a Dark Time: The Apocalyptic Temper in the American Novel of the Nuclear Age*. West Lafayette, IN: Purdue University Press, 1990.

Dickinson, Emily. "The Bible is an Antique Volume—." *The Poems of Emily Dickinson*. Ed. Thomas H. Johnson. Vol. 1–3. Cambridge: Harvard University Press, 1958. 1: 1065–67.

Disch, Thomas. *The Dreams Our Stuff Is Made Of: How Science Fiction Conquered the World*. 1998. New York: Touchstone, 2000.

—. "Getting Down to Basics." Review of Kurt Vonnegut, *Galápagos*. *Times Literary Supplement* 8 November 1985: 1267.

Donne, John. "Valediction Forbidding Mourning." *The Complete Poetry and Selected Prose of John Donne and The Complete Poetry of William Blake*. New York: Modern Library, 1941. 33–34.

Dorris, Michael, and Louise Erdich. "Bangs and Whimplers: Novelists at Armageddon (Post-Apocalypse Worlds in Modern Fiction)." *The New York Times Book Review* 13 March 1988: 1, 24–25.

Doxey, William S. "Vonnegut's *Cat's Cradle*." *Explicator* 37 (1979): 6.

Doyle, Rodger. "Why Do Prisons Grow? For the Answers, Ask the Governors." *Scientific American* 285.6 (2001): 18.

Edelstein, Arnold. "*Slaughterhouse-Five*: Time Out of Joint." *College Literature* 1 (1974): 128–39.

Elliott, Robert C. *The Shape of Utopia: Studies in a Literary Genre*. Chicago: University of Chicago Press, 1970.

Emerson, Ralph Waldo. *Ralph Waldo Emerson: Essays & Lectures*. Ed. Joel Porte. New York: The Library of America, 1983.

—. "The American Scholar." *Essays & Lectures*. 53–71.

—. *The Heart of Emerson's Journals*. Ed. Bliss Perry. Boston: Houghton Mifflin Co, 1926.

—. "The Poet." *Essays & Lectures*. 445–68.

—. "Self-Reliance." *Essays & Lectures*. 255–82.

Erikson, Erik H. *The Life Cycle Completed*. Extended Version. New York: Norton, 1998.

Fekete, John. "Doing the Time Warp Again: Science Fiction as Adversarial Culture." Review of Carl Freedman, *Critical Theory and Science Fiction*. *Science Fiction Studies* 28.1 (2001): 77–96.

Fiedler, Leslie A. "The Divine Stupidity of Kurt Vonnegut." *Esquire*. September 1970: 195–97, 199–200, 202–04. Reprinted in Leeds and Reed, *Images*. 5–18.

Fitzgerald, F. Scott. *The Great Gatsby*. 1926 New York: Penguin, 1950.

Freedman, Carl. *Critical Theory and Science Fiction*. Hanover, NH: Wesleyan University Press, 2000.

Freese, Peter. "Surviving the End: Apocalypse, Evolution, and Entropy in Bernard Malamud, Kurt Vonnegut, and Thomas Pynchon." *Critique* 36 (1995): 163–76.

—. "Vonnegut's Invented Religions as Sense-Making Systems." Reed and Leeds, *Chronicles*. 145–64.

Frick, Thomas. "Either/Or." *Antioch* Review (1996). Reprinted in Birkerts, *Tolstoy's Dictaphone*. 200–21.

Frost, Robert. "Fire and Ice." *The Complete Poems of Robert Frost*. New York: Holt, Rinehart, and Winston, 1967. 268.

—. "Forgive, O Lord." *In the Clearing*. New York: Holt, Rinehart, and Winston, 1962. 39.

Frye, Northrop. "Varieties of Literary Utopias." Manuel, *Utopias*. 25–49.

Fussell, Paul. *Killing in Verse and Prose and Other Essays*. 1988 London: Bellew, 1990.

—. "Thank God for the Atom Bomb." *Killing in Verse and Prose*. 13–37.

—. *Wartime: Understanding and Behavior in the Second World War*. New York: Oxford University Press, 1989.

—. "Writing in Wartime: The Uses of Innocence." *Killing in Verse and Prose*. 51–79.

Gardner, Martin. "Introduction." Lewis Carroll. *The Annotated Alice: Alice's Adventures in Wonderland and Through the Looking Glass*. 1960. New York: Meridian, 1963. N.p.

Giannone, Richard. "Violence in the Fiction of Kurt Vonnegut." *Thought* 56 (1981): 58–76.

—. *Vonnegut: A Preface to His Novels*. Port Washington, NY: Kennikat Press, 1977.

Giddens, Gary. "Vaporizing Midland City." Review of *Deadeye Dick. The Nation* 13 November 1982: 500–02. Reprinted in Mustazza, *Response*. 251–53.

Gifford, Don. *The Farther Shore: A Natural History of Perception*. New York: Atlantic Monthly Press, 1990.

Gill, R. B. "Bargaining in Good Faith: The Laughter of Vonnegut, Grass, and Kundera." *Critique* 25 (1984): 77–91.

Giraudoux, Jean. *The Madwoman of Chaillot*. Trans. Maurice Valency. In *Jean Giraudoux: Four Plays, Adapted, and with an Introduction by Maurice Valency*. New York: Hill and Wang, 1958.

Godshalk, William L. "Vonnegut and Shakespeare: Rosewater at Elsinore." *Critique* 15 (1973): 37–48. Reprinted in Mustazza, *Response*. 99–106.

Goodwin, Barbara. "The Perfect and the Perfected." Review of Krishan Kumar, *Utopia and Anti-Utopia in Modern Times*. N.d. Oxford: Blackwell. *Times Literary Supplement* 24 July 1987: 786.

Gottlieb, Adolph, and Mark Rothko. Statement printed in the column of Edward Alden Jewell. *The New York Times*, 13 June 1943. Reprinted in Chipp, *Theories of Modern Art*. 544–45.

Gould, Stephen Jay. *Full House*. New York: Three Rivers Press, 1996.

Grady, Denise. "A Glow in the Dark, and a Lesson in Scientific Peril." *The New York Times* 6 October 1998: B14.

Greer, Creed. "Kurt Vonnegut and the Character of Words." *Journal of Narrative Technique* 19 (1989): 312–30.

Greiner, Donald J. "Vonnegut's *Slaughterhouse-Five* and the Fiction of Atrocity." *Critique* 14 (1973): 38–51.

Gunn, James. "The Horror." *The Road to Science Fiction: From Wells to Heinlein*. Ed. James Gunn. New York: NAL, 1979. 134–37.

—. "Science Fiction and the Mainstream." *Science Fiction Today and Tomorrow*. Ed. Reginald Bretnor. New York: Harper & Row, 1974. 183–216.

Haley, Alex. *Roots*. New York: Dell, 1977.

Hartwell, David. *Age of Wonders*. 1984. New York: McGraw Hill, 1985.

Hawking, Stephen. *A Brief History of Time: From the Big Bang to Black Holes*. New York: Bantam, 1988.

Hayles, N. Katherine. *How We Became Posthuman: Virtual Bodies in Cibernetics, Literature, and Informatics*. Chicago: University of Chicago Press, 1999.

Hearron, Tom. "The Theme of Guilt in Vonnegut's Cataclysmic Novels." *The Nightmare Considered: Critical Essays on Nuclear War Literature*. Ed. Nancy Anisfield. Bowling Green, OH: Popular Press, 1991. 186–92.

Hendin, Josephine. "Experimental Fiction." *Harvard Guide to Contemporary Writing*. Ed. Danuel Hoffman. Cambridge, MA: Belknap Press, 1979.

Hollinger, Veronica. "Specular SF: Postmodern Allegory." *States of the Fantastic: Studies in the Theory and Practice of Fantastic Literature and Film*. Ed. Nicholas Ruddick. Westport, CT: Greenwood, 1992. 29–39.

Howe, Irving. "The American Voice—It Begins on a Note of Wonder." *New York Times Book Review*. 4 July 1976: 1–3.

—. *Politics and the Novel*. New York: New American Library, 1987.

Høeg, Peter. *The Woman and the Ape*. Trans. Barbara Haveland. London: Harvill, 1996.

Hughes, David Y. "The Ghost in the Machine: The Theme of *Player Piano*." *America as Utopia*. Ed. Kenneth M. Roemer. New York: Burt Franklin, 1981. 108–14.

Hume, Kathryn. *American Dream, American Nightmare: Fiction Since 1960*. Urbana: University of Illinois Press, 2000.

—. *Fantasy and Mimesis: Responses to Reality in Western Literature*. New York: Methuen, 1984.

—. "The Heraclitean Cosmos of Kurt Vonnegut." *Papers on Language & Literature* 18 (1982): 208–24. Reprinted in Merrill, *Critical Essays*. 216–30.

—. "Kurt Vonnegut and the Myths and Symbols of Meaning." *Texas Studies in Literature and Language* 24 (1982): 429–47. Reprinted in Merrill, *Critical Essays*. 201–16.

—. "Postmodernism in Popular Literary Fantasy." *The Dark Fantastic*. Ed. C. W. Sullivan III. Westport, CT: Greenwood Press, 1997. 173–82.

—. "Vonnegut's Melancholy." *Philological Quarterly* 77 (1998): 221–38.

—. "Vonnegut's Self-Projections: Symbolic Characters and Symbolic Fiction." *Journal of Narrative Technique*. 12 (1982): 177–90. Reprinted in Mustazza, *Response*. 231–43.

Hutcheon, Linda. "Historiographic Metafiction: Parody and the Intertextuality of History." *Intertextuality and Contemporary American Fiction*. Ed. Patrick O'Donnell and Robert Con Davis. Baltimore: Johns Hopkins University Press, 1989. 3–32.

Huxley, Aldous. *Brave New World*. 1932. Harmondsworth: Penguin, 1955.

Irving, John. "Kurt Vonnegut and His Critics: The Aesthetics of Accessibility." *The New Republic* 22 September 1979: 41–49. Reprinted in Mustazza, *Response*. 213–25.

—. "Vonnegut in Prison and Awaiting Trial." Review of Kurt Vonnegut, *Hocus Pocus*. *Los Angeles Times Book Review* 2 September 1990: 4, 10.

Jackson, Rosemary. *Fantasy: The Literature of Subversion*. New York: Methuen, 1981.

Jamison, Kay Redfield. *Touched with Fire: Manic-Depressive Illness and the Artistic Temperament*. New York: Free Press, 1993.

Jamosky, Edward, and Jerome Klinkowitz. "Kurt Vonnegut's Three *Mother Nights*." *Modern Fiction Studies* 34 (1988): 216–19.

Jefferson, Thomas. "Letter to John Adams, 28 October 1813." *The Adams-Jefferson Letters: The Complete Correspondence Between Thomas Jefferson and Abigail and John Adams*. Ed. Lester J. Cappon. 2 Vols. Chapel Hill: University of North Carolina Press, 1959. 2:387–92.

Job. *The New Oxford Annotated Bible with Apocrypha*. Revised Standard Version. Ed. Herbert G. May and Bruce M. Metzger. 1952. New York: Oxford University Press, 1971.

Johnson, George. "The Brain Eater." Review of Richard Rhodes, *Deadly Feasts: Tracking the Secrets of a Terrifying New Plague. The New York Times Book Review* 16 March 1997: 9.

Joyce, James. "James Clarence Mangan." *The Critical Writings of James Joyce*. Ed. Richard Ellmann and Ellsworth Mason. New York: Viking Press, 1959.

Juvenal. *The Satires of Juvenal*. Trans. Rolfe Humphries. Bloomington: Indiana University Press, 1958.

Kaku, Michio. *Hyperspace: A Scientific Odyssey through Parallel Universes, Time Warps, and the Tenth Dimension*. New York: Oxford University Press, 1994.

Karon, Jeff. "Science and Sensibility in the Short Fiction of Kurt Vonnegut." Boon, *At Millennium's End*. 105–117.

Kaufman, Will. "Vonnegut's *Breakfast of Champions*: A Comedian's Primer." *Thalia: Studies in Literary Humor* 13 (1993): 22–33.

Kearney, Richard. *Poetics of Imagining: Modern to Post-Modern*. 1991 Rev. ed. Edinburgh: Edinburgh University Press, 1998.

Kemenov, Vladimir. "Aspects of Two Cultures." *VOKS Bulletin* (Moscow), USSR Society for Cultural Relations with Foreign Countries, 1947, 20–36. Reprinted in Chipp, *Theories of Modern Art*. 490–95.

Kenner, Hugh. *Dublin's Joyce*. Bloomington: Indiana University Press, 1956.

Kernan, Alvin B. *Modern Satire*. New York: Harcourt Brace and World, 1962.

Ketterer, David. "Vonnegut's Spiral Siren Call: From Dresden's Luna Vistas to Tralfamadore." *New Worlds for Old*. New York: Anchor Books, 1974. 296–333.

Kierkegaard, Søren. "The Ancient Tragical Motive as Reflected in the Modern." *Either/Or* Trans. David F Swenson and Lillian Marvin Swenson. 1959. Rev. Ed. Vol. 1. Princeton: Princeton University Press, 1971. 113–23.

Kirkwood, Tom. *Time of Our Lives: The Science of Human Aging*. New York: Oxford University Press, 1999.

Klee, Paul. "Creative Credo." 1920. Trans. Norbert Gutterman. *The Inward Vision: Watercolors, Drawings and Writings by Paul Klee*. New York: Abrams, 1959. 5–10.

Klinkowitz, Jerome. *Kurt Vonnegut*. New York: Methuen, 1982.

—. "Kurt Vonnegut's Ultimate." *The Nightmare Considered: Critical Essays on Nuclear War*. Ed. Nancy Anisfield. Bowling Green, OH: Popular Press, 1991. 193–98.

—. "Review of *Slapstick* by Kurt Vonnegut." *The New Republic*, 25 September 1976: 40–41. Reprinted in Mustazza, *Response* as "A Review of *Slapstick*." 187–88.

—. "Vonnegut in America." *Vonnegut in America*. Ed. Jerome Klinkowitz and Donald L. Lawler. New York: Delacorte Press, 1977. 7–36.

—. "Vonnegut the Essayist." Boon, *Millennium*. 1–16.

Klinkowitz, Jerome, and Donald L. Lawler, ed. *Vonnegut in America*. New York: Delacorte Press, 1977.

Klinkowitz, Jerome, and John Somer. *The Vonnegut Statement: Original Essays on the Life and Work of Kurt Vonnegut, Jr*. New York: Delta, 1973.

Kopper, Edward A., Jr. "Abstract Expressionism in Vonnegut's *Bluebeard*." *Journal of Modern Literature* 17.1 (1991): 582–84.

Kramer, Hilton. "The Crisis in Abstract Art." Review of Frank Stella, *Working Space. The Atlantic* October 1986: 94–98.

Kuttner, Robert. "Buying into America." Review of Martin and Susan Tolchin, *Buying into America: How Foreign Money Is Changing the Face of Our Nation. The New York Times Book Review* 21 February. 1988: 9.

Leeds, Marc. "Beyond the Slaughterhouse: Tralfamadorian Reading Theory in the Novels of Kurt Vonnegut." Reed and Leeds, *Chronicles.* 91–102.

—. *"Mother Night*: Who's Pretending?" Leeds and Reed, *Images.* 81–92.

—. *The Vonnegut Encyclopedia: An Authorized Compendium.* Westport, CT: Greenwood Press, 1995.

Leeds, Marc, and Peter J. Reed. *Kurt Vonnegut: Images and Representations.* Westport, CT: Greenwood Press, 2000.

Leff, Leonard. "Utopia Reconstructed: Alienation in Vonnegut's *God Bless You, Mr. Rosewater.*" *Critique* 12 (1971): 29–37.

Le Guin, Ursula K. "American SF and the Other." *Science Fiction Studies* 7 (1975). Reprinted in *The Language of the Night: Essays on Fantasy and Science Fiction.* Revised Edition. Ed. Usula K. Le Guin. New York: HarperCollins, 1992. 93–96.

—. "Introduction." *The Left Hand of Darkness.* 1969. New York: Ace Books, 1987. N.p.

Leonard, John. "Black Magic." Review of *Hocus Pocus. The Nation* 15 October 1990: 421–25. Reprinted in Mustazza, *Response.* 301–07.

Lessing, Doris. "Vonnegut's Responsibility." *The New York Times Book Review* 4 February 1973: 35. Reprinted in Mustazza, *Response.* 45–47.

Leuchtenburg, William E. *A Troubled Feast: American Society Since 1945.* Boston: Little, Brown, 1983.

Leverence, John W. *"Cat's Cradle* and Traditional American Humor." *Journal of Popular Culture* 5 (1972): 955–63.

Lewis, C[live] S[taples]. "On Science Fiction." *C. S. Lewis: On Stories and Other Essays on Literature.* Ed. Walter Hooper. New York: Harcourt, Brace, Javanovich, 1982. 55–68.

Lin, Maya. "Making the Memorial." *The New York Review of Books* 57.17 (2 November 2000): 33–35.

Louis, Dolores K. Gros. "The Ironic Christ Figure in *Slaughterhouse-Five.*" *Biblical Images in Literature.* Ed. Roland Bartel. Nashville: Abington Press, 1975. 161–75.

Lundquist, James. *Kurt Vonnegut.* New York: Ungar, 1977.

Machado de Assis, Joaquim Maria. *The Posthumous Memoirs of Brás Cubas.* Trans. Gregory Rabassa. New York: Oxford University Press, 1997.

Manuel, Frank E., ed. *Utopias and Utopian Thought.* Boston: Houghton Mifflin, 1966.

Maslow, Abraham H. *Toward a Psychology of Being.* 1962. 2nd ed. Princeton: Van Nostrand, 1968.

Matthew. *The New Covenant Commonly Called the New Testament.* Revised Standard Version. 3 vols. New York: Thomas Nelson, 1946. 1: 1–69.

May, John R. "Loss of World in Barth, Pynchon, and Vonnegut: The Varieties of Humorous Apocalypse." *Toward a New Earth: Apocalypse in the American Novel.* Notre Dame: University of Notre Dame Press, 1972. 172–200.

Mayo, Clark. *Kurt Vonnegut: The Gospel from Outer Space.* San Bernardino, CA: Borgo Press, 1977.

McCarthy, Cliff. *"Bluebeard* and the Abstract Expressionists." Reed and Leeds, *Chronicles.* 165–77.

McConnell, Frank. "Stalking Papa's Ghost: Hemingway's Presence in Contemporary American Writing." *Ernest Hemingway: New Critical Essays.* Ed. Robert A. Lee. Totowa, NJ: Barnes & Noble, 1983. 193–211.

McGinnis, Wayne D. "The Arbitrary Cycle of *Slaughterhouse-Five*: A Relation of Form to Theme." *Critique* 17 (1975): 55–68. Reprinted in Mustazza, *Response.* 113–22.

—. "The Source and Implications of *Ice-Nine* [sic] in Vonnegut's *Cat's Cradle.*" *American Notes & Queries* 13 (1974): 40–41.

McHale, Brian. *Postmodernist Fiction.* New York: Routledge, 1987.

McInerney, Jay. "Still Asking the Embarrassing Questions." Review of *Hocus Pocus*. *The New York Times Book Review* 9 September 1990: 12. Reprinted in Mustazza, *Response*. 309–11.

McNelly, Willis E. "Science Fiction the Modern Mythology [Vonnegut's *Slaughterhouse-Five*]." *America* 5 September 1970: 125–27. Reprinted in *SF: the Other Side of Realism*. Ed. Thomas D. Clareson. Bowling Green, OH: Popular Press, 1971. 193–98.

Melville, Herman. "Bartleby." *The Portable Melville*. Ed. Jay Leyda. New York: Viking Press, 1952. 465–512.

Merrill, Robert. "Kurt Vonnegut as a German American." *Germany and German Thought in American Literature and Cultural Criticism*. Ed. Peter Freese. Essen: Blaue Eule, 1990. 230–43. Reprinted in Reed and Leeds, *Chronicles*. 73–83.

—. "Vonnegut's *Breakfast of Champions*: The Conversion of Helliogabalus." *Critique* 18 (1979): 99–109. Reprinted in Merrill, *Critical Essays*. 153–61.

Merrill, Robert, ed. *Critical Essays on Kurt Vonnegut*. Boston: G. K. Hall, 1990.

Merrill, Robert, and Peter A. Scholl. "Vonnegut's *Slaughterhouse-Five*: The Requirements of Chaos." *Studies in American Fiction* 6 (1978): 65–76. Reprinted in Merrill, *Critical Essays*. 142–51.

Messent, Peter B. "*Breakfast of Champions*: The Direction of Kurt Vonnegut's Fiction." *Journal of American Studies* 8 (1974): 101–14.

Meyer, William E. H., Jr. "Kurt Vonnegut: The Man with Nothing to Say." *Critique* 29 (1988): 95–109.

—. "The Unwelcomed Presupposition of *American* Philosophy—Eye-Epistemology: An Essay Far Beyond the Bounds of Current Interdisciplinary Scholarship." *Weber Studies* 12 (1995): 83–94.

Miller, J. Hillis. *Fiction and Repetition: Seven English Novels*. Cambridge: Harvard University Press, 1982.

Mills, John. "Return of the Dazed Steer." *Queen's Quarterly* 88 (1981): 145–54.

Mistichelli, Bill. "History and Fabrication in Kurt Vonnegut's *Hocus Pocus*." Mustazza, *Response*. 313–25.

Morrow, James. *The Eternal Footman*. San Diego: Harcourt, 1999.

Morse, Donald E. "Bringing Chaos to Order. Vonnegut Criticism at Century's End." Rev. of *Chaos Theory and the Interpretation of Literary Texts: The Case of Kurt Vonnegut* by Kevin Boon, *Sanity Plea: Schizophrenia in the Novels of Kurt Vonnegut* by Lawrence R. Broer, *Vonnegut in Fact: The Public Spokesmanship of Personal Fiction* by Jerome Klinkowitz, *The Vonnegut Encyclopeia: An Authorized Compendium* by Marc Leeds, *Critical Essays on Kurt Vonnegut* by Robert Merrill, *The Critical Response to Kurt Vonnegut* by Leonard Mustazza, *Forever Pursuing Genesis: The Myth of Eden in the Novels of Kurt Vonnegut* by Leonard Mustazza, *The Short Fiction of Kurt Vonnegut* by Peter J. Reed, *The Vonnegut Chronicles: Interviews and Essays* by Peter J. Reed and Marc Leeds. *Journal of the Fantastic in the Arts* 10 (2000): 395–408.

—. "Kurt Vonnegut: The Antonio Gaudi of Fantastic Fiction." *The Centennial Review* 42.1 (1998): 173–83.

—. *Reader's Guide to Kurt Vonnegut*. Mercer Island, WA: Starmont, 1992.

—. "Repetition and Generalities." Rev. of *The Short Fiction of Kurt Vonnegut*, by Peter J. Reed. *Science-Fiction Studies* (25) 1998: 371–77.

Mumford, Lewis. *Technics and Civilization*. New York: Harcourt, Brace, 1934.

Mustazza, Leonard. "A Darwinian Eden: Science and Myth in Kurt Vonnegut's *Galápagos*." *Journal of the Fantastic in the Arts* 3 (1991): 55–65. Reprinted in Mustazza, *Response*. 279–86.

—. *Forever Pursuing Genesis: The Myth of Eden in the Novels of Kurt Vonnegut.* Lewisburg: Bucknell University Press, 1990.

—, ed. *The Critical Response to Kurt Vonnegut.* Westport, CT: Greenwood Press, 1994.

Napier, James J. "Voltaire and Vonnegut." *The CEA Forum* (October 1975).

Nelson, Kay Hoyle. "*Jailbird*: A Postmodern Fairy Tale." Reed and Leeds, *Chronicles.* 103–12.

Nichols, Peter. Review of *Bluebeard* The BBC World Service 5 May 1988.

O'Brien, Flann [Brian O'Nolan]. *At Swim-Two-Birds.* 1939. New York: New American Library, 1976.

O'Neill, Eugene. *The Iceman Cometh.* 1940. New York: Vintage, 1957.

O'Sullivan, Maurice J., Jr. "*Slaughterhouse-Five*: Kurt Vonnegut's Anti-Memoirs." *Essays in Literature* 3 (1976): 244–50.

Parrinder, Patrick. "Science Fiction and the Scientific World View." *Science Fiction: A Critical Guide.* Ed. Patrick Parringer. New York: Longman, 1979. 67–88.

Paulson, Ronald. *The Fictions of Satire.* Baltimore: The Johns Hopkins University Press, 1967.

Perry, Ralph Barton. *Puritanism and Democracy.* 1944. New York: Harper & Row, 1964.

Phillips, Robert. "Fiction Chronicle." *Hudson Review* 44 (1991): 133–41.

Pierce, John J. *Foundations of Science Fiction: A Study in Imagination and Evolution.* Westport, CT: Greenwood Press, 1987.

Pinsker, Sanford. "Fire and Ice: The Radical Cuteness of Kurt Vonnegut, Jr." *Between Two Worlds: The American Novel in the 1960's* [sic]. Troy, NY: Whitson, 1980. 87–101.

Poirier, Richard. *The Renewal of Literature: Emersonian Reflections.* New Haven: Yale University Press, 1987.

Rabe, David. *The Basic Training of Pavlo Hummel. Famous American Plays of the 1970s.* Ed. Ted Hoffman. 1981. New York: Dell, 1988.

Rackstraw, Loree. "Dancing with the Muse in Vonnegut's Later Novels." Reed and Leeds, *Chronicles.* 123–43.

—. "Quantum Leaps in the Vonnegut Mindfield." Boon, *Millennium.* 49–63.

—. "Vonnegut the Diviner and Other Auguries." Review of *Jailbird. North American Review* 264 (1979): 75–76. Reprinted in Merrill, *Critical Essays.* 47–53.

Rampton, David. "Into the Secret Chamber: Art and the Artist in Kurt Vonnegut's *Bluebeard.*" *Critique* 35 (1993): 16–26.

Reddy, K. Satyanaryana. "Structure of Consciousness in the Major Fiction of Kurt Vonnegut, Jr." *The Literary Endeavour: A Quarterly Journal Devoted to English Studies* 9 (1987–1988): 91–96.

Reed, Peter J. "Appendix: The Graphics of Kurt Vonnegut." Reed and Leeds, *Chronicles.* 205–22.

—. "Hurting 'til It Laughs: The Painful-Comic Science Fiction Stories of Kurt Vonnegut." Leeds and Reed, *Images.* 19–38.

—. *Kurt Vonnegut, Jr.* New York: Warner, 1972

—. "Kurt Vonnegut (1922–)." *Postmodern Fiction: A Bio-Bibliographic Guide.* Ed. Larry McCaffery. Westport, CT: Greenwood Press, 1986. 533–35.

—. "Kurt Vonnegut's Fantastic Faces." *Journal of the Fantastic in the Arts* 10.1 (1998): 77–87.

—. "Lonesome Once More: The Family Theme in Kurt Vonnegut's *Slapstick.*" Reed and Leeds, *Chronicles.* 113–22.

—. "The Responsive Shaman: Kurt Vonnegut and His World." Reed and Leeds, *Chronicles.* 47–57.

—. *The Short Fiction of Kurt Vonnegut.* Westport, CT: Greenwood Press, 1997.

Reed, Peter J., and Marc Leeds, eds. *The Vonnegut Chronicles: Interviews and Essays*. Westport, CT: Greenwood Press, 1996.

Roethke, Theodore. "The Waking." *The Collected Poems of Theodore Roethke*. Garden City, NY: Anchor, 1975. 104.

Rorty, Richard. *Achieving Our Country: Leftist Thought in Twentieth-Century America*. Cambridge: Harvard University Press, 1998.

Rose, Ellen Cronan. "It's All a Joke: Science Fiction in Kurt Vonnegut's *The Sirens of Titan*." *Literature and Psychology* 29 (1979): 160–68. Reprinted in Mustazza, *Response*. 15–23.

Rosenfield, Israel. *The Invention of Memory: A New View of the Brain*. New York: Basic Books, 1988.

Sachs, Oliver. "Foreword to the Paperback Edition." Israel Rosenfield. *The Invention of Memory: A New View of the Brain*. New York: Basic Books, 1988. xiii–xviii.

Saltzman, Arthur M. "The Aesthetic of Doubt in Recent Fiction." *Denver Quarterly* 20 (1985): 89–106.

Sayers, Valerie. "Vonnegut Stew." Review of *Timequake*. *The New York Times Book Review* 28 September 1997: 14.

Schatt, Stanley. *Kurt Vonnegut, Jr*. Boston: Twayne, 1976.

—. "The World of Kurt Vonnegut, Jr." *Critique* 12 (1971): 54–69.

Schöpp, Joseph C. "*Slaughterhouse-Five*: The Struggle with a Form That Fails." *Amerikastudien* 28.3 (1983): 335–45.

Schulz, Max F. "The Unconfirmed Thesis: Kurt Vonnegut, Black Humor, and Contemporary Art." *Critique: Studies in Modern Fiction* 12 (1971): 5–28.

Segal, Howard P. "Vonnegut's *Player Piano*: An Ambiguous Technological Dystopia." *No Place Else: Explorations in Utopian and Distopian Fiction*. Eds. Eric S. Rabkin, Martin Greenberg, and Joseph D. Olander. Carbondale: Southern Illinois University Press, 1983. 162–81.

Shakespeare, William. *The Tempest. Shakespeare: The Complete Works*. Ed. G. B. Harrison. New York: Harcourt, Brace, 1952. 1475–1501.

Sheppeard, Sallye J. "Kurt Vonnegut and the Myth of Scientific Progress." *Journal of the American Studies Association of Texas* 16 (1985): 14–19.

—. "Signposts in a Chaotic World: Naming Devices in Kurt Vonnegut's Dresden Books." *The McNeese Review* 312 (1986): 14–22.

Shriver, Donald. "Bonhoeffer Remembered." *Union News*. New York: September 1984: 2.

Sigman, Joseph. "Science and Parody in Kurt Vonnegut's *The Sirens of Titan*." *Mosaic* 19 (1986): 15–32. Reprinted in Mustazza, *Response*. 25–41.

Skinner, B. F. *Walden Two*. New York: Macmillan, 1948.

Slouka, Mark. "In Praise of Silence and Slow Time: Nature and Mind in a Derivative Age." Birkerts, *Tolstoy's Dictaphone*. 147–56.

Snepp, Frank. "The Last Days of Saigon." *Newsweek* 1 May 2000: 32–51.

Spiegelman, Willard. "Criticism at Century's End." *The Yale Review* 88 (2000): 133–50.

Stevens, Wallace. "Sunday Morning." *Wallace Stevens*. 5–8.

—. *Wallace Stevens: The Palm at the End of the Mind: Selected Poems and a Play*. Ed. Holly Stevens. New York: Vintage, 1972.

—. "The Well Dressed Man with a Beard." *Wallace Stevens*. 190.

Stone, Brad. "Vonnegut's Last Stand." *Newsweek* 29 September 1997: 78, 80.

Stoppard, Tom. *Rosencrantz & Guildenstern Are Dead*. 1967. New York: Grove Press, 1968.

Stuart, Francis. *The Abandoned Snail Shell*. Dublin: The Raven Arts Press, 1987.

Sullivan, Walter. "Researchers Cast Doubt on Finding that Water Can Be Converted to a Dense, Vaseline-Like Form." *The New York Times* 2 April 1970: C30.

Swartley, Ariel. "So It Went." *The Boston Globe* 5 October 1997: C1–C2.

Swift, Jonathan. "The Partridge-Bickerstaff Papers." *Satires and Personal Writings by Jonathan Swift.* Ed. William Alfred Eddy. 1932. London: Oxford University Press, 1956. 159–91.

Tanner, Tony. *City of Words: American Fiction, 1950–1970.* New York: Harper & Row, 1971.

—. *The Reign of Wonder: Naivety and Reality in American Literature.* Cambridge: Cambridge University Press, 1965.

Thomas, Evan. "Coming to Terms with a Tragedy." *Newsweek* 7 May 2001: 56–57.

Thoreau, Henry David. *Walden and Civil Disobedience.* Ed. Sherman Paul. Boston: Houghton Mifflin, 1960.

Tichborne, Chidiock. "Tichborne's Elegy, Written with His Own Hand in the Tower Before His Execution." *Renaissance England.* Eds. Roy Lamson and Hallett Smith. New York: W. W. Norton, 1956. 577.

Tillich, Paul. "Critique and Justification of Utopia." Manuel, *Utopias.* 296–309.

Trout, Kilgore [Phillip José Farmer]. *Venus on the Half-Shell.* New York: Dell, 1974.

Twain, Mark [Samuel Langhorne Clemens]. "Dinner Speech: Atlantic Monthly *Dinner, Seventieth Birthday of John Greenleaf Whittier.*" *Mark Twain Speaking.* Ed. Paul Fatout. Iowa City: University of Iowa Press, 1976. 110–15.

—. *Adventures of Huckleberry Finn. Adventures of Huckleberry Finn: An Annotated Text, Backgrounds and Sources, Essays in Criticism.* Eds. Scully Bradley, Richmond Croom Beatty, and E. Hudson Long. New York: Norton, 1961. 1–226.

"Unnatural Water." *Time* 19 December 1969.

Uphaus, Robert W. "Expected Meaning in Vonnegut's Dead-End Fiction." *NOVEL: A Forum on Fiction* 8.2 (1975). Reprinted in Mustazza, *Response.* 165–74.

Vanderbilt, Kermit. "Kurt Vonnegut's American Nightmares and Utopias." *The Utopian Vision: Seven Essays on the Quincentenniel of Sir Thomas More.* San Diego: San Diego State University Press, 1983. 137–73.

Whitlark, James S. "Vonnegut's Anthropology Thesis." *Literature and Anthropology. Studies in Comparative Literature.* 20. Eds. Philip Dennis and Wendell Aycock. Lubbock: Texas Tech University Press, 1989. 77–86.

Wicker, Tom. *A Time to Die.* New York: Quadrangle, 1975.

Wiener, Norbert. *Cybernetics: Control and Communications in the Animal and the Machine.* 1948. New York: MIT Press and Wiley, 1961.

—. *The Human Use of Human Beings.* Cambridge, MA: Riverside Press, 1950.

Wittgenstein, Ludwig. *Tractatus Logico-Philosophicus.* Trans. D. F. Pears and B. F. McGuinness. London: Routledge & Kegan Paul, 1961.

Wolfe, G. K. "The Encounter with Fantasy." *The Aesthetics of Fantasy, Literature and Art.* Ed. Roger C. Schlobin. Notre Dame, IN: University of Notre Dame Press, 1982. 1–15.

—. "Vonnegut and the Metaphor of Science Fiction: *The Sirens of Titan.*" *Journal of Popular Culture* 4 (1972): 964–69.

Wolfe, Tom. *The Painted Word.* 1975. New York: Bantam Books, 1976.

Wood, James. "The Wrecked Generation." Review of *Fates Worse Than Death. Times Literary Supplement* 15 November 1991: 8–9.

Yarmolinsky, Jane Vonnegut. *Angels without Wings: A Courageous Family's Triumph over Tragedy.* New York: Fawcett, 1987.

Yeats, W. B. *The Collected Poems of W. B. Yeats.* 1950. London: Macmillan, 1971.

Zinn, Howard. *A People's History of the United States: 1492–Present*. Rev. Ed. New York: HarperCollins, 1995.

Zins, Daniel L. "Rescuing Science from Technocracy: *Cat's Cradle* and the Play of Apocalypse." *Science Fiction Studies* 13 (1986): 170–81. Reprinted in Mustazza, *Response*. 67–77.

WORKS CONSULTED

Abádi-Nagy, Zoltán. " 'The Skilful Seducer': Of Vonnegut's Brand of Comedy." *Hungarian Studies in English* 8 (1974): 45–56.

—. "Ironic Messianism in Recent American Fiction." *Studies in English and American* 4 (1978): 63–83.

Alastrué, Fernando Plo, and María Antonia Soláns García. " 'From Timid to Timbuktu': Temporal Parameters in Kurt Vonnegut's *The Sirens of Titan*." *Science, Literature, and Interpretation: Essays on Twentieth-Century Literature and Critical Theory*. Zaragoza: University Zaragoza Press, 1991. 141–56.

Attebery, Brian. *The Fantasy Tradition in Literature: From Irving to Le Guin*. Bloomington: Indiana University Press, 1980.

Barnes, Clive. "Stage: 'Happy Birthday, Wanda June.' " *The New York Times* 9 October 1970: 43.

Beauchamp, Gorman. "Zamiatin's *We*." *No Place Else: Explorations in Utopian and Dystopian Fiction*. Eds. Eric S. Rabkin, Martin H. Greenberg, and Joseph D. Olander. Carbondale: Southern Illinois University Press, 1983. 56–77.

Bosworth, David. "The Literature of Awe." *Antioch Review* 37 (1979): 4–26.

Buck, Lynn. "Vonnegut's World of Comic Futility." *Studies in American Fiction* 3 (1975): 181–98. Reprinted in Mustazza, *Response*. 151–64.

Campbell, Felicia. "Two Gurus—Vonnegut's Bokonon and Narayan's Raju: Teachers Outside the Classroom." *West Virginia University Bulletin* 36 (1990): 77–81

Cooley, John R.. "The Garden in the Machine: Three Postwar Pastorals." *The Michigan Academician* 13.4 (1981): 405–20.

Cordle, Daniel. "Changing the Old Guard: Time Travel and Literary Technique in the Work of Kurt Vonnegut." *The Year Book of English Studies* 30 (2000). "Time and Narrative." Ed. Nickola Bradbury. Leeds: Modern Humanities Research Association. 166–186.

Crump, G. B. "Magic, *Foma*, Madness, and Art in the Fiction of Kurt Vonnegut, Jr." *Pleiades* 12 (1991): 64–82.

Cunningham, Valentine. "The Dilemmas of a Liberal Humanist." Review of *Palm Sunday*. *Times Literary Ssuppliment* 19 June 1981: 692.

Dimeo, Stephen. "Novel into Film: So It Goes." *The Modern American Novel and the Movies*. Eds. G. Peary and R. Shatzkin. New York: Ungar, 1978: 282–92.

Faris, Wendy B. "Icy Solitude: Magic and Violence in Macondo and San Lorenzo." *Latin American Literary Review* 13 (1985): 44–54.

Fiene, Donald M. "Kurt Vonnegut's Popularity in the Soviet Union and His Affinities with Russian Literature." *Vonnegut in America*. Eds. Jerome Klinkowitz and Donald L. Lawler. New York: Dell, 1977. 166–190.

Finch-Reyner, Sheila. "The Unseen Shore: Thoughts on the Popularity of Fantasy." *Journal of Popular Culture* 18.4 (1985): 127–34.

Freese, Peter. "Laurel and Hardy Versus the Self-Reflexive Artifact: Vonnegut's Novels Between High Culture and Popular Culture." *High and Low in American Culture*. Ed. Charlotte Kretzoi. Budapest: ELTE, 1986. 19–38.

Heller, Joseph. *Catch-22*. 1961. New York: Dell, 1962.

Hoagland, Edward. "Kurt Vonnegut Singing in the Bath." Review of *Palm Sunday*. *The New York Times* 15 March 1981. *Sunday Book Review*: 3.

Hoffman, Thomas P. "The Theme of Mechanization in *Player Piano*." *Clockwork Worlds: Mechanization Environments in SF*. Eds. Richard D. Erlich and Thomas P. Dunn. Reprinted in Mustazza, *Response*. 5–14.

Horton, Andrew. "Unstuck in Time: *Slaughterhouse-Five*." *The Films of George Roy Hill*. New York: Columbia University Press, 1984. 81–98.

Issacs, Neil D. "Unstuck in Time: *Clockwork Orange* and *Slaughterhouse-Five*." *Literature/Film Quarterly* 1 (1973): 122–31.

Jones, Fiona K. "The Twentieth Century Writer and the Image of the Computer." *Computers and Human Communication: Problems and Prospects*. Washington: University Press of America, 1974. 167–80.

Klinkowitz, Jerome. "Kurt Vonnegut, Jr. and the Crime of His Times." *Critique* (12) 1971: 38–53.

—. "Kurt Vonnegut: Public Spokesman." Reed and Leeds, *Chronicles*. 59–71.

—. "A Review of *Slapstick*." *The New Republic* 25 September 1976: 40–41. Reprinted in Mustazza, *Response*. 187–88.

—. *Vonnegut in Fact: The Public Spokesmanship of Personal Fiction*. Columbia: University of South Carolina Press, 1998.

Kropf, Carl. R. "Douglas Adam's 'Hitchhiker' Novels as Mock Science Fiction." *Science Fiction Studies* 15 (1988): 61–70.

Lazar, Mary. "Sam Johnson on Grub Street, Early Science Fiction Pulps, and Vonnegut." *Extrapolation: A Journal of Science Fiction and Fantasy* 32 (1991): 235–55.

Lee, Cremilda Toledo. "Fantasy and Reality in Kurt Vonnegut's *Slaughterhouse-Five*." *English Language and Literature* 37.4 (1991): 983–91.

Lundquist, James. *Kurt Vonnegut*. New York: Ungar, 1977.

Manlove, Colin. *The Impulse of Fantasy Literature*. Kent, OH: Kent State University Press, 1983.

—. *Modern Fantasy: Five Studies*. Cambridge: Cambridge University Press, 1975.

Martin, Robert A. "*Catch-22* and *Slaughterhouse-Five*." *Notes on Contemporary Literature* 15 (1985): 8–10.

—. "*Slaughterhouse-Five*: Vonnegut's Domed Universe." *Notes on Contemporary Literature* 17 (1987): 5–8.

Matheson, T. J. " 'This Lousy Little Book': The Genesis and Development of *Slaughterhouse-Five* as Revealed in Chapter One." *Studies in the Novel* 16.2 (1984): 228–40.

McConnell, Frank D. *Four Postwar American Novelists: Bellow, Mailer, Barth and Pynchon*. Chicago: University of Chicago Press.

McGinnis, Wayne D. "Vonnegut's *Breakfast of Champions*: A Reductive Success." *Notes on Contemporary Literature* 5 (1975): 6–9.

Moore, Lori. "How Humans Got Flippers and Beaks." *The New York Times Book Review* 6 October 1985: 7. Reprinted in Mustazza, *Response*. 271–73.

Mustazza, Leonard. "The Machine Within: Mechanization, Human Discontent, and the Genre of Vonnegut's *Player Piano*. *Papers on Language and Literature* 25.1 (1989): 99–113.

Nelson, Joyce. "*Slaughterhouse-Five*: Novel and Film." *Literature/Film Quarterly* 1 (1973): 149–53.

Parshall, Peter F. "Meditations on the Philosophy of Tralfamadore: Kurt Vonnegut and George Roy Hill." *Literature/Film Quarterly* 15 (1987): 49–59.

Persica, Dennis. "Vonnegut: Free Speech rights Hard to Defend." *The Times Picayne* February 1986.

Pieratt, Asa B., Jr., Julie Huffman-klinkowitz, and Jerome Klinkowitz. *Kurt Vonnegut: A Comprehensive Bibliography.* Hamden, CT: Archon, 1987.

Rackstraw, Loree. "The Paradox of 'Awareness' and Language in Vonnegut's Fiction." Leeds and Reed, *Images.* 51–67.

—. "The Vonnegut Cosmos." Review of *Deadeye Dick. North American Review* 267 (1982): 63–67. Reprinted in Merrill, *Critical Essays.* 53–61.

Rapf, Joanna E. " 'In the Beginning Was the Work': Steve Geller on *Slaughterhouse-Five.*" *Post Script* 4 (1985): 19–31.

Reid, Susan. "Kurt Vonnegut and American Culture: Mechanization and Loneliness in *Player Piano.*" *Journal of the American Studies Association of Texas* 15 (1984): 46–51.

Sandels, Robert. "UFOs, Science Fiction and the Postwar Utopia." *Journal of Popular Culture* 21 (1986): 141–51.

Samuels, Charles Thomas. "Age of Vonnegut." *The New Republic* 164 (12 June 1971): 30–32.

Scholes, Robert. *Fabulation and Metafiction.* Urbana: University of Illinois Press, 1979.

Schriber, Mary Sue. "Bringing Chaos to Order: The Novel Tradition and Kurt Vonnegut, Jr." *Genre* 10 (1977): 283–97. Reprinted in Mustazza, *Response.* 175–85.

Seed, David. "Mankind vs. Machines: The Technological Dystopia in Kurt Vonnegut's *Player Piano.*" *Impossibility Fiction: Alernativity—Extrapolation—Speculation.* Eds. Derek Littlewood and Peter Stockwell. Amsterdam: Rodopi, 1996. 11–23.

Shaw, Patrick W. "The Excremental Festival: Vonnegut's *Slaughterhouse-Five.*" *Scholia Satyrica* 3 (1976): 3–11.

Sieber, Sharon. "Unstuck in Time: Simultaneity as a Foundation for Vonnegut's Chrono-Synclastic Infundibula and other Nonlinear Time Structures." Leeds and Reed, *Images.* 147–53.

Tunnell, James R. "Kesey and Vonnegut: Preachers of Redemption." *A Casebook on Ken Kesey's* One Flew Over the Cuckoo's Nest. Ed. George J. Searles. Albuquerque: University of New Mexico Press, 1992. 127–33.

Updike, John. "All's Well in Skyscraper National Park." Review of *Slapstick. New Yorker* (1983). Reprinted in Merrill, *Critical Essays.* 40–47.

Vonnegut, Kurt. "About This Play." *Happy Birthday, Wanda June.* New York: Dell, 1971. vii–xvi.

Watts, Philip. "Rewriting History: Céline and Kurt Vonnegut." *The South Atlantic Quarterly* 93 (1994): 265–78.

Wiedemann, Barbara. "American War Novels: Strategies for Survival." *War and Peace: Perspectives in the Nuclear Age.* Eds. Ulrich Goebel and Otto Nelson. Lubbock: Texas Tech University Press, 1988. 137–44.

Williams, Raymond. "Utopia and Science Fiction." *Science Fiction: A Critical Guide.* Ed. Patrick Parrinder. New York: Longman, 1979. 52–66.

Wineapple, Brenda. "God Bless You, Mr. Vonnegut." *Current Perspectives in Social Theory.* 2 vols. Eds. S. G. McNall, et al. Greenwich, CT: JAI Press, 1981. 2:233–45.

Wymer, Thomas L. "Machines and the Meaning of Human in the Novels of Kurt Vonnegut, Jr." *The Mechanical God: Machines in Science Fiction.* Eds. Thomas P. Dunn and Richard D. Erlich. Westport, CT: Greenwood Press, 1982. 41–52.

Index

About the Author

DONALD E. MORSE is Professor of English and Rhetoric, at Oakland University, Fulbright Lecturer at Kossuth University, Hungary, 1987–1988, and Conference Chair for the International Association for the Fantastic in the Arts.

**Recent Titles in Contributions to the
Study of Science Fiction and Fantasy**